THE RELUCTANT ABBESS

THE
RELUCTANT
ABBESS

Angélique Arnauld of Port-Royal
(1591–1661)

By

MARGARET TROUNCER

SHEED AND WARD   **NEW YORK**

Biography 922

To my two friends
Marquise de Gourmont
and
Kathleen Chesney

"To know all the grandeur of humanity, one must know Port-Royal."

> —Roger Collard, quoted by Sainte-Beuve

"Pure as angels, proud as devils."

> —Hardouin de Péréfixe, Archbishop of Paris,
> speaking of the Port-Royal nuns

"The profligate abuses, the Puritan refuses, the Catholic uses."

> —Frank Sheed

CONTENTS

THE RELUCTANT ABBESS

PROLOGUE

THE ABBEY IN THE VALLEY OF SIGHS

FROM EARLY dawn, that July day of 1598, the chef had hired porters to bring his provisions from the quay-sides and markets of Paris. Monsieur Marion, Baron de Druy, a rich barrister, was entertaining his old friend Dom de la Croix, the Master General of the Cistercians and the Abbot of Cîteaux.

"You'd think he were provisioning the whole Order," grumbled the butler as he laid the silver dishes and spoons in the dark dining-room. The house was at the angle of the rue de la Verrerie and the rue du Renard. Through the open windows could be heard the chimes of St. Merri.

The chef appeared in the doorway with red roses to decorate the crisp and crunchy game pie which the caterer had just delivered: "Seems our master's going to ask the Master General to find an abbey for Mademoiselle Jacqueline. A shame I call it, and she not seven years old yet."

"You don't say!" exclaimed the butler, pausing as he arranged the silver goblets on the side table. "So that's why I had to go panting up to the Montmartre vineyards yesterday, to order the best local wine: as if our Argenteuil wouldn't do. I thought something was afoot, like the day we entertained his Majesty and I had to scour the market gardens for the best melons."

"Yes, Monsieur called me up to his study and said everything must be of the best quality, and no trouble spared." The cook

3

laughed drily. "His only regret is that he's got none of those new-fangled forks yet: but he doesn't seem to realize that they're only for the nobility."

"Sh," whispered the butler, putting out soft milk-and-butter rolls. "He *does* call himself Baron de Druy. Though, I suppose if he were quality, natural like, he wouldn't need to read books on table manners on the quiet."

"For all that," laughed the cook, "you did tell me yourself that when he's alone with the family he blows his nose into his table napkin, licks his fingers and forgets to wipe his spoon before putting it into the common dish."

"Ho! Which reminds me," whispered the butler, "he said the Master General must be given several changes of table napkins. I must get our mistress to unlock the linen cupboard. Tell me the menu again, there's a good fellow; all this fuss for one guest puts me off my stride: feel as if I'm serving the Holy Father himself."

The cook recited: "A rich poultry broth to start with, the pie, then some nice mushrooms I picked myself near Notre Dame, a good dish of frogs, tender as babies' bottoms, artichokes, asparagus —the last this season, the master brought them himself from Andilly—"

"What's the dessert?"

"Well, it's too early for the new greengages or the bergamot pears which he likes, so I got him some fine Tours prunes and several punnets of wood-strawberries from Corbeil."

"Got the cream?"

"Yes, but no sugar: still too expensive for our pockets. Finishing up with cherry conserve and muscat wine."

"Well, I foresee it's going to be a ceremonial banquet: I must go and change into my best hat and sword. I'm sure, if he had them, the master would peel the oranges before presenting them to his guest and offer them covered again with their peel. It's in his book. *Ciel!* I must fetch some rose water for the bowls: he's to be allowed to dabble his fingers after every course, it seems. And all this to make little Mademoiselle Jacqueline into an abbess!"

The feast, which began at midday, went on for two hours. Monsieur Marion, although he shared his house with his daughter and her husband, Antoine Arnauld, had insisted on entertaining the Master General alone, in case the children should interrupt their important conversation. Monsieur Marion kept on his large feathered hat. The white-robed Master General sat back in his leather chair and fingered the china lizards in an immense green Palissy dish at his side. He had a coarse, flushed face and a sensual mouth.

"Well, well, well. So you want me to find an abbey for your granddaughter?"

"I do. You see, the financial situation is becoming critical: her mother is only twenty-six and she's already had ten children."

"H'm," laughed the Master General, stroking a china frog encrusted on the dish. "Frog spawn! In a few more years she may have twenty—who knows?"

"Yes, indeed," replied Monsieur Marion. "Ah, my dear friend, you are not drinking." He made a sign to the butler, who whisked his napkin off his shoulder. "Try a little of this Frontignan: I can recommend it."

The Master General drank it down at one gulp: impossible to savour the bouquet lingeringly, when a servant was at your elbow waiting to take your goblet back to the side table.

"Excellent!" and he smacked his lips.

Monsieur Marion continued: "Well, as I was saying, I am sure the Lord will bless my daughter with many more olive branches. She is not elegant, she prefers visiting the poor to wasting hours at the tailor's. She's just the kind of woman who likes managing a nursery, and a large one at that. But even with my son-in-law's earnings, which are by no means meagre, he cannot afford to give all the girls marriage dowries. And up to date, they seem to go in for girls, rather than boys. He'll settle a lump sum on Catherine when she marries, but Jacqueline and Agnès must both enter religion. It is much cheaper that way."

The Master General sucked a strawberry rather noisily. He spat out the stalk, wiped his mouth and proclaimed: "You must be more optimistic, my friend. Look at the way the King loves Antoine

Arnauld's speeches. He is always in his good books; if you look out of the window now, you can see all the nobles in their coaches queueing up to ask his advice."

"Ah," said Monsieur Marion, "but nobles sometimes don't pay their accounts. The middle classes always remember to pay. I assure you, he's known the pinch when he was exiled at Tours and he doesn't want to sample it again. Let me help you to some more cream."

"Well, well, well!" exclaimed the Master General, replete with good victuals, "I will have to go into this. I must call on the old Abbess, Dame Boulehart, this afternoon at Port-Royal des Champs. You know, about six leagues away, in the valley of Chevreuse. My chaplain is coming too. I might ask her to take a coadjutrix, though she'll think your Jacqueline a trifle young."

"Yes, that's true," replied Monsieur Marion, looking anxious, "but Dame Boulehart could reserve the place for her. Try and tempt her—explain that we will restore the estate. I suppose it's crumbling, like all the others."

"Aha," replied the Master General, "if you only knew how hard up they were, those poor nuns. It is a very unhealthy spot, surrounded by marshland. What will Mademoiselle[1] your daughter say when she hears of it? I'm sure she will imagine it most unsuitable for her child. The enclosure walls are in ruins—in fact the nuns don't seem to keep to the enclosure at all, so far as I know. They visit other abbeys and have theatrical performances. Which reminds me," he added with a laugh, "you should have seen the Paris St. Antoine nuns the other day, dressed up as men in a play called 'Cleopatra.' Most diverting! They know how to entertain their Master General when he makes a visitation!"

Monsieur Marion interrupted. "I am not asking you to find an abbey where Jacqueline will live a strict life. She's too—er—impetuous to bear the yoke for long. As for the climate, she is very strong and can endure a great deal. What I am asking you to find, my dear old friend, is a stable situation for her, as she is not going

---

[1] A married woman of the middle classes was always called Mademoiselle. St. François de Sales always referred to Madame Arnauld thus.

to marry. How many nuns are there in this community?" he added.

"Oh," replied the Master General, "let me see—about eleven[1] in all. Most of them afflicted with rheumatism and swollen limbs, owing to the damp, and—oh yes, there is an imbecile. What makes me anxious is that the old Abbess may live a long time yet. She may refuse to see your Jacqueline at all. I think she is frightened of her own relations, who are plotting to seize the place when she dies."

"Oh, that's easily dealt with," said Monsieur Marion airily, "we can bring in a troop of guards and make the nuns do as we wish, eh, my old friend? You mustn't admit defeat when mere women are concerned. I'm sure you've got a hold on them. And we, of course, are prepared to contribute towards their well-being."

"All right," exclaimed the Master General, slapping his large thigh, "that's a bargain. It's clinched. Well, I'll leave you now. Ho," he called to his chaplain, "off we go to Port-Royal. Have the horses saddled immediately."

Three hours later the Master General and his chaplain, a distinguished young monk called Dom Bernard, had left Versailles behind them. Versailles, of course, in those early days was nothing more than a hillock crowned by a tiny red brick château and a windmill belonging to monks. It was surrounded by the woods and almost impenetrable thickets in which the kings of France loved to hunt.

It was a close July afternoon. The sun had turned an ominous red, the sky was a sultry yellow. If Dom Bernard had not been so holy, he would have despised his Superior. Obedience was more perfect when given to an unworthy being. He had gone into the Cistercian Order at sixteen, in all the enthusiasm of youth, inspired by reading a life of the great St. Bernard. He had been horrified to witness the corruption of this great Order. Only his strong sense of vocation had induced him to remain after the disillusions of his novitiate. He determined to keep his Rule. He would not

---

[1] Names of the nuns: Elisabeth de Mauternes; Catherine Dupont; Madeleine Mulot; Claire-Martine Pinot; Charlotte de Hérelle; Isabelle Agnès de Châteauneuf; Magdeleine de Ste. Candide Le Cerf; Goulas; Morel; Marie Baron de St. Paulin.

hunt with the others, or see plays performed by nuns. He refused
to eat meat, and he wore a hair shirt under his white habit.

The Master General had chosen him as his secretary because
he never complained of hard work and his handwriting was very
beautiful. Therefore, instead of chivvying him for his austerity,
which secretly he found exasperating, he humoured him in order
to be assured of his continued allegiance.

The face of the Master General had turned reddish purple with
the effort of digesting Monsieur Marion's large meal. Also, he was
anxious because he had not mentioned to his host that the Prioress
at Port-Royal, young Dame Elisabeth de Mauternes, had a bad
reputation. The Arnaulds, for all their grasping, middle-class ambitions, were a clean-living family. Although irreligious and un-
learned, they still wished to keep the externals respectable. They
might have something to say, when they knew about the Prioress.
Ah well, they would find out in good time, and then she would
probably be sent elsewhere. He was lenient to the erring nuns
under his jurisdiction. They had so often been driven into these
abbeys by avaricious and hard-hearted parents: straight from
nursery to cloister. At first, things would go fairly well, for they
were too much afraid to complain. But then, in adolescence, these
little girls grew up and discovered that they were women. During
the annual masquerades at Candlemas, he had observed plenty
of unedifying jollifications, but he'd winked an eye. After all, who
was he to stand in judgment on his brothers and sisters?

They both ambled slowly up the hill leading southwards out of
Versailles, turned right and soon reached a vast, desolate plain.
A gust was blowing the corn which a roughly dressed peasant
was reaping with a sickle. He glanced up in surly fashion at the
white-cloaked monks. As the Abbot blessed him, the peasant
looked greedily at his enormous amethyst ring, and then went on
with his work, mumbling under his breath.

The monks set their horses to a canter. It was a long white road
full of dust. In the far distance could be seen the trees of a farm-
house, Les Granges, which belonged to Port-Royal. It was on a hill-
top overlooking the Abbey, which lay in the hollow of a deep
valley. The monks and nuns of St. Bernard always loved to choose

a well-watered hollow for the site of their abbeys,[1] as so many of the place names will show—Clairvaux, Clairefontaine and so on. They must always be assured of a plentiful supply of water. But here it seemed as if they had exaggerated. Not only did the river flood the fields and turn them into unhealthy quagmires and marshlands in wintertime, but both river and fish pond seeped into the Abbey infirmary, which was at a lower level. Nuns sick with marsh fever and tuberculosis felt that they were relegated to a damp and pestilential cellar. It is not surprising, then, that they did not tell their infirmarian of their ills, but preferred to keep to their own cells for as long as possible. The infirmary was the antechamber of the tomb. Water everywhere. Even the well for domestic use was in the cloister garth, where the nuns were buried, and the water must have been filthy. It is not surprising that the richer nuns had no liking for the drinking water and often asked their friends and relations to bring them wine.

Even from a distance the croaking of thousands of frogs could be heard. The fields were alive with frogs, toads and snakes.

They stopped cantering. The chaplain felt overcome by a strange, indefinable sensation of terror. He crossed himself.

At length they left the plain and reached the farm of Les Granges. Here the road sloped downhill steeply. On the right, in the hollow, was the twelfth-century church, surrounded by all the Abbey buildings and dependencies, hallowed by memories of St. Louis. The encircling wooded mountains looked as if they were toppling onto them, and smothering them. They shut out any view beyond: one had to look heavenward. The hollow seen from the heights was like a vast, dark emerald, from which arose the mists of the bogs. The red sun was reflected in these weirs, which now looked like pools of blood.

The atmosphere did not seem to have affected the Master General. He muttered under his breath, "Yes, quite an extensive place; three hundred and eighty acres of plough land, nine hundred and twenty-five wooded copses and forty acres of meadowland, all in one piece. That ought to suit my Paris friend." Aloud he exclaimed,

[1] There are the Latin verses which tell us that: "Bernard loved the valleys, Benedict the hills, Francis the citadels, Ignatius the great cities."

"But I'm sure the Pope won't allow a child of that age to be Abbess. However, we'll just have to—ahem—add to her age on the documents."

The chaplain looked suitably shocked.

In that year 1598 there were still plenty of trees around the estate, but the year after, there was a very severe winter which killed off many of them. The result was that with nothing to absorb the humidity of air and soil, the place became damper than ever. Dom Bernard observed the birches, aspens, oaks hung with mistletoe and the trembling, solitary poplars. Doves cooed near the twelfth-century dovecot.

In the distant woods, hounds were baying. "Who can that be?" asked the Master General. "It isn't the King. Oh, I know," he said, "it's the chaplain. He's always out hunting. Doesn't read his breviary, poor chap, but he certainly knows a good hound when he sees one."

When at length they got to the foot of the hill, they turned to the right along a very badly kept private road. From there they could see the mud walls enclosing the Abbey. On the left, up a flight of grassy steps, was a glade called La Solitude, with a great cross in the middle. The nuns used to spin there at recreation. The monks turned to the right again and at length reached the enclosure door.

After they had hammered for some time, it was opened by a lay sister, who looked amazed when she saw the Master General.

"How now, my good Sister, don't look at me like that, openmouthed. I'm not Saint Louis. Go and tell your Reverend Abbess that I wish to speak to her. Is she up?"

"Yes, my Lord, no my Lord—at least she's in her room. She isn't very well. She's hardly ever up nowadays."

"Yes, I know, I know," he said impatiently.

An unkempt-looking farm menial slouched up and took the horses. All of a sudden from the garden appeared an aged nun lugging a watering can. She wore a mask and gloves and carried a fan. The Master General greeted her gleefully.

"Ah, still looking after your idol—your private garden, Dame Morel? You've renounced everything except that, haven't you?"

"Ah, my Lord," she replied, tearing off her mask. "I will give you a bunch of such beautiful roses and Madonna lilies to take home with you. Who but myself would provide flowers for our chapel?"

"Quite so, quite so," he said absent-mindedly, and he clambered up to the Abbess's private suite.

In the meantime the chaplain went into the chapel to say his Office. He thought there was no one in it. There hardly ever was. And then in the half light, upright in her magnificent sixteenth-century carved stall, he saw the imbecile. She was deaf and afflicted with an incomprehensible stammer. She went to confession by making signs to some other nun. Her appearance was very neat and she had a sweet, devout expression. Apparently she was almost the only nun there who really spent some time in the chapel. As she had not heard the chaplain, she thought she was alone. He noticed that she had a bunch of wild flowers in the crook of her left arm, and with her right hand she picked up one flower at a time and offered it to a crucifix with a look of indescribable happiness. It was a madwoman's medley: great sword flags snatched up from the banks of the pond, plaintain, herb Robert, water mint, black hellebore, buttercup, toad flax, goose grass, wild white clover, bog myrtle, spotted orchis, marsh cranesbill, ragged robin and mallow —all the treasures of marshland.

This afflicted nun who had lived there from early childhood, unwanted by her family, was offering to God the only due she could, like Our Lady's tumbler. She could not pronounce her Office, so one by one she gave the flowers she had picked.

The chaplain began to lose the feeling of horror which had assailed him on the height. Yes, there was something magnetic about the place. It had once been holy ground. In here had prayed St. Louis and St. Thibault and Mathilde de Garlande, the foundress, and holy abbesses and benefactors. If only a new abbess could come now, freely elected, and reform them all, and bring them back to the pristine splendour of the days when the Rule of the great St. Bernard was fully kept. Saint Bernard had ordained that his monks and nuns should rise every day two hours after mid-

night, and stay up, but these nuns rose at four, and several of them
were dispensed even from that.

He recalled his own early days in the novitiate at Cîteaux. He
was not very strong but he was stouthearted, and he had managed
to get through the first year. He was now almost used to austerities,
though they had greatly declined in his Order.

Much too distracted to continue his Office, he looked at the habit
of the poor idiot nun. The ample white robe was pleated, the white
cloak was very long, both of relatively thin serge. He noted the
hooded cowl, which was thrown back. The black veil was made of
coarse muslin, the wimple was white. He recalled the gloves and
fan of Dame Morel, and the mask to protect her complexion. Oh,
the vanity of these women! He remembered the Venetian nuns of
St. Laurence, very disorderly, their bosoms barely hidden by transparent gauze. Here at Port-Royal, they found ways and means of
eluding the regulations. The rich nuns with private incomes indulged in jewelled crucifixes and pearl rosaries. Two or three of
them even wore precious jewels. Their chemises were of real linen,
instead of the wool ordained by the Rule.

The chancel was crowded with thirteenth-century tombs of
abbesses; one Marguerite de Lévy wore exactly the same habit as
the nun in the choir stall. So many of the tombs were of strange
Byzantine style. There were recumbent crusaders too, on green
flagstones with black fleur-de-lys in honour of the abbesses from
the noble house of Marly Montmorency. The cloister, he recalled,
was paved with crimson tiles splashed with rosettes and stars.

After a while he left and wandered alone in the garden. He
looked up at the great hill, on the top of which was the farm, and
he could descry the stags and does which peopled that charming
solitude and prevented it from being too horrible a desert. Willow
warblers sang sweetly in the oaks.

In the meantime, crouching over a fire which was never allowed
to go out, bent double by rheumatism, the old Abbess was complaining to the Master General. She was a baffling blend of obstinacy and feeble wits. She had ruled there for nearly five and
twenty years. Most of her present nuns were very young. She kept

them in subjection by frightening them, and in her presence they behaved like children.

Now after complaining about her health, she went on to the next chapter, groaning about the small revenues of the Abbey. The Master General interrupted her impatiently:

"But with all these acres, you ought to be able to farm the place properly. Look at the trees for kindling: they alone represent quite a small fortune. And the fruit."

"Oh," she said, "fruit. We never seem to see much of it. The agent helps himself and never lets me look at the accounts."

"Ah," he said briskly, "you are too ill at the moment to cope with all this. I know that you are courageous, dear Abbess. What you need is an assistant."

She rapped her stick against the stone floor and nearly shouted at him.

"An assistant—no, Master General! I am capable of ruling here. I have ruled for a quarter of a century, and I can go on, like my predecessors, until I reach the half century." Then she eyed him with her cold, shrewd eye. "Now, what are you trying to tell me?"

He came to the point at once, as she had meant him to, and explained how his great friend, the powerful Monsieur Marion, patronized by Henri Quatre, wished to give her his granddaughter Jacqueline Arnauld as coadjutrix. Again she rapped her stick.

"No, no, no. I won't have her in the place. You might care to appoint her—you, after all, are the Master General of the Order, and I have to obey. But I was legally elected Abbess of Port-Royal, and I won't have any interference. I will not have her in my presence. And then, if she were to come, look at all my nieces! They would rush over here and make my life torture. My nieces seem to think that abbeys are inherited from aunts."

"Ah," he said, "we'll protect you from them. I'll just send some guards—er—to keep the doors and the enclosure. We won't allow anybody in. *You* need the finances, the Arnaulds have them. They are very rich. You are being robbed right and left here by your agent and servants. I have noticed that, in the depths of winter, you never have enough logs for your fire, but there are plenty for the servants. You want somebody to build up the wall, to drain the swamp, to pay the wages, to win your lawsuits. Monsieur Arnauld is a famous barrister. Just think how wonderful it is to have the law on your side! You'd never lose a lawsuit with his daughter here."

And after wrangling with her for two good hours, and persuading her that she had nothing to fear, as Jacqueline was not yet seven, he won her over.

That night at recreation, the Abbess said to her nuns, "I have done a good stroke of work for you today, my children, and one day you will live to thank me."

1. *AN UNHAPPY CHILDHOOD*

THE MASTER General and his chaplain spent the night with Dom Nicolas Brissonet, the chaplain of the nuns at Port-Royal. He regaled them with endless stories of his hunting exploits and a dish of *lapin sauté*. They were nearly asleep when he had finished sucking the last garlicky bone and wiped his fingers on his white habit.

In the morning the Master General overslept. His chaplain rose at four, just as the hilltops were suffused with the first flush of dawn. He went to the chapel, hoping to hear the community sing Matins. After he had waited for some time, two or three young nuns scrambled in, looking dishevelled and tired. They yawned audibly. The hideous cacophony of their chant appalled and dismayed him so much that he nearly left. It was obvious that they understood nothing of the meaning of the great words. They looked around and scratched their heads as if they were alive with lice. Later, the Master General chanted Mass for the community. Only two sisters came to receive Holy Communion.

The two monks rode back to Paris that evening before twilight fell. They passed the Clocheton des Trépassés, or bellringer of departed souls, a sinister figure under an immense black felt hat, clothed in a black dalmatic painted with skulls and crossbones interlaced. He carried an enormous bell, and when night fell, he would cry in his sepulchral voice: "Awaken, all ye who sleep, pray to God for the departed."

Very soon their horses' hooves were clattering in the narrow dark

street near the Church of St. Merri. Servants and grooms met them.
The house at the angle of the rue de la Verrerie and the rue du
Renard was tall, narrow and dark. While the Master General bent
to reassure Monsieur Marion in a whisper, the chaplain paid his respects to Madame Arnauld, who was as usual expecting another
child. Not wishing to perturb her in her present condition by re-
counting his premonitions about Port-Royal, he told her a pious
legend about St. Thibault, the saint of Port-Royal, and how he
had presented St. Louis with a basket of flowers from which sprang
eleven stems of lilies, a symbol of the number of children who
would be born to him through his intercession. But young
Madame Arnauld with the long, thin, rather dour face was really
not listening. She was planning to have her housekeeper up and
scold her that evening for some imagined misdemeanour.

Dom Bernard finally sensed that she was not very anxious about
the place for Jacqueline. She made no enquiries at all.

Half an hour before supper, he excused himself, as he wished to
say Compline in the church of St. Merri. The second church of that
name was then being built, but the workmen had left for the day.
The doors were open and the street children were still playing on
the steps. The admirable sixteenth-century glass—since destroyed
—glowed in the twilight.

He groped his way to the Arnauld chapel, which was filled with
their ancestral tombs. He opened his breviary and, by the light of
one guttering taper, was just reading: "your adversary the Devil
. . .", when he got the fright of his life. He heard a sigh coming
from a dark corner, quite near. Peering, he saw a girl of about
seven crouched with her face on a tomb. She was clutching to her
breast a child's silver rattle. She lay quite still, and occasionally
she sighed. He was just about to go up to her and see if she were
ill when his sleeve was tugged by another little girl of eight whom
he recognized as Catherine, the beautiful eldest daughter of the
Arnaulds.

"Please come out and talk to me," she said in a hoarse whisper.

She led him to the end of the church and they sat down on two
chairs next to each other.

"You mustn't take any notice of Jacqueline. Every evening she

goes to pray that she won't be parted from Simon, our baby
brother. She loves him so much, and he can't live without her.
Mother could never bear to have her in the room until he was born.
But he would not take his food unless Jacqueline were there. Our
governess, Madame Pichotel, would whip her if she knew she
had taken his rattle. She hides it and I hide it for her sometimes.
We come in here every evening and say our prayers. Poor Jacqueline. She doesn't want to be a nun."

The chaplain sighed. "I think she will catch a chill if she stays
there any longer. Ah, here she is."

And he saw little Jacqueline Arnauld for the first time. She had
large dark, deeply set eyes, under hooded lids; her eyebrows rose
at the ends, giving her a critical, almost sardonic expression, most
unpleasing in a child. Her nose was like her father's, long, clever
and well-formed; her mouth was a sensual Cupid's bow, and her
chin dimpled yet determined. Her dress was plain and a little
neglected. She had hidden the rattle beneath her apron. She said
in rather a loud voice, like a boy's:

"Good evening, Dom Bernard. You have been to the Abbey, have
you?" And without waiting for an answer, she said: "Today my
sister Agnès[1] said to Monsieur Marion, my grandfather: 'Since
you wish me to be a nun, I wish it too, but on condition that I shall
be an abbess.' Later, she came to him again and said, 'Grandfather,
I have come to tell you that I do not want to be an abbess, as I
have heard it said that abbesses must render account to God for
the souls of their nuns and I have enough to do to care for my
own.'"

"Admirable, admirable," exclaimed the chaplain.

Beautiful little Jacqueline burst out laughing and said: "I told
my grandfather: 'I want to be an abbess, Grandfather. I shall take
care to make my nuns do their duty.'"

They all smiled. Jacqueline continued:

"Oh, it is unusual for Agnès to have these scruples. She is always
very pleased with herself. Now if I were *her* abbess, I would
humble her pride. She always likes to wear such neat clothes. I

---

[1] Her name in the world was Jeanne, but to avoid confusion I have called
her Agnès throughout, as this was her name in religion.

would put her into a filthy dirty habit and make her keep it on for a long time."

"Aha," laughed the chaplain, as they neared the house, "but your sister Agnès will never be in your novitiate. She is going to be Abbess of Saint Cyr, quite near Port-Royal, and a very magnificent abbey it is, too. They wear clean, beautiful habits."

On learning this, the child looked surprisingly disconcerted, jealous and sullen.

Jacqueline Arnauld was the fourth child and second daughter of Monsieur Antoine Arnauld and Mademoiselle Marion. She came into the world at Tours in 1591, when her mother was only eighteen. For some reason which is not clear, neither parent could endure her. Perhaps it was because she had an iron will. But it is not farfetched to say that in that childish despair engendered by their dislike her woeful destiny was born.

Perhaps Madame Arnauld's unkindness was due to her own fragile health. She had been a premature child. She had married at twelve and started bearing her long line of children at fifteen. She had borne and lost her first son in the January of 1585, but by the end of that selfsame year she had borne her second son, whose name was Robert d'Andilly. Moreover, she lived in her parents' house; she was the sole heiress and had to care for her mother, who was a querulous and exacting invalid. Her whole existence was spent in confinements, funerals of the children who did not survive, christenings of the children who survived, visiting the poor in her parish, humouring her mother and trouncing the servants. As a young twelve-year-old bride, she had learned to rule. She even had the pluck to smack a servant of twenty who had been kissed by a man and had not resisted sufficiently. From the very beginning, she had made the old housekeeper quail by railing at her because her account of the linen room was not to her liking. She had had little childhood to speak of herself, and so she treated Jacqueline with the unconscious cruelty of a frustrated girl.

When her father, Monsieur Marion, had first heard the great Antoine Arnauld speaking at the bar, he was so transported with admiration that he literally carried him away in his coach and brought him home to dine. And very soon afterwards he offered him his daughter. Young Mademoiselle Marion, hardly out of the nursery, was too much overcome by the great orator to speak. His gestures, his bearing, and above all his beautiful, mellifluous voice reduced her to silence. Oh, that moving golden voice which he used as a weapon to impose his iron will! Throughout his married life, he always imposed his desires on her. His words, his endless flow of words, somehow drowned her resistance in every way. Even her natural desire to be prettily dressed as a young bride was ridiculed by his clever speeches. He would mock the silly farthingales and ruffs and slashed sleeves of the court beauties, eloquently deride their locks twisted into serpentine shapes, spread out like bats and crimped like Moors.

"No, my dear, not for you. You go and visit your poor." And he would say to his friends: "My wife is not elegant: she visits the poor."

She might make out that she was not the one to rule in that household. In later life she betrayed herself by saying: "How, having begun to command since the age of twelve, could I learn to obey after fifty?"

Hers was a rule of severity. She never appealed to the heart or the soul. Indeed she hardly knew her Bible or missal. Like most people of the middle classes, all her concern was for outward decorum. She could not teach her daughters about religion, as she did not know much herself. So she kept strictly to her duties and always went to her parish priest for confession. Later she became, in the words of Saint-Cyran, "a soul truly solid and built on rock." At that time her living children were: her eldest son, Robert, and her younger son, Henri, who was to become the Bishop of Angers; her eldest girl, Catherine, who had a religious vocation which she was not allowed to fulfil, but instead was forced to marry a Monsieur Le Maître, who physically ill-treated her and was unfaithful; next, Jacqueline, then Anne-Eugénie, then Agnès. After Jacqueline had entered the Order, two other girls were born, Marie-Claire and Madeleine Christine. All five girls were destined to enter Port-Royal—even the unhappy Catherine after her husband's death.

In appearance, Catherine was very like her younger sister, Jacqueline, but with a much sweeter expression. Anne-Eugénie, we know, was very beautiful, and, as a girl, romantic, proud and haughty; Agnès, extremely plain and homely, very middle-class, redeemed however by that expression of serenity which we see in the great Louvre picture by Philippe de Champaigne.

All the girls were delightful, touching and interesting characters, and they all came under the spell of their sister Jacqueline. Just as the great St. Bernard himself had drawn thirty of his friends and relations into Cîteaux, so Jacqueline's imperious will and magnetic personality swept all her sisters after her.

Very shortly after their marriage, the Arnaulds had fled from Paris to Tours, for Henri de Navarre (who was to be Henri IV in 1589) had made that town his headquarters. It was at Tours, away from the rich clientèle of the capital, that the Arnaulds first tasted the bitterness of being poor, and it was not to their liking. Quite soon they began to acquire their reputation for being covetous birds of prey, avid for pensions. They were so proud and conventional that they would not resign themselves to poverty. An enemy of theirs, whom Antoine had once humiliated, revenged himself by looking up all their pension claims in the records, and found that they had even claimed money for children in the cradle, who could offer no services to the State. That little revenge cost them much.

They went to live in the great house near St. Merri with forty-five-year-old Monsieur Marion, Madame Arnauld's father. He called himself the Baron de Druy and was chief Counsel at the Bar. He was highly thought of in his day, and indeed likened to Cicero. Jacqueline's nephew, Antoine Le Maître, wrote of her childhood, after hearing her speak of it. She said that from early morning, her mother would send her away, out of her room, to her grandfather. He often played with her. Even if old Marion was a crafty, unscrupulous and irreligious man, he certainly had the art of being a grandfather: how unhappy the child would have been without him.

Clinging to the end of his large sleeve, Jacqueline would trot after him from room to room in his part of the house. Her brothers and sisters were kept at home by her parents, "who felt tenderness for them and an aversion for me." She was thrown out to her grandfather directly she was dressed. "To revenge myself in some way because she chased me out in this way, I used to close the little door of the lodging of Monsieur Marion with a bolt as soon as I'd passed through it, wishing to prevent my brothers and sisters from entering and coming to share with me the affection of my grand-father, with whom I always remained, following him almost every-where either in his room or in his study and holding him ordinarily by one of his sleeves. I was proud from those early days onwards, and behaved with caution. . . . When I found any one of my sisters at Monsieur Marion's, I would chase them out and say, 'You go home to your own place. This is my house and not yours.' " She insisted on being called Jacqueline Marion when she was with her grandfather, and Jacqueline Arnauld when she was with her father. ". . . wishing always to pass for a daughter of the master of the house in which I was, so that I should be more highly con-sidered. The guests would laugh gently."

When Jacqueline left home and entered the Cistercian Order in the autumn, her mother saw to it that she went to confession. Even as a child she must have had a very strong sense of the Divine Presence, for she knelt down in the middle of the courtyard to make her act of contrition. She says: "This was the first instance in which I acted with reason and discernment." Like many unhappy children neglected by their parents, she would turn to the thought of the anguish of Jesus. In her grandfather's house she found a Book of Hours which spoke of the Passion. She wept a great deal when she read it, but afterwards returned to her naughty ways, tricks and pranks.

Jacqueline's handwriting was legible enough, not exquisite like some of her nuns' handwritings. Her spelling is typical of other nuns of her day. Her style is laborious, with enormously long sen-tences. She does not aim at charming. The fact remains that Jac-queline was illiterate, she never really had any proper education. She always speaks of the world as a horrible place, and that so soon after the Renaissance and in an age when many women knew several languages and played musical instruments. In reality, she did not know the world at all. She knew no history, no geography, she had read no literature or poetry, she thought music was evil,

probably because she had not listened to good music in her parents'
house. She said that she loved beautiful things. It is very hard to
imagine how she acquired that love, for her parents could not have
had very many beautiful objects in their house.

To walk in the Paris streets of the day was an education in itself.
There were some horrible things to see and hear. The Arnaulds
were quite near the Place de Grève, where criminals were tortured and executed. (A criminal awaiting execution on the scaffold
at the foot of the gallows impressed himself on Jacqueline's childish imagination: she recalled him many years later when she saw
herself as a criminal before the Eternal Judge.) When the Arnauld
girls went for walks with Madame Pichotel, their strict governess,
it was not far to the pont Notre Dame, and from there they could
see Notre Dame and the thin spire of the Sainte Chapelle. The map
of the times gives some delightful street names—rues des Singes,
Poirier, Brisemiche, Trousse Vache, Foureur, des Lavandières,
Pain Mollet, Place aux Chats. In her day the rue Renard was named
rue du Régnard-qui-Prêche,[1] and there was still swinging in the
breeze the old street ensign of a fishing fox. The district was
crowded with smart new houses, for in 1550 the old hovels had
been demolished to make place for spacious grand houses for
State Counsellors and Parliamentary Presidents. At the end of the
fourteenth century, the street had rather an ill reputation because
of its brothels, but at the beginning of the fifteenth century the
courtesans were turned out to the Cours Robert, despite all the
protests of the rapacious landowners who argued that they should
live near the church in order to save their souls!

It is delightful to think that Madame de Sévigné was to come
often to that house to see Arnauld's grandson, the Marquis de
Pomponne. A precious sketch of Trémolet's in 1880 shows us this
ancient rue Renard—depressing, dark, with tall houses and narrow
pavement, old paving blocks, and with milestones against the
houses. The Arnaulds' house had very high storeys with high windows. Inside was a spacious staircase with an ancient handrail. The
great entrance was quite imposing, and it opened onto a courtyard,
beyond which was the house. The garden overlooked the rue

[1] Not *Pêche.*

Renard. Afterwards, when it was no longer in private ownership, the house became the office for stage coaches going to Germany and Eastern France. In 1763 it became the public baths. Quite near lived the Queen's rich obstetrician, Michel Marescot, in a great house surrounded by a garden. From the engravings of the time it is easy to reconstruct a middle-class interior under Henri IV. There were heavy fringed curtains hanging from the windows, fringed cloths flung across the tables, immense pieces of carved oak furniture, leather-covered chairs (no armchairs, of course); on the walls, old tapestry and books in dark calf bindings. In the hearth in winter, great log fires, and of course everywhere rush lights and candles. The middle-class interior gave one the impression of a house for men, adapted for their needs and pleasures and above all, their work. No birds, pet cats or dogs. No flowers. Jacqueline did not love flowers—a bad sign.

At meal times, Jacqueline was used to hearing her father discuss his speeches against the Jesuits, who had been under suspicion of trying to murder the King. As a result of these eloquent tirades, the Jesuits were dismissed from France. This has been called "the original sin of the Arnaulds."

In looking upon an abbey as a source of income, unmindful of whether a child had a vocation or not, Antoine Arnauld was no better and no worse than most fathers of families in his time. What had made this sort of thing possible was the Concordat signed near the beginning of the century—1516 to be precise—between Pope Leo X and the French King Francis I. Its general effect was that the King could nominate bishops for every see in France as it fell vacant, and abbots and abbesses to all the great monasteries. It was an extraordinary concession to the royal power, and the Pope made it only for fear that if he did not sign, Francis would take the whole of France out of the Church (as Henry VIII was to take England so soon after). There were certain limitations to the King's power of nomination—bishops must be at least twenty-seven, abbots at least twenty-three—but these did not apply to relations of the King or members of the high nobility; and where they did apply, there was always the possibility of falsification. Jacqueline Arnauld was far below the minimum age requirement, and her father simply added the necessary years in the official documents.

It is difficult to form any idea of the plunder of abbeys which en-
sued from the Pope's permission to the King of France. The court
would give abbeys to children still in their cradle, to men at arms,
to courtiers. Henri IV placed on the episcopal throne at Metz his
illegitimate child, Henri de Verneuil, at the age of eleven.

The statistics of religious houses are amazing. There were more
than a million and a half monks and nuns in religious houses. They
formed a tenth part of the Catholic population and owned a third
of the kingdom. Though paying no tax on their revenues, they
raised tithes from the poorer classes which amounted to something from thirty to one hundred million livres per year. The great
princes of the Church were like the *grands seigneurs,* with their
own households and courts, their luxuries, hunts, pleasures, mistresses and—authentic proof of nobility—their debts. It was very
unusual for priests to know how to read or write, or to be seen in
church, and as M. Jaccard has said: "This prodigious ignorance
was accompanied by a life so scandalous that all persons of quality
would think themselves degraded in their nobility to enter the
ecclesiastical state if they were not at the same time provided with
some rich living. Avarice, drunkenness and impurity had now become second nature to most of them. They were heard swearing
even at the altar. Some had several children, others would auction
church possessions and sell holy things to the highest bidder. Many
installed themselves in cures which they then handed on, for very
small fees, to ignorant, vicious and sometimes excommunicated
and interdicted vicars."

Bourdaloue, the great Jesuit preacher of the seventeenth century, storms against forced vocations. He rails against the avarice,
ambition, sensuality and blindness of the parents: ". . . throwing
yourselves into a pit and leading your children to it.

"If there are two or three daughters in a family to provide for,
you will not fail to destine one of them to the cloister, even from
her cradle. But if she is not called thereto? No matter! Monsieur
and Madame desire it to be so. But why? There is no other eligible
match for her. But if she does not possess the grace of vocation?
Measures will be taken thereto. But if her inclination does not lie

that way at all? She will do all that she can when she will be there.
But if she is not disposed that way? She *will* be, when she has been
clothed with a habit! This is how one drags to the foot of the altar
the poor victim, bound hand and foot, who dares not complain for
fear of exposing the passion of the father and the obstinacy of the
mother. Execrable sacrifice which has no other motive than avarice,
than a sordid interest, reprehensible scheming, criminal and damn-
able ambition. Be assured that nothing less is involved than your
damnation and the damnation of your children."

Before he left the hospitable roof of the Arnaulds with his Master
General to return to Cîteaux, Dom Bernard asked Madame
Pichotel to show him round the Church of St. Merri. They were
accompanied by the delightful Catherine.

Catherine had been telling Dom Bernard about a country an-
chorite under the rule of Charles V, who was called Guillemette de
la Rochelle, when Jacqueline, who had been trailing along in the
distance, not listening very much, exclaimed with a scoffing, un-
childlike laugh: "Do you really believe that story of Guillemette,
the anchoress of Saint Merri? That little legend is just as true as the
one about blessed Agatha's bones, which are also supposed to be
here."

"Hold your tongue," said Madame Pichotel, "or I will smack
you."

The child skulked away, looking very sullen. Dom Bernard
whispered to her: "You mustn't speak like this if you are going to
become an abbess."

She drew him aside, and looking up at him most earnestly, she
said, "I don't want to become an abbess. I don't want to leave my
little brother. What would he do without me? I know he would
die."

It was extremely hot on this last evening. Dom Bernard had left
the Master General talking to Monsieur Marion. They were drawing up a petition to the Pope in which Jacqueline would be made
much older than she was. Feeling rather disgusted, Dom Bernard
eventually slipped off to Notre Dame to say his Office, for he knew

he would have no further opportunity that evening. A cool breeze was blowing up the river, dispelling the noisome odours from the narrow, overcrowded streets near St. Merri. Walking along the Quai de la Grève, he crossed the first part of the pont au Change, and was just going towards the place Dauphine, to get a little air, when he again met Madame Pichotel, accompanied by all the Arnauld girls. He greeted them gravely and was about to leave them for Notre Dame when Jacqueline begged him to come with them to that green part on the Ile de la Cité looking towards the west. On it nowadays is the equestrian statue of Henri IV. It was a cool, delicious place from which to get a good view of the river.

The four girls, Catherine, Jacqueline, Agnès and Anne-Eugénie, all clustered on a fallen tree trunk while he rested on a tree stump opposite them. They were seated in order of age, and he could not help smiling at their youthfulness and high spirits. Madame Pichotel asked him to tell the children a story. He thought for a moment and then began.

"I think as there are the two of you here who are entering the great Order of Saint Benedict, I ought to tell you briefly a little about Saint Bernard, who entered the reformed branch of the Cistercians."

"Oh, please do!" they all exclaimed. "We love a good story."

"And this is a true one," added Agnès.

Jacqueline exclaimed flippantly, "Well, as long as I'm not expected to imitate Saint Bernard, I'll listen."

"Don't be impertinent," exclaimed Madame Pichotel, annoyed at the behaviour of her charge.

Dom Bernard smiled. "I don't think there is any fear of Mademoiselle Jacqueline imitating our incomparable saint. Why, he ruined his digestion very early in his monastic life by his austerity, and a little hole had to be provided for him in the choir into which to be sick."

They all laughed.

"And then, although he was the Abbot and Master General of that immense Order and could have had a cell suited to his rank and requirements, at Clairvaux, he chose an obscure little nook at the top of the staircase, very dark and small and inconvenient

—which, by the way, I have seen with my own eyes. In there he loved to meditate about the child Jesus, for you know the Holy Child had appeared to him in a dream when he was a little boy."

At these words Jacqueline's eyes became expressive. "I must tell my brother Simon about that," she murmured.

The monk was glad to have found a way to her heart.

Catherine asked: "But what did Saint Bernard look like as a young man, before he left the world?"

"Oh," he replied, "he was tall, slender, with fair hair and blue eyes. He was extremely handsome. He was the flower of knightly chivalry. A great career at arms was open to him, but no, he left the family castle at Fontaine-lès-Dijon, he renounced the world with all its beauties to hide in the marshlands of Cîteaux. There the reformed Rule of Saint Stephen Harding was so strict that, for some time, no new men had asked to be admitted to the novitiate. Saint Bernard brought with him almost all his brothers, brothers-in-law, uncles and friends. Thirty in all."

"Ah," exclaimed Jacqueline, looking threateningly at Agnès, "I will drag you in with me."

"Oh no," answered Agnès, "I am going to be Abbess of Saint Cyr when I am twenty. I don't want to go to Port-Royal, thank you. Anyway I don't want to obey *you*."

"Now, girls," exclaimed Madame Pichotel, crossly, "don't quarrel, and please listen."

And so the monk continued to tell them something of that golden legend of the early twelfth century, that life of mingled contemplation and action. This saint who loved to be alone in his cell was obliged to preach Crusades, pursue heretics like Abelard, found abbeys, and ceaselessly to ride up and down the roads of Christendom. And yet he was so withdrawn within himself that he never noticed the wondrous landscapes unfurled before him. He was completely absorbed in his love, his immense love for the Beloved within his soul. And it is in this spirit that he wrote his mystical treatise on the Canticle of Canticles.

At this point, the monk saw that the attention of the younger ones was straying. Alone the eldest girl, Catherine, listened intently, her eyes aflame. She turned to Jacqueline impulsively.

"If only *you* could remain in the world, and I could take your place at Port-Royal, how happy I should be."

"Ah," said Jacqueline, "no hope. And I who want to marry and have children, I who want to be with my little Simon always, *I* have to leave all that just to say those musty, dreary Offices, to get up at dead of night, to fast—oh, dear, how dreadful."

"Now then, that will do, else I will tell your parents," threatened the ever prompt Madame Pichotel.

Just then a street girl with bare feet came past, carrying a hod of brilliant red cherries.

"*Cerises de Montmorency,*" she called out.

For a moment St. Bernard was forgotten. Jacqueline groped in her reticule to find a groat or two.

"I must buy some cherries for Simon. He likes them so much."

After this little interlude, they were all attention again.

"But," asked Madame Pichotel, "why did Saint Bernard choose an Order that was so strict? He was very pure and did not have to expiate any sins."

"Ah," replied Dom Bernard, "he said: 'My soul is so sick that it needs a stronger medicinal potion than that found at Cluny.' You see," he explained, "Cluny was the mother house of the unreformed Benedictine Order—an immense place with a great abbey church much larger than Saint Peter's at Rome."

Catherine asked, "Were they very good?"

"Oh yes," he replied, "excellent monks, but they liked to concentrate more on the liturgy. Also they loved the beauties of architecture. Saint Bernard liked simplicity in his abbeys—white, square, plain buildings which did not distract the mind from contemplative prayer. And then, he loved the poor so much, that he could not endure to pray in rich churches while there were beggars in need."

Again Jacqueline's interest was reawakened. She loved the needy and would spend her all to give to a beggar.

"Will I be able to distribute alms at Port-Royal, and can I have a dispensary for the sick?" she asked.

"I don't know," he replied hastily. "You see, those nuns are very poor."

And then he realized that he should not have let that remark slip out. The Master General had begged him to be discreet and not put the child off.

"Oh, but Mamma will help us. She's always going to visit the parish poor in their hovels."

Glancing at Jacqueline's complacent expression, Dom Bernard began to wonder if he would not be wasting his time to speak so eloquently about this magnificent Order. She looked so critical, so pleased with herself. He tried not to feel superior, but when he thought of the Order in which so many great men, lords of far-flung acres and professors in universities who had left all, indeed who had sacrificed a great deal more than a fisherman's nets to follow Christ, he did not feel like speaking to smug little Jacqueline Arnauld. How could a child who only opened her mouth to say something ironical appreciate the effect of perpetual silence on a monastic soul? However, he had seen her face become more expressive when he spoke of the Child Jesus, or of the poor.

He pondered on how great intellects in the Order had acquired a remarkable appreciation of nature. The monk did not believe there was much love of nature in any of those Arnaulds. They seemed totally devoid of any aesthetic sense. They would not know how to appreciate the male and almost virile poetry and sobriety of Cistercian architecture, the severity of white stone devoid of all ornament. Behind the windows, bare of stained glass, he remembered seeing the white light of dawn unfold among the moving branches. Then the daylight after Matins revealed his brethren in their white cowls. The naves were bathed in serenity. As he had watched a handful of them grow in perfection—and indeed there were still a few of that kind left at Cîteaux even in these degenerate times—he noticed that each monk participated in the ceremonies with a preoccupation for beauty which moderated his gestures and the sound of his voice when he intoned the night Office.

"What makes you love Saint Bernard so much?" asked Madame Pichotel.

"Chiefly his understanding of the Passion of Our Lord. Do you know, Saint Bernard defined a monk as a donkey who carries the Lord? And then, he was so tenderhearted! Yes, it is indeed, or it should be, an austere Order, but still it is a very tender one—and mostly because of him. Great austerity and great tenderness often go together."

Jacqueline rose and smoothed her dress, just like a grown-up person.

"Thank you very much for your talk," she said primly, "but I think we'd better go home before these cherries start wilting."

The lights were twinkling at all the windows of the Louvre, across on the other bank.

"I wonder if King Henri is eating his dinner now," said Catherine.

"I hope he comes to see me when I become an abbess," said Jacqueline.

"And me too," added Agnès.

Jacqueline said: "His Majesty told Papa that the Order is an ornament to the kingdom of France."

She turned to Dom Bernard and added politely: "When you come to see me at Port-Royal, I will entertain you. I suppose you will accompany your Master General when he comes to see me there as Abbess? I wish all monks were like you. The ones I have met so far, I haven't liked much."

Fortunately Madame Pichotel was not attending, or she might have reproved the child again. And then, to his amazement and horror, Jacqueline said to him quite calmly:

"I think your Master General is very ill-born and has little merit."[1]

"Do you usually criticize your elders like that?" said the monk frigidly. "A child so young should not express her opinions so freely."

"Huh," she laughed. "They throw me out of home without asking if I want to go or not. And they think I'm old enough to be an abbess."

They walked home in silence.

At supper, a nursemaid suddenly came in carrying young Simon, who was howling: "Jackee, I want Jackee!"

The nursemaid said to Madame Arnauld, "He won't eat his meal unless Mademoiselle Jacqueline gives it to him."

---

[1] Quoted from her autobiography.

"All right, then. Put him at the table near the window, apart from the others."

Dom Bernard could not help overhearing the conversation between brother and sister. Indeed the love talk was delightful.

"Now look, I've got a little silver bowl of cherries with the stones taken out. You will have one or two if you're very good and drink up your broth."

"But I don't like it, Jackee, I don't like it."

"Do you know, this afternoon on the river, I saw a fly catcher feeding her baby. She made him open his beak just like this—now you open your beak—and in popped the worm." She tipped a spoonful into his mouth before he could utter a word. And she went on charming and delighting him by her stories until his porringer was empty. She never knew she had been overheard.

After a while, she crushed him in her arms. And then, quite audibly for all to hear, she looked out of the window and said, "When I become an abbess, I will be damned by man and God."

2. *AT THE ABBEY OF MAUBUISSON*

Monsieur Arnauld cheated about Jacqueline's age. But even so, permission from Rome was slow to come. So, after a family confabulation, it was thought more prudent for her to enter the novitiate. She was clothed with the white Cistercian habit in September 1599 at St. Antoine des Champs. The Master General, Abbot of Cîteaux, whom she disliked so much, performed the ceremony.

Jacqueline temporarily forgot her despair because all the festivities were for her. She won all hearts by her gay and charming ways, and she was ever after much beloved by the nuns of that house. At the end of October, she left them and went to the Abbey of St. Cyr[1] near Versailles with her sister Agnès. She was there for the winter of 1599 and spring of 1600. Nothing much is known of what she did there or of what happened to her.

The two little future abbesses had quarrels. Agnès said to her one day, that she did not wish to have her in her house and she could very easily drive her out of it when it pleased her. Perhaps Agnès remembered the times when Jacqueline had driven her out of her grandfather's apartment. However, in spite of these quarrels, this short time together helped them to form an intimate friendship which lasted all their lives.

Alas, in February 1600 a terrible tragedy happened to Jacqueline. Her beloved little brother, Simon, died. It is easy to imagine her feelings at that time. Perhaps she felt that life would never smile on her again, and she became dully resigned to her

---

[1] Madame de Maintenon destroyed it to build her girls' school.

fate. After all, she was not wanted at home: she had only been tolerated because of Simon. Now there was nothing left to keep her at home. Nothing.

On June the 24th, the feast of St. John the Baptist, Agnès was clothed as a Benedictine nun, and the day afterwards, June 25th, Jacqueline went to the Abbey of Maubuisson.

The history of this thirteenth-century abbey founded by the mother of St. Louis is so entrancingly interesting that it is impossible not to pause for a moment, and reveal some of its history.

The Abbess, Angélique d'Estrées, had been appointed to Maubuisson at the instigation of her sister, Gabrielle d'Estrées, Henri Quatre's mistress, the one who induced him to become a Catholic.

The Abbess of Maubuisson had twelve bastards by twelve different fathers. She treated each one according to the father's rank. She kept four of her daughters at Maubuisson to serve her as ladies-in-waiting. She was completely without shame, and she used to boast about these twelve illegitimate children. So immodest was she, that even her own sister, the King's courtesan, used to reproach her about her ways. On the day that she was enthroned as Abbess, an old gentleman of the court, observing her behaviour, predicted that she would die in squalor and shame.

A curse seemed to lie on the place and its surroundings. Indeed, its name, Maubuisson—Evil Shrub—had something sinister about it, like Malmaison. It was so called because many cutthroats hid in the quarries and behind the copses near the path of the pilgrims going to St. James of Compostella. In vain had Blanche de Castille tried to get her foundation called The Abbey of Notre-Dame-La-Royale: the old name, Maubuisson, seemed to stick.

The Abbey was now no more than an elegant club for the surplus daughters of the nobility. As they had no ideals, but just a love of comfort, they certainly had little to complain of when Angélique d'Estrées assumed her charge in May 1579.

She never appeared for night Office. Oh, no, the chapel was far too cold. She left a few ardent nuns to freeze there.

In the morning when she woke, she passed long hours at her toilet, trying various headdresses and wimples in fine gauze and having her hair curled. Most of the nuns kept their hair uncut. (Indeed there was one with beautiful long golden tresses which she combed every day. Great was her surprise when, many years afterwards, a nun trained by Jacqueline slipped into her cell one morning with a pair of scissors and snipped them off before she could say a word.)

Dame d'Estrées would have her midday meal served in her Abbess's lodging. It was always abundant and delicious. Her arms were engraved on her pewter and silver and emblazoned over the entrance to the Abbey. In the early afternoon she would walk to the church, holding her crosier. Perhaps some subservient cleric would carry her train. (This habit was observed by Jacqueline and it horrified her.) Dame d'Estrées would say Vespers with the nuns, giving up chant for the sake of speed. And then they would all foregather: in the summer in the garden, in the winter by the blazing hearth in her own room, which had been transformed into a drawing-room filled with beautiful *objets d'art*. And there they talked with country gentlemen of the neighbourhood, who often came to spend the afternoon at the Abbey. They composed rhymes, they had refreshments, they exchanged billets-doux. On Sundays, their Vespers gabbled off, the Abbess and her daughters, leaning on the arms of the most brilliant cavaliers, would walk through the delightful park till they reached the pond under the great elms. In the evening Dame d'Estrées would summon violins, and they danced till night fell. This example was a temptation to the monks of the Monastery of St. Martin of Pontoise. They hastened to join their religious sisters at Maubuisson in their jigs.

What must Jacqueline have thought of the cavaliers, young men with pointed beards and puffed breeches, half strangled in their goffered ruffs? What would her mother have thought? But there is no record of her appearing at Maubuisson. Without consulting the mother, Monsieur Arnauld and Monsieur Marion between them had decided to send Jacqueline to Maubuisson as a subtle compliment to the King. They knew the Abbey was very richly endowed, and there Jacqueline would not feel the intolerable burden of monastic life too early. It is recorded that Madame Arnauld did not dare to voice her disapproval.

Angélique d'Estrées had a very lively character and was extremely pretty. She did not like constraint of any kind, either for herself or others. Passionately devoted to pleasure, she was addicted to gambling, to gourmet's delights, to visiting other abbeys and country houses. The conversation of men was her ordinary pastime. She had a special Abbess's lodging built for her, and this soon became the meeting place of high society of the dissolute kind.

Many noblemen began to think she was a great asset to the neighborhood. She certainly enlivened the dullness of country life. They enjoyed seeing how well-dressed she was and admiring her new furniture and trinkets, which were indeed those of a woman of the world rather than of a nun. One thing one can say about her: she was never a hypocrite, and, as long as her nuns did not complain, she gave them a good time.

Some of the holders of the greatest names of France have been abbesses at Maubuisson: Isabeau de Montmorency, Charlotte de Bourbon-Soissons, Catherine d'Orléans Longueville, Princesse Palatine de Bavière. If the abbess were highborn and powerful, the confessors and chaplains were obsequious. The monks of Cîteaux, usually so impudent, so bold, seemed to be suitably cowed and impressed by Dame d'Estrées. Jacqueline records that "when the abbesses are proud and haughty, their confessors become their valets. And that is so true that I saw one who would busy himself planting out the Abbess's flower beds and putting her arms and monograms on them." If the confessors were to her liking, the Abbess rewarded them in her own way. The confessors' table was a very good table d'hôte, and even the nephews of these clerics found good cheer there, and sometimes their University expenses were paid from the Abbey funds.

Years later, Jacqueline wrote: "The grandeur of the house I had just left has taught me so well that these unhappy thorns choked the word of God, and I had seen such . . . detestable monuments of vice . . . that I loved poverty the more tenderly."

But on that June afternoon, when the Master General and her father were taking her in a coach to Maubuisson, she was far from considering the dangers of monastic riches. She was remembering her clothing of the previous autumn. Apparently she had inspired compassion in the congregation, for she heard them whispering among themselves, "The poor child doesn't know what she's doing," and she had said to herself, "Am I then so mad? They say I don't know what I'm doing. I know very well."

Afterwards she was to have strange scruples about her vocation, and said, "I looked upon this vow not as a gift which I had made to God, of which I was not yet capable because of my age, but as an extreme honour which He had conferred upon me, to take me so soon for His daughter and His bride, and I would deserve to be reprobate in His eyes if I refused to remain in so glorious a state."

"Yes," the Master General was saying to Monsieur Arnauld in the coach, "quite a commendable extent, this place: a hundred acres of woods, fields, vines, orchards, kitchen gardens; not to mention pools and a rivulet under the building of the latrines which, further on, turns the mill-wheel. However, the nuns are always complaining that they have to go quite far to fetch their water."

They soon passed Pontoise, the little mediaeval city which St. Louis had loved so much because it reminded him of the holy city Jerusalem, set on a hill. Indeed, it was whilst staying at his royal manor of Maubuisson that he had a vision in his sleep in which God called him to his last crusade.

"Hurry," called the Master General to the coachmen, "hurry through this part." Then, turning to Monsieur Arnauld: "I don't like it much. I've heard of too many rich merchants and poor jugglers who've had their throats cut on this very spot. Yes, the bravest are seized with a strange premonition of disaster when passing this way."

To the right they saw the lowlands near Aulnay—wide meadows dotted with elms, and a narrow stony path which wound its way through copses of brushwood. That was the danger spot. Very soon, however, they were within sight of a great shady park full of magnificent trees.

"Ah, we'll soon be there. Do you see the vineyards? The Abbey still has the right to recruit the labours of the local peasants at the time of the grape harvest."

"What is the wine like?" asked Monsieur Arnauld.

"Well, the Emperor Julian, when he lived in Paris, used to say that the grape of Lutetia was exquisite, and I daresay it has not changed much since his day. Anyway, you will see for yourself, as I am sure we will be offered a drink and a collation. Yes, wine from grapes harvested on the estate. In the old days the serfs had to come—a hundred of them—three times a day, directly they heard the Abbey bell ring. They had to obey, and indeed up to this very day, the Abbess has the right of administering justice on her domain."

Soon they arrived at the enclosure, and the footman knocked on the great entrance door surmounted by its stone cross. The Abbey porter bowed low on seeing that he was admitting a distinguished prelate. The Master General pointed out to Monsieur Arnauld the large shady alley with other roads forking out of it. The road to the left led to the farm and the kitchen garden and the others, to the right, to the Abbey itself, which was built in the sober style of pure primitive Gothic. The buildings and dependencies clustered around the church. Far out, beyond the Abbey, was a great pool, the monastic fish preserve, a windmill on its banks. The gardens were very beautiful, in the French style, conventional, with straight alleys and neat flower beds. Henri IV loved melons, and the Abbess had taken care that his cravings should be provided for in a large melon bed.

A whole crowd of servants flocked to greet the guests. The Master General and Monsieur Arnauld went to pay their respects to the Abbess, while Jacqueline, still feeling a little clumsy in her elegant white habit, was seized upon by four merry-looking young girls in secular clothes who were the Abbess's so-called maids-in-waiting—really, her bastards. They pestered her with many questions. How many brothers and sisters had she got? Was she going to like Port-Royal? Did she enjoy monastic life? Did she play hopscotch? Did she know any Latin? Could she dance? Could she play any musical instruments? Had she been made to do any lessons at home? Jacqueline, with her usual aplomb and self-mastery, replied with a dignity and truthfulness far above her years:

"I do not wish to become an abbess. I have no vocation. I do so because I am frightened of my parents."

They all roared with laughter, as if it were a great joke.

"What a pity," they said, "you're not like Blanche the daughter of Saint Louis, whom he destined for Maubuisson. Before she was twelve years of age, she took precautions against being cloistered without her permission. She obtained a letter from the Pope allowing her to leave the cloister and return to the world when she was older, if she wanted to."

"I wish I could write to the Pope," sighed Jacqueline.

"What would you do if you weren't a nun? I suppose your father, with such a large family, hasn't got enough money to give you a marriage dowry. I suppose you'd like to marry?"

"I don't know," said Jacqueline, truthfully again. "The lot of a wife seems hard, but it is good, I think, to have children. I have loved to watch my younger brothers and sisters in their cradles. What a pity one can't have children without a husband."

"Oh, but you can," declared Emerance, the most brazen of the young hussies.

Just then a kindly-looking nun called Dame Le Vasseur appeared and took Jacqueline to have a look round the Abbey.

"It just so happens that I have a free afternoon, my dear child. And, anyway, our good Mother Abbess, who thinks of everything, has put you under my care. You must come to me for everything you need. I will look after you. I don't think you will find the yoke of religion too hard to bear here. Now let us go and look at the church, as it is only right and proper that we should visit the Lord's house first."

"What abbess is that in the middle of the choir?"

"Oh, that's not an abbess, my dear child. That's our foundress, Queen Blanche de Castille, the mother of Saint Louis. Isn't she beautiful, surrounded by her angels? When she knew she was going to die, she asked to be clothed in our Cistercian habit, and she lay on ashes, just as they all did then. They brought her to Maubuisson wearing her crown and her royal robes, though she

wore a Cistercian habit underneath. And here is her effigy. Saint
Louis loved her more than anybody else in the world, perhaps even
more than his wife, and that, alas, caused trouble between them."

Jacqueline's attention began to wander. She looked at another
recumbent effigy of an abbess whose epitaph had been half
scratched out.

"Why has this been scratched out?"

"Ah," laughed the nun, this is the tomb of the Abbess Guillau-
mette II, who left so few regrets that her nuns erased the conventional praises from her monument. They ought to have done the
same to Antoinette de Dindeville, who used to send insubordinate
nuns to the dungeons. And she was abbess here for forty-three
years."

Just at that moment a troup of little children from the neighbouring hamlet trotted in, carrying provisions of apples, nuts and
sweetmeats.

"What are they going to do ?" asked Jacqueline.

"Oh, those naughty children, how tiresome they are. However,
you might as well come and watch them putting sweetmeats into
the mouths of the hermits—you see those wooden hermits around
Our Lady's statue?

"Now I will show you the library. Do you like reading? You
know how to read?"

"Not quite," answered Jacqueline.

"Very well, then, I will have to teach you. What is the use of an
abbess who can't read?"

It is a good thing that the revolutionaries have left us a long inventory of the library, so we know what books were there in Jacqueline's day. It is surprising that she made so little use of them.
There were the works of St. Augustine, Lives of the Saints, *The
Golden Legend*, the Homilies of St. Gregory and St. Bernard, the
Summa Theologica of St. Thomas Aquinas, the Life of St. Eliza-
beth of Hungary (which indeed Jacqueline does seem to have read,
as she quotes from it). And apart from all these holy tomes, there
were works of literature, history, science, law and medicine, a book
against the Jesuits which must have slipped in afterwards, pamphlets on the celebrities of the time, and even a whole pile of im-

moral novels. The nun tiptoed up when she saw them, and tried
to push them further out of reach.

The child was no fool and she noticed that those novels were
much more worn than the other books. In fact some of them were
beginning to fall to pieces. The brevity and discretion with which
Jacqueline speaks of this abbey in her later years are most indica-
tive. Her silence is more eloquent than words.

"And now, dear child, we will go up and see the sacristy, where
we keep our greatest treasures—the ones we have to hide under-
ground when there is a war or a foreign invasion. Our Abbess has
kindly allowed me to take the keys, so that you can have a look
round."

(When a new abbess comes into possession of her abbey, a very
complete inventory is made up in the presence of a Superior of the
Order and signed by the whole community. It is in case an abbess
suddenly takes it into her head to leave with some of the abbey's
treasures!)

"Look at this lovely crosier in crystal and silver with a design
in thistles, with fleur-de-lys on its shaft.[1] It's for solemn ceremonial occasions. There are plainer ones for everyday."

And then she displayed before Jacqueline's amazed eyes all the
glorious treasures of this ancient and rich abbey—arras of silk and
gold, Persian gold cloths with angels embroidered on them, lovely
gold dalmatics and chasubles, tunics in blue cloth sprinkled with
gold fleur-de-lys and lined with violet silk. A tunic embroidered
with beasts and golden birds lined with vermilion. A satin chasuble
embroidered with leopards and flying serpents in Cyprus gold
lined with green.

Just then a bell rang for the midday meal.

"I suppose today you will eat in the refectory, because I know
our Abbess is entertaining the Master General and your father in
her private apartment. I think afterwards, as you are going to be
an abbess, you will probably eat with her and some of her ladies-
in-waiting. I hope you have enjoyed this little trip through our
glorious house. You can imagine how very proud we are of it."

[1] This exquisite crosier is now in the Lambinet Museum of Versailles.

This meal,[1] at which the Abbess did not preside, was an eye-opener for Jacqueline. There was a nun called Dame de Ricarville who came in singing a fashionable ditty, and when she was reproved by the presiding Prioress she said:

"Madame, I have nothing to occupy me, and it is far preferable to sing than to think evil thoughts."

Old Dame du Meng had just come from the chapel, where she had been admiring the stained-glass window of St. George riding full tilt against the Evil One and piercing him with his lance. She was in high spirits and she nudged Dame Candide with her elbow and said quite audibly, "You see, my good friend, I'll tell you something. Saint George is a capital fellow." And before the lay sisters could prevent her, she had whisked a pig's head off a platter destined for an ancient and wealthy nun who had all her meals sent up to her private apartments. She held it up to her face as if it were a mask and went from one nun to the other, sometimes giving it a surreptitious bite as if it were an apple, and with so insolent an air of buffoonery that the Prioress, who was usually somewhat indifferent, looked at her severely, and eventually told her to stop.

In the early days, the Pope had ordered that this great abbey should house a hundred and forty nuns. There were certainly very, very few here that day, for many of the rich ones ate apart. The poor nuns down in the refectory had humble fare. When they were on the point of starvation, they had to flatter the rich ones to get a morsel of food. (In fact, the day was not far off when a starving lay sister would go out of the enclosure to the town and beg a peasant for a piece of bread, in reward for which she gave him one of the Abbey treasures, a picture of St. Mary of Egypt painted by an abbess.)

Jacqueline, much to her confusion, was given a special dessert for herself alone. She could not help observing that some of the shabbier nuns glanced at her greedily and enviously; they looked quite displeased, and there were murmurs and whisperings.

The nun reading aloud at the lectern was barely audible. Hardly anybody kept the monastic silence. Some of them began to leave

[1] These incidents are transposed from a later date, though the nuns in question were there during Jacqueline's childhood.

before grace at the end of the meal, and there were audible hic-
cups and burps. Never had she seen such bad behaviour.

Jacqueline spent much of her time at Maubuisson playing in
the Abbess's apartment with one or other of her girls. Later she
said of all this: "Often during that time I was with the Abbess,
where one learnt more than anywhere else."

How significant that is! How alarming to think of the sights and
sounds that assailed the child's chastity. Her guardian angel must
have been looking after her, for the only effect on her in later life
was a very strong reaction, particularly against the bad monks who
haunted the Abbey. If they were not openly immoral, they were
jovial, hearty eaters, loving good company and laughter; some
had wide red faces; they were great hunters and knew all about
hounds and horses. These braggadocios, who never knew their
breviaries, made a lot of noise in their hunting boots and spurs,
cracking their whips.

But Jacqueline did not go to the Abbess's apartment that day.
Dame Le Vasseur had to break the news to her that her father had
left without saying good-bye to her. The child was a little taken
aback, then heavily resigned, as ever.

Her four little friends came to fetch her to play in the park,
which was deserted, for the Abbess had driven off with her cronies
to the high road to Pontoise, where they were to meet the good
monks of St. Martin for a dance.

That night, Jacqueline slept in a room near the Abbess. It was
very difficult to get to sleep. There were heavy footsteps up and
down the turret stairs all night, and singing and other strange
noises. She was terribly homesick and kept thinking of Simon's
tomb in the church near home. Towards dawn she heard the bell
sound for Matins, but no footsteps trailing towards the chapel.

She rose and looked out of her window. To her amazement, she
saw a man on horseback going through the park, and the door of
the enclosure being opened for him by the night porter. "How
very strange," she thought, and went back to bed.

3. MADAME DE PORT-ROYAL PLANS TO ELOPE, BUT IS CONVERTED BY AN EVIL MONK

JACQUELINE'S ELECTION as coadjutrix at Port-Royal was not confirmed at Rome, much to the annoyance of the Arnauld menfolk.

"I wonder if an enemy has been telling tales," said Monsieur Marion.

The Arnaulds had plenty of enemies, and were indeed to have more in a few years' time when Henri Quatre brought back the Jesuits, who had been dismissed from his kingdom greatly owing to the speeches of Antoine Arnauld. And it was also most annoying that the old Abbess of Port-Royal, Dame Boulehart, was growing more suspicious and querulous in her old age. She still completely refused to have Jacqueline, if only for a few days, and in fact she was beginning to question the legality of having the girl at all, even after her own death.

Madame Arnauld, who was expecting still another child, having just had one, said nothing. As usual, like patient Griselda, before her husband's forcefulness, she took refuge in silence.

"I have it!" exclaimed Monsieur Marion. "I've got it! This will do the trick. Let us suggest to Dame Angélique d'Estrées when she takes Jacqueline for a visit to her old abbey near Amiens, that she have her confirmed and then change her name from Jacqueline to Angélique. Not only will it be flattering to her, and to the King, but if we again asked the Pope for a Bull confirming Jacqueline's election we could do it under this new name, and His Holiness won't suspect it's the same nun. You see what I mean?" he said, smiling into his whiskers.

45

And so it came to pass that Jacqueline had her name changed to Angélique de Sainte-Madeleine. The most famous of seventeenth-century abbesses took the name of a sister of the King's mistress.

Angélique's time at Maubuisson dragged on. She was kind to the lay sisters (who always remembered it), she made some friends among the old nuns, who loved little attentions from the young. She saw a few plays acted by the monks and the younger nuns. She got some amusement, but not a great deal, from playing with the ladies-in-waiting of the Abbess. Here the difference of class was too greatly accentuated. They were all little aristocrats and therefore free and easy in their speech, whereas Angélique had been brought up in conventional middle-class tradition, and was often easily shocked. She did no lessons, she learnt hardly anything. She did not read much, she did not even learn to recite her Office. In fact she had a great antipathy to Offices and holy books. She spent her time playing hide-and-seek, bowls and skittles and nursing her dolls. She certainly was not trained to wash or to keep herself neat and clean, as she would have done, had she lived at home under the vigilant eye of a good mother or a strict governess.

But this one thing she did above all, and this helped to ruin any childlikeness in her nature: secretly and quietly, without a word, she judged everyone she saw. The idle, hunting, flattering monks, the greedy monks, the monks with nephews who wanted meals, the frightened monks who picked bouquets for the Abbess. But above all she judged the Abbess herself. She lived so near her that she could almost read her thoughts. Straight through the high pomp and circumstance of a great Cistercian abbess of noble birth, she saw the moral squalor within, and she sensed the impending doom.

One early dawn in July 1602, Monsieur Arnauld appeared at Maubuisson and asked to see Angélique at once. He refused to call on the Abbess, who anyway was fast asleep, or the Prioress or the novice-mistress, and he refused to explain to the very curious lay sister.

He looked edgy and irritable, so the lay sister hurried off to find Angélique.

"And he says you're to bring your cloak. No, you're not to pack anything. You're going away, I think, but you haven't time to pack."

"I wonder what has happened—I wonder if anybody is ill at home."

She greeted him respectfully. He gave her no explanations but insisted on her getting into his coach at once and driving off to St. Cyr. On the way, he told her he did not wish any rumours to get about, but the Abbess of Port-Royal was on her deathbed. Any moment now, Angélique would be elected in her stead.

"But I haven't said good-bye to all my old friends at Maubuisson, *Monsieur mon père*," said the child, not yet eleven.

"Never mind, never mind. You'll go back quite soon after you've been installed as Abbess, and say good-bye to them all properly, and thank them for having been so kind to you. You look very strong, I declare. They seem to have fed you well."

"Oh yes, *Monsieur mon père*, the food was excellent and the wine too."

"Which reminds me," he said, looking at the baskets at his feet, "I brought a few hampers of victuals for your nuns at Port-Royal. When you are Abbess, they'll be only too grateful for a little food. They're quite poor, you know. You mustn't expect the riches and luxury you've had at Maubuisson."

"No, *Monsieur mon père*, I expect nothing."

"Your mamma has been most thoughtful: she's had a few spiced hams prepared and some stuffed capons, and there are good white loaves and flasks of Burgundy. Also a cheese or two. I hope the old Abbess will not tarry—er—in her passing. The cheese won't last in this heat."

Angélique and the cheese did not have to wait long. The news was brought to her at St. Cyr the next afternoon that Dame Boule-hart had gone to her reward. "And high time too," muttered the impatient Monsieur Arnauld, who thought he was losing clients by hanging about in this way at St. Cyr, looking after his daughter's affairs.

The nuns at St. Cyr explained to Angélique exactly what she must do when she took possession of her abbey. She was to go to the great entrance door, put her hand on it, and from that moment onwards it belonged to her. Writers have exclaimed on this decisive gesture when that little hand pushed the door open, to doom, disaster and immortality! They slipped an amethyst ring on her finger and made her practise holding it out to be kissed. "Your father had it taken off Dame Boulehart's hand, immediately after her death."

"But it's too big for me," exclaimed Angélique, "it will fall off!" As she drove towards the Abbey, she was chilled by vague apprehensions.

"There it is," said her father at last, as he pointed to the right. "Now you can see the church spire above the woods."

"The valley is like a cup," she murmured, "with mist steaming out. I wonder what it is like in winter? How closed-in I will feel there! Oh, I don't know that I am going to like it."

Her father exclaimed impatiently, "You're not asked whether you're going to like it or not, my girl. You've just got to behave yourself and not pass on your unfavourable impressions to me or your mamma. Is that understood? Your mamma is coming in two or three days to have a look round the place with me. I think there will be many matters to set in order. She hasn't quite recovered from her last confinement: indeed, she is expecting another child at the end of the year. So you see, she's been too busy to visit Port-Royal."

And he thought: "I'm afraid she will get an unpleasant surprise when she does see it."

Suddenly bells began to ring through the valley. Peasants and harvesters appeared from all sides, doffing their caps and bowing very low to these newcomers who were supposed to be so rich and openhanded. A few of them, however, were a little apprehensive, especially the dishonest steward and his underlings who had kept the nuns so short of food and wood all these years: these men had brought nearly all the fruit to market and kept the money, and they had collected the wood for themselves so that the nuns shivered in winter and had to go out gathering meagre firewood. Ah well, the Abbess was very young, not yet eleven, they whispered, although her family tried to make out that she was a good deal older. Perhaps she could be as easily hoodwinked as the infirm old Abbess. On the other hand, rumours were spreading that Madame Arnauld would be on the spot quite soon, and that she was a highhanded and masterful housewife of great experience. Another person who was feeling worried was the young Prioress, Dame Elisabeth de Mauternes, who was living an immoral life.

As for the other eleven young nuns, they had lived there since early childhood. They had been crushed by the Abbess and had all lost their health. Many of them were crippled with rheumatism and their limbs were swollen. Being so hungry, they were delighted at the prospect of a feast very soon.

Soon Angélique and her father descried the surgery, washhouse, pharmacy, joinery, forge, a tannery for making the nuns' shoes, a mill for grinding flour, some beehives, the kitchen gardens and a poultry yard with a few mouldy-looking hens scratching in the dust. But everything was in disrepair and the mud walls of the enclosure were crumbling.

Angélique's heart began to beat. As they turned into the lane on the right which led to the Abbey, they passed the little leafy wood called La Solitude,[1] in the centre of which stood a great cross. A rustic bridge spanned a rivulet.

As they neared the church, Angélique saw an abundant and limpid spring. (It was afterwards to be called "Angélique's fountain.") Around it were some dwarf trees which formed a charming little walk. Monsieur Arnauld was not impressed with the solemnity and gravity of the moment. All that occupied him was his relief that Pope Clement VIII, after all the prevarication, had at last given permission for Angélique's installation at the beginning of this year. The old Abbess had died just at the right time.

It was a hot, drowsy afternoon and again, as on the Master General's visit, the sun was a ball of red fire. There was a mist everywhere and a dank, oppressive atmosphere. Frogs croaked in the marshes. A great black crow winged his way slowly towards a hill called Les Mollerets. This hill was to play a great part in Angé-

---

[1] Much later, this was divided into a number of avenues all called by different names, the Strawberry Avenue, the Elm Avenue, the Espalier, the Gooseberry Lane.

lique's inner life; she remembered it on her deathbed, for she had
seen it in the only dream of mystical import she ever had.

But on that day, as she looked up at it, she felt it was going to
fall on her. She felt closed-in, as if all the hills were slowly drawing
near and looming over her: soon she would be a speck crushed
under their weight.

A lot of blandly obsequious farm servants came crowding
around the coach. The bells continued to ring. Her father lifted
her down. A kindly, sensible, neatly dressed nun called Dame
Dupont came towards Angélique. She knelt and kissed her amethyst ring, much to Angélique's surprise. If Dame Dupont thought
she looked very young and small, she never let her thoughts appear
on her face. She was all politeness and subservience. Angélique began to feel as if she were indeed a personage. Dame Dupont
handed a beautiful jewelled crosier to her and said, "I'm sure you
know what to do, Mother Abbess."

"Yes, thank you. I have learnt the rite," she replied calmly.

She walked slowly and with great dignity towards the entrance
and made that historic gesture of touching the door. Then she
came into the beautiful little thirteenth-century church. The
corpse of Dame Boulehart had been taken away for the occasion.
(In due time, the Arnaulds were to pay for her tomb.)

The eleven nuns were waiting in their choir stalls. They all
looked up curiously as their young Abbess touched the lectern
and put her hand on the high altar in token that now the Abbey
was hers. But she was beset by the niggling little fear that canoni-
cally it was not her abbey at all, that all her vows were null and
void, for her father had deceived Rome about her age. If she
wanted to run away, she could do so without offending God and
His Church. Yet she knew inwardly that she could never escape,
that she *would* never escape. She knew that if she went into the
world, her nature was such that she would lose her soul. True, she
hated the life of being a nun, but she would hide her distaste from
them all. She would be proud and secretive. If her temperament
gave trouble, she would smother it. She would never let them see
her moods of ill humour: she would keep these all to herself, for
she had been bred to heroism. She was damned, anyway. Oh

Simon! She had once whispered of her damnation into his baby ear.

A few days afterwards, Madame Arnauld appeared on the scene. She had never seen Port-Royal before and she was appalled. Angélique hoped her mother would be impressed by seeing her in her proud situation as an abbess, but not at all. Madame Arnauld remained the *terre-à-terre*, domineering mamma throughout. She certainly did not kiss her daughter's ring or ask her permission for anything. Boldly she sailed into the enclosure with her husband, and between them they began to set everything to rights. Angélique seethed. They dismissed the Prioress, for they had heard about her flagrant immorality. Through the influence of the Master General, she was sent off to another abbey.

Monsieur Arnauld engaged in and won a lawsuit to reclaim some land which had been filched from the Abbey. Then they dismissed the thieving servants: the ones who had not been caught out yet began to leave of their own accord because they were frightened of those powerful, all-seeing Arnaulds. In the meantime, the poor little nuns had their feast and Angélique was made much of.

After her parents had left, everyone breathed more freely. Dame Dupont, now Prioress, continued to be very subservient and correct to Mère Angélique, and always asked her permission for everything and insisted that everybody else should do the same. And this helped to keep some kind of outward order. Angélique went to as few Offices as decently possible, and certainly avoided four o'clock Matins if she could. She never liked reading holy books either, though indeed there were very few in the library.

Soon Madame Arnauld returned to arrange all the festivities, and the banquet celebrating Angélique's installation as Abbess. To this were invited Dame d'Estrées and two other abbesses of ill repute. The ceremony was to coincide with Angélique's first Communion. It is significant and pathetic that Madame Arnauld, busied as she was in bustling, worldly preparations (about which she never consulted her daughter), should still have found no time to instruct Angélique about this great sacrament, which usually makes a profound impression on young minds. So complete was

Angélique's ignorance that a cobbler on the estate took pity on her and lent her a little manual of preparation.

She had her own apartments now, and Soeur Marie Baron, a lay sister, was her servant, and a very nice girl too. Angélique used to give her some of her white bread, because she knew the girl preferred it to coarse brown. They all spent their evenings out of doors. Indeed, the Master General on one of his visitations had advised the Abbess to take the nuns walking in the grounds after Vespers, and in summer they would play all kinds of childish pranks and get extremely hot. At night, Mère Angélique would interrupt her games and say: "Let us all go and bid good night to Dame Dupont."

They would all follow her, and then return afterwards to their frolics.

One fine day, when Mère Angélique was looking over her estate, she went to the coach-house and found a dilapidated old coach which had belonged to the last Abbess. It was probably no better than a glorified sixteenth-century cart with leathern curtains and wooden seats. Haughtily she called a carpenter, and without allowing any argument she said it must be repaired, oiled and put in order by the next day. At first, the man looked impudent, but after one glance at the Abbess's set chin and sarcastic eyebrows, he touched his cap and went away to collect the necessary material and recruit local labour.

The day after that, Angélique gathered three or four of her younger friends and said: "Let us go and pay a few calls in the neighbourhood."

They were all delighted and clapped their hands.

"One moment please, dear Mother Abbess. May I go and fetch my cloak, and may I go and tidy my hair a little?"

"And I fetch my gloves and fan?"

"And I my mask?"

They were incurably vain, all of them, and Angélique rather despised them for that, as she always affirmed that no nun could ever look as smart as the lowest of maidservants.

"Will you come with us, Dame Morel?" she said, as she waited for them.

"No, thank you very much, Mother Abbess. I must water my garden. We need rain. I've got such lovely lilies for the altar," she added quickly, seeing Angélique's face.

Angélique shrugged her shoulders. She knew all about that garden of Dame Morel's. It was her idol. Very often she missed Office in order to water it. She had a private key, for it was locked up in a little arbour, and Heaven help any nun or servant who tried to peep over and see what was happening inside. She was a keen gardener, and indeed she had the green thumb. But she had far too great a sense of private property. She knew nothing of the spirit of religious poverty.

"I think we will go and call on my sister Agnès at Saint Cyr, and bring her back here for one or two days. Perhaps my sister Anne-Eugénie is with her. I think it would do them good."

The Abbess returned from St. Cyr with her sisters. Agnès was just as elegant as ever, with a little gold crucifix at the end of her rosary, her spotless pleated surplice over her white habit, and her thin veil beautifully arranged. She held a breviary in her gloved hands.

"What do you want that for?" snorted Angélique, giving her sister's veil a vicious tweak.

"Why, aren't we going to say Vespers?"

"*You* can if you like," she said, "I don't."

"But how dreadful! And you're the Abbess."

"Oh, don't start lecturing me. I hate it all."

"Hush," said Agnès, glancing at the other nuns.

"Oh, they know, they know. They understand."

The young nuns all burst out laughing.

"Well," said Soeur Marguerite de Ste. Blandine, "that doesn't prevent our Mother Abbess from being very, very kind to us, and looking after us like a true mother."

"Oh," said Angélique, "I will reform in my old age and then I'll go to some very severe Order like the Feuillantines of Toulouse, and become a lay sister to atone for the evil behaviour of my youth."

"No!" cried Agnès, "what should I do without you? Don't think of such a thing, please."

"All right, then," said Angélique, "but you're not to scold me about Offices and suchlike. Let's make a bargain: if you don't talk to me about saying my Office, I won't say anything more about entering some other Order. Is that understood?"

"Very well, very well." Agnès still had her old self-sufficient, smug look. "Odd, this mixture of pious fanaticism and conceit," thought Angélique to herself. "She is a peculiar nun, I must say. However, no queerer than myself. I suppose she has what you call a vocation. I wonder whether Anne-Eugénie has one."

Anne-Eugénie was the beauty of the family, and probably destined to marry, unless smallpox marked her for life. Oh, these abbeys, crowded with girls whose complexions were like orange peel! Angélique had not forgotten the snubs she had received from Agnès at St. Cyr, and she was very anxious to impress her with her abbey.

Angélique was just going to show her sister the sacristy, when she noticed that the lay sister who was putting away the altar linen was gossiping with a visiting Cistercian monk.

"Ah, ha," she said to herself, "I will teach them a lesson." And she locked them in. Then she turned to Agnès and said:

"She'll learn that she's not to behave in this manner. That's the sort of thing that goes on at Maubuisson."

"How severe you are," said Agnès, admiring and a little surprised.

After a while, the trapped lay sister began to knock violently on the door. Angélique opened, and trounced her like a grown-up abbess, not like a child under eleven.

"And never let this happen again. Bread and water for your supper tonight. Do you understand?"

"Yes, Mother Abbess," she said in floods of tears, for she was very hungry.

Angélique could look quite alarming when she was angry, even Agnès became a little afraid of her. She had a presence like her father's, and she certainly had a voice which nothing could quell, neither high position nor religious decorum. It was the loud voice of a Paris guard. One day, St. François de Sales was to quieten it a little, but to the end of her life it was beyond her control.

In 1605, unwittingly, Angélique received an immoral monk from St. Antoine. One afternoon when he was feeling very bored, he suggested that they both go and call on a neighbouring abbess, Mère Odette. A few days afterwards he came again, and this time he brought two lay gentlemen into the enclosure against Angélique's wishes. She said:

"*Mon Père,* you make the rules. When you are here, I must keep them."

The priest replied: "Madame, but there is no danger," and so Angélique was not cross. And from then onwards, more and more men called on the Abbess. And thus she began to waste a lot of time in worldly and perhaps not quite innocent chatter. If Agnès reproved her, she would again threaten to repent in old age and become a lay sister in some stricter Order.

Angélique herself confessed that at that time she was extremely "alert and frolicsome beyond anything that one could conceive."

In February, 1605, when Angélique was nearly fourteen, her old grandfather, Monsieur Marion, died. At Carnival time Catherine, her beautiful eldest sister who was so like her in appearance, and who had hesitated a long time to accept the attentions of a Monsieur Le Maître, because she thought she had a religious vocation, was at length persuaded to marry him. He had just lost his first wife.

Angélique, not knowing as yet how evil this Isaac Le Maître was to prove, boiled with envy and anger. She had hidden a looking glass in her coffer. She would look at her reflection very often now as she grew into girlhood. She saw that her eyes were magnificent, that her hair, which she allowed to peep through her veil, was dark and beautiful. Why hadn't she been allowed to marry, and why hadn't Catherine come here in her place? Why had her parents arranged everything against their desires? Yet she did not want to have an affair like the Prioress, Elisabeth de Mauternes. She wanted to marry and have children. As she actually said of herself:

"A family which was very chaste and strongly opposed to all impurity had made me always inaccessible to every temptation of this kind, although my lack of piety and the relaxation of my giddy and libertine life in such extreme youth and the discourses I was accustomed to hear from our Bernardine monks, may well have made those think the contrary who did not know the depths of my heart."

And among those who "did not know the depths" of Angélique's heart was her own mamma, who now took to coming to Port-Royal unexpectedly and unannounced and at the most unusual hours of day or night, hoping to catch her daughter at fault. She would just break into the enclosure and be there before Angélique could listen for her coach wheels along the lane. Angélique ground her teeth and determined to put a stop to all this as soon as she was a little older.

Indeed her mother, seeing her so lively and so alert, was horribly afraid because of the men who came in and out of the Abbey so freely. Angélique said: "And she thought that I had listened to discourses of love and that I had linked myself in some kind of understanding with some man."

In fact, Madame Arnauld prided herself on knowing her daughter. She said to Catherine: "I know my daughter very well."

And Angélique afterwards explained: "My mother did not put great trust in me."

One fine autumn morning, when both Monsieur and Madame Arnauld had come to spend the day in the Abbey, they suddenly heard the hunting horn in the distant woods, and hounds were baying. It was not the confessor, for he was asleep in the garden, after eating honey.

"Well, I do believe it is his Majesty!" exclaimed Monsieur Arnauld. "Quick," he said to Angélique, "put on your pattens. You're so short, he mustn't see you at the height you are or he'll get suspicious. Quick, do as I say."

Angélique hated this deceit, but there was no arguing with her father.

Very soon this romantic and dearly loved French king was near the walls of the enclosure. He doffed his great plumed hat and cried out:

"The King kisses the hands of Madame the Abbess."

A servant of Monsieur Arnauld rushed up and said: "Monsieur

Arnauld is in the enclosure, and I am sure that the Abbess would receive you with great pleasure."

"Indeed, indeed, I would like it."

He recalled that the child had been at Maubuisson where his beloved mistress was buried, and her child too, who had brought her to this end. He had a sardonic, shrewd and not unkindly smile, and a fascinating swagger about him which explained the extraordinary hold he had on the fair sex and on his army. He was a king so excellent and so capable in every respect save his private life, that the French have forgiven him his immorality, as they have never forgiven other kings who behaved like him. He had brought prosperity to a country wrecked by the wars of religion and the wars of the Ligue. His desire that every Frenchman should have a hen for his Sunday meal had now become proverbial—"*La poule au pot.*" He had forced the French to found industries such as silk spinning and Gobelins tapestry, even against their will, and so had been the founder of national prosperity. He knew his minister, Sully, could not endure those Arnaulds, but he found good uses for them, for in their day, they had served him well when it was not sure that he would ever be King. He never forgot that kind of thing, and he was glad to be able to do good Monsieur Arnauld a service in placing his girl at Port-Royal.

He dismounted in the courtyard, threw his reins to his squire, and with a great clatter of spurs came into the guest parlour, which in those days had no iron grille or curtain.

There was the little Abbess, looking surprisingly tall, and yet her face was very young. Why, she was only in her early teens. He bowed low and said: "Madame, I didn't know you were so tall."

The squire sniggered in the background and Monsieur Arnauld looked round angrily. The King turned to Monsieur Arnauld and said: "I wouldn't have called unless I'd known that you were here, Monsieur Arnauld."

Angélique then said: "Sire, I hope that you will honour us with your presence at a meal."

"Delighted, Madame, delighted. Supposing I come tomorrow?"

It can be imagined what a to-do there was in that abbey, preparing the King's repast, and how the Arnaulds rushed about trying to get good fare. But, alas, on the morrow, the King merely passed by on his horse and excused himself. He could not come, the hunt was too far away. Secretly, he didn't like the place. He felt dragged down and depressed in it. He failed to see how the Arnaulds could have relegated their daughter there. Poor child, how she must miss the gaieties and pleasure of Maubuisson. Well, well, that wasn't his affair.

In 1607 Madame Arnauld had her fifteenth and sixteenth children, twins who did not survive the birth. She was very unwell after that; consequently she could not come and pry on her daughter for some time. So Angélique continued enjoying herself. When she did come, Angélique, seeing her look so exhausted, was in a mood to listen to her reproaches. In floods of tears, her mother appealed to her not to receive the men who called at the Abbey, nor to allow monks to bring other men in their train, nor to call on the frivolous, overdressed abbesses of the neighbourhood.

"But, Mamma," cried Angélique, almost in tears herself, "what will I do all day? I'll die of boredom. You don't know how heavily time hangs here."

"But you're the Abbess, you must set a good example. You've got your Office to say."

"Office? I hate it. Besides, I don't understand Latin."

"You can get some books. Aren't there any books in the library?"

"Oh, yes, *Plutarch's Lives*."

"Well, that should suit you. You must try and be more heroic, my child. Look what I have to bear."

"Yes, but it was your vocation to be married and have children. It is not my vocation to be here."

"Hold your tongue," said Madame Arnauld sharply; "hold your tongue or I will smack you."

Angélique became icy.

"May I remind you that if you hit a nun you will be excommunicated."

"Hold your tongue anyway," said Madame Arnauld. "And listen, you really must promise me"—she started weeping again—"to mend your ways. It's causing such talk in the neighbourhood. Besides, it's

unsafe. Just think: supposing you had an affair. It would bring disgrace on us all."

"Yes, that's all you mind about," thought Angélique to herself.
"Outward disgrace. The offence to God wouldn't enter your head
at all."

"Oh promise me, Angélique. I'm only thinking of your own happiness. Please promise me."

And Angélique, who in those early days could always be appealed to through her heart, promised. Her mother left for Paris
very soon afterwards.

Her young friends surrounded her. "May we all go out in the
coach now?" they asked.

"No, I'm afraid we can't. You see, I promised my mamma—" But
to hide her tears, she walked slowly away from them towards the
meadow.

They looked at each other in dismay. If only the elder Arnaulds
would keep away from the Abbey, how happy they would all be
with their Abbess. They all had attacks of hero worship for her. She
had a kind of magnetic attraction for those surrounding her. To
begin with, she had a great deal of charm, and her nuns said she
was charitable and discerning, and thus they were the more ready
to do her will. And those poor hungry little nuns were grateful for
the food.

On that hot afternoon, alone in the meadow, Angélique began
to realize that her life was really an intolerable burden. As one of
her best modern biographers has said about her, "her ardent temperament showed clearly in her face and in her handwriting." And
temperament was beginning to burgeon.

Now on the brink of womanhood, she realized what she had lost.
She sat down under the hedge smothered in cow-parsley and
watched the mare who had just had a foal. Oh, what a delicious
creature, on its long unsteady legs. And there he was, nuzzling
his way for his meal and the mare looking round at him and licking
his rump.

All of a sudden her thoughts turned to Simon, her little brother
whom she lost, oh so long ago now. She would never have a child
like him. How cruel everything was! And here was her mother

overburdened by her many children, and Catherine expecting a child. . . .

Everything was alive. The wild vetch was wreathing the hedge-rows, the air was heavily scented with pollen, the birds had built their nests and were teaching their young to fly, a hen was cluck-ing over her brood of chicks, the pools were swarming with deli-cate jumping frogs, and here was the mare playing with her foal. Everything was alive, abundant, creative, and she alone was doomed to sterility.

From the bag at her side she took a book she had found in the library. Ah yes, *Plutarch's Lives*. She sat down and thought of Rome and the Vestal Virgins. Poor girls, like herself vowed to perpetual virginity, and if they lost their maidenhood, they were burnt alive. In ancient Rome, they lived in regal pomp and mag-nificence, attended by slaves. They always had the best places at the games, they wore beautiful clothes, but they were doomed, like herself, to barren days. She must be heroic like them. She must not let the others have an inkling of what she was enduring.

Woefully she opened the book, and read the immortal love story of Antony and Cleopatra. She could picture it all—this siren of ancient Egypt, sailing along the river Cydnus in her magnificent purple-sailed galley. . . .

Angélique flung the book from her, frightening some magpies on the hedge. How much longer!

Inexorably it would go on, year after year after year. She re-called her great-uncle Arnauld, who had lived to be a hundred, who had died the year she was born. Alas, she came from a long-lived race. How terrible if she too lived to be a hundred! Eighty-five or so more years doomed to nothingness—no children, no grandchildren, afflicted with all the ills of the inhabitants of this horrible Port-Royal des Champs, her limbs swelling with rheuma-tism. Already she was beginning to find kneeling difficult. What would it be like in a few years? She would become an idiot like poor Soeur Anne-Marie Johannet. Or she would become like cranky old Dame Morel who dreamed of nothing else but man-uring, hoeing and watering. And then the thought occurred to her again: her vows in the eyes of Rome were illegal; she could escape.

She could go in the coach to La Rochelle to one of her Protestant uncles and aunt. So often they had come to call on her here and tell her that her vows were null and void, that she was not bound to stay. "Don't tell your parents, of course, that I said so." And then her aunt, la Présidente de Druy, very richly dressed, had said to her:

"Why don't you come to La Rochelle for a time? You need not ask your parents' permission, of course. We would find you a husband."

She wanted a husband only that she might have children. She wanted children more than anything else in the world. And then she cried to God: "Oh God, lock me up in a prison where I will see neither heaven nor earth, and where I will be freed from all the temptations and all the occasions in which I offend Thee."[1]

And after her prayer, her thoughts strayed to the world which she loved and which she was supposed to have forsworn. She loved so much in the world, beautiful things, rich houses and lovely clothes in the latest mode. Clothes such as her other sisters wore, and beautifully appointed houses and linen and feastings and lavish hospitality for one's friends. And hunting—to think that she would never hunt! She recalled the squire who had attended the King when he called on her. Tall and slender, and a gay look about him, and he wore such well-cut trunk hose.

On that unnaturally hot summer afternoon, she was devoured by passion and desire, and she had no friend in whom she could confide.

For several days after, she began secretly to plan to elope. Two or three times she went to the coach-house and inspected the coach very carefully; then she would go to the stables and look at the horses. One day, she asked the coachman:

"I wonder how far they could go?"

He looked at her sharply, and did not reply.

She left him before his suspicions were aroused.

Yes, she would collect the funds, she knew where Dame Dupont had hidden them. She would pack her casket with lay clothes and hide it in the coach the night before. She would pretend to call

[1] Her actual words.

on some other abbess—and then, what would she do? Dismiss the
coachman? Bribe another servant? Somehow or other she would
eventually get to La Rochelle.

Her mother was expecting another child, so she couldn't pos-
sibly pursue her. As for her father, she would choose a time when
she knew he was engaged in an important lawsuit. How she would
enjoy discarding her Abbess's white habit! How wonderful to
throw it into a ditch. She was not at all afraid of being attacked on
the way. She decided to take a knife with her in order to defend
herself against robbers.

"Perhaps, after all, I ought to keep my habit. That is a form of
protection, for anyone who attacks a nun in her habit will be tortured and executed at once."

Had Angélique read the Dialogues of Cassian, she would have
known that she was being afflicted by a terrible ill, *accidie*, "the
noontide devil"—that vague boredom which assails contemplatives
all over the world, but which did not attack the jovial religious who
lived according to Rabelais.

She was on the brink of eloping when, on the Feast of St. James
in July, she fell very gravely ill: marsh fever and threatened menin-
gitis. Her parents were informed. Much alarmed, they came at
once to fetch her away in a litter to their Paris house.

Her mother seemed completely transformed from the cold and
rather irritable person she had known. She put Angélique in her
own room and tended her throughout the night. If ever Angélique
wanted anything, her mother came, even before the nurse. She
received every care, every attention. Physicians surrounded her.
Throughout that long time, no priest came near her, and nobody
spoke to her of religion. Her married sister, Catherine, who had
gone away to take the waters, hurried back to look after Angélique.
She was excellent at tending the sick, for she had a heart of gold.

Angélique could not help observing in her lucid moments that
matrimony had certainly not improved Catherine's looks or spirits.
When she thought no one was observing her, the young woman
looked very downcast. Perhaps, after all, married women were not
always very happy, thought Angélique.

Her Protestant aunts and uncles called in their rich silks and brocades. When she was a little improved they crowded round her bedside and chatted about the latest court news, that entertaining court of Henri IV. Angélique would lie there and feel she had been excluded for ever from an impossible paradise.

. In September, when she had improved still more, she was brought to Andilly, near Montmorency, the beautiful estate and parkland which her mother had inherited from her father. Angélique had not been there before, but she was delighted with such a lovely rural place and thought that "one always ought to live in such surroundings." And yet the prospect of returning to Port-Royal loomed ahead. She had been defeated by the unexpected kindness of her parents. She knew she could no longer pursue her plan for eloping. In Paris, she had asked the maid to sew whale-bones into her bodice, so that it would show up her figure, lest she compare too ill with her delightfully dressed and tightly laced aunts.

Hardly anything escaped Madame Arnauld's eye. When she saw her daughter trying to make the best of herself, she said to her husband: "I think Angélique is in love. Who knows? There are so many men going in and out of Port-Royal. She has been too free, visiting all those disreputable abbesses. Now, you stay with her here for the day and I will drive to Port-Royal and look through her papers."

"But you can't do that! She's an abbess. You're only a secular. That would be most improper," he said, "and she would be extremely angry."

"I suppose she would be angry, but she is still my child and I must protect her from herself. Don't breathe a word before I go. Afterwards, I will get hold of a Dame de Jumeauville from Saint Cyr to supervise her. But we needn't put it like that. I will just say she is there to look after her health. She will be very useful. She could report to us if she noticed anything peculiar."

"I don't know," replied Monsieur Arnauld. "Angélique is no fool, and she would very much resent this. Just look—she *is* an abbess. She has power over her nuns. And here you are putting her in subjection to a nurse."

"Never mind," said his wife, quite determined for once in a while.

When she had left, Monsieur Arnauld broke the news to his daughter. Angélique smouldered with resentment. She said to her father: "She will find nothing there."

Then he gave her an illegibly written piece of paper, and, without allowing her time or opportunity to read it, said firmly: "Sign your name here."

She was still so much in awe of him—indeed, so frightened of him—that she signed the document which committed her irrevocably, against her will, to being a nun. This paper can be seen in the Bibliothèque Nationale. It is not in the usual high, clear, proud handwritting of Monsieur Arnauld, but made purposely illegible. But she still had time to glance at one or two of the words which revealed her fate to her. And she was boiling over with suppressed fury.

At length, in December, she returned to Port-Royal. She was sixteen, still unwell and weak. Her young nuns were all delighted to see her, for they were greatly devoted to her.

To her dismay she found Dame de Jumeauville installed. A petty female persecution began. The spy insisted that Angélique should go to bed to sleep, not read, so she gave orders to her servant, Marie Baron, that the Abbess was not to be allowed any wax candles. But so supreme was Angélique in the lay sister's esteem, that she managed to smuggle in some tallow candles for her. And so, after a while, Dame de Jumeauville insisted on sleeping in Angélique's cell. She wrote reports to the anxious Arnaulds and very soon she had a few things to tell them.

Angélique, it appeared, would rise in the middle of the night and moan and cry. Yes, she was sure there was something afoot. But she would be on the lookout.

Angélique had brought back her eight-year-old sister, Marie-Claire, who was very fond of her. She had not seen Marie-Claire in childhood, for the child had been born when she was at Maubuisson.

Winter closed in with its fogs and mists. All the nuns fell ill in turn. And then dawned the year 1608, which was to herald a complete change in Angélique's destiny and transform her from a discontented nun into an ardent reformer who fired many with her enthusiasm.

On the Feast of the Purification, at the beginning of February, the chaplain and the menservants took part in the traditional frolics, which were called "the good traditions of the Order"; at Port-Royal, these were taking place for the last time.

Near Lady Day, in one of those lovely March twilights, Angélique was returning from a walk in the woods with her nuns when a lay sister announced that a Père Basile was at the door, asking whether he might preach a sermon to the nuns.

Night was falling fast, and servants were lighting torches. Angélique exclaimed:

"But this is an unusual hour. It is getting dark. No, I think I had better refuse." Then she changed her mind. "Perhaps a sermon would do instead of spiritual reading before Compline. Yes, ring the bell."

She went to her Abbess's stall in the cold chapel. A young white-clad Cistercian monk climbed the little pulpit and started preaching. He chose as his text a sermon by St. Bernard.[1] He spoke of the humiliation of Our Lord when He was born in a manger. He said that in becoming flesh, He had made Himself the fodder of beasts, for all flesh is grass.

Angélique had been brought to a spiritual desert by the sufferings of the last months, so she listened. And then, it seemed as if God were speaking to her. (Many years afterwards, when recalling this eventful evening, her niece said "that hour was like the dawn of a day, which has been crescent in her until it reached the fullness of noontide.")

The humility of Christ's birth in a stable had always meant much

---

[1] "On the day of the nativity, the Word was made flesh and we know that 'all flesh is grass.' Let us become like beasts in the pious sense after the example of him who says 'I am become a beast before Thee, and I am always with Thee.' For beasts of this kind know their 'owner' and their 'master's crib' in which He Himself who is the Bread of angels is offered them for their food as sweetest hay. He is the Living Bread on which man ought to live. But since man is 'compared to senseless beasts and made like to them' the Bread has become Hay, so that even thus he might live thereon."—From St. Bernard's "Sermon for the Octave of the Feast of the Circumcision."

to her. The tender vision of the Christ child was entwined with her longing for children and her love for her brother Simon. Suddenly, that night, she felt full of joy because she was a nun. All her being leapt forward to God. She wrote afterwards:

"I don't know what I would not have done for God, if He had continued giving me the grace He bestowed on me at that moment."

In a flash, the glory of her vocation as a Cistercian contemplative became clear to her. She saw the necessity of obedience and contempt of the flesh; above all, she realized the merit of true poverty: "And God gave me so much affection for these virtues, that I lived only in the hope of finding means of practising them."

She would have torn herself to pieces for the love of God. Dame de Jumeauville, ever on the lookout for signs, noticed her exalted expression, her flaming eye and cheek, her hands tensely clasped, and she thought, "Oh, ho! What is all this?" She, unlike Angélique, must have heard of the evil reputation of Père Basile. He had only preached because he needed alms. He was young and handsome, and endowed with a glib tongue when talking of mystical prayer. But he had led a very immoral life and had done all manner of unseemly things in religious houses, with nuns. He oscillated between repentance and impurity. (Some years later, he apostatized from the Faith altogether.)

Angélique had an inkling that she must not ask his advice, so she took another nun with her when she went to the parlour to thank him for this sermon. She prevented her nuns from seeing him.

There was little sleep for her that night. She felt her religious life had really begun, and now she would serve God wholeheartedly. But she could not go on being an abbess. She knew she had no right to be here. She would go to an Order where she would be far away from her relations. She would become a lay sister and live to expiate her days of frivolity, here and at Maubuisson.

To escape the watchful eye of Dame de Jumeauville, she would go to an attic. For the first time, she began praying: "I prayed to God as much as I could."

Once, some other nun who was sleeping in her room overheard a noise. She peeped through her curtains, and there was Angélique, trickling scalding hot wax down her arms and legs. When later she was upbraided for this, she replied smilingly, "In those early days, everything served."

In the meantime, at Whitsuntide, she asked advice from a Père Bernard. He dissuaded her from leaving her Order.

Unfortunately he spoke of all this to the new Vicar General of Cîteaux, Dom de Morimond, a friend of Monsieur Arnauld. Naturally the Vicar General told Monsieur Arnauld. Husband and wife became greatly alarmed at this new turn of events. What? To leave, after all the trouble they had taken to hoodwink Rome! True, they had not wished their child to be frivolous; but, on the other hand, it did not suit them for her to become an austere nun. They had not perjured their souls for that. And then, they were afraid of losing her, if she injured her health. They had already lost too many children. They clung to those who were left. They ordered her to come and stay again at Andilly, during the grape harvest in September.

Angélique consented to go, so that she could persuade her father to confess his fault and get new dispensations from Rome. She appeared at Andilly looking as haggard as ever. The morning after her first night, the maid who swept her room glanced at her bed and rushed down to Monsieur and Madame Arnauld with a shriek of dismay.

"Madame," she cried, "Monsieur, monsieur, something awful has happened!"

"What—what? Speak, my good girl!"

"Madame Angélique's poor legs are scalded with deep red marks, and her arms too."

"Why, was she not wearing hose?"

"No, she had got no linen hose as usual. She went to bed in her day habit. And I'm afraid the cloth, which wasn't very clean, is crawling with lice."

Madame Arnauld cried out with anger: "Filthy! It will spread to the rest of the household."

Husband and wife rushed upstairs and began upbraiding the young abbess.

"Does devotion consist in filth? Did they never teach you to wash at Maubuisson?"

Her father stormed. He was very highly strung. His voice went up and up and up. Her little sister, Claire, who was lying ill in bed next to her, began to sob. Angélique also started crying.

Monsieur Arnauld, who really had a kind heart, did not know which of his daughters to console first. He cursed the Capuchin monks, who had lately been advising Angélique in place of the Cistercians.

"They're sneaks—they're sanctimonious sneaks. I'll tell the Master General to keep them away from Port-Royal."

"But it is for me, *Monsieur mon père,* to choose what monks will come and speak to my nuns. I am the Abbess."

"Hold your tongue," he said. "I am your father and you owe me obedience."

"Excuse me," she said, "I do not owe you obedience, but my nuns owe *me* obedience. I wish you would not interfere in my private affairs. And Mamma," she added, "you will never come into the enclosure again, as you did before, and pry into my private papers."

At that, Madame Arnauld lost her temper. She opened the windows, ordered the maids to bring hot water, and commanded Angélique to wash.

"The stench in this room is unendurable. We will have lice all over the children's heads. Disgusting! I don't know how you could be so selfish. Do you call that being religious? Faugh!"

Angélique returned to Port-Royal in October 1608, again with her sister Claire. On the Feast of All Saints Père de Vauclair, a young, ardent Cistercian, preached on the text: "Blessed are those who suffer persecution for justice's sake."

Angélique's lay sister, Marie Baron, said to her afterwards: "You could, if you wished, be of that number."

But Angélique snubbed her harshly: "You're very insolent to say that."

M. Joly, in *"Génies sains et malsains,"* says that Angélique was merely an ambitious and imperious woman who wanted to play a role and impose her will on others. He thinks that she loved wielding authority so much that, when she chose her nuns, she always selected them among docile, simple, humble girls. No one with a temper or a personality. He says that when Angélique was very young, she learnt nothing, and when she was prematurely Abbess, she hovered between the reading of mystical books and despising all intellectual pursuits in order to lose herself in dumb contemplation of the eternal, and in this eternal she found the eternal feminine which is called the desire of supremacy and of perfection. Therefore, because she knew her innate pride, she rushed to infinite humility, and in this she did nothing but look at herself all the time. At first she congratulated herself on having done very well, and then she was afraid of having been too proud of her action, and so went into a spiral of looking at herself and filling herself and others with spiritual terror.

In *Enthusiasm*,[1] Mgr. Ronald Knox speaks of this terrible self-consciousness of the early Jansenists, and says there is no doubt that Angélique inspired a great deal of it by her own behaviour and example.

But to hint, like M. Joly, that she was insincere in her desire for perfection is untrue. She was very sincere in those early days. No one can explain the nature of that spiritual experience of hers, on Lady Day of 1608, when she was listening to that unworthy monk, but that strange experience altered her whole life.

These things are very difficult to keep to oneself, especially when one is only a girl of seventeen. She confided first of all in Soeur Marguerite de Ste. Blandine de la Grange, and afterwards in Soeur Goulas, whom ever afterwards she loved most particularly.

To escape the watchful eye of Dame de Jumeauville, Angélique would drag her two friends out into the wintry garden, and together they would talk their hearts out. Angélique, who had listened a great deal more than may be imagined to Dom Bernard's long talk by the banks of the river Seine when she was a child in 1598, began to drag some of his words from the limbo of memory. Now *he* was a true Cistercian, she told the others. He lived according to the spirit of our Father, St. Bernard. She spoke of the way they recited Office at Cîteaux, of poverty, of fasting:

"The original Cistercian Rule excommunicates any nun or monk

[1] Oxford University Press.

who has private possessions, and here we all have our own little collection of clothes and books, rosaries and even jewels. We are allowed to accept anything our parents offer us when they come to see us. How can we be the true nuns of the Christ child shivering in straw, if we behave like this?"

And very soon, because Angélique was a magnetic personality with a tongue as persuasive as her father's, she filled her friends with enthusiasm, although they were both older than she. Soon these two friends won over more disciples. One day Angélique painted texts and hung them on the Abbey walls:

"He who perseveres to the end will be saved."

"Many are called but few chosen."

And in the passage leading to the church, she put: "The Lord is in His temple, let all the earth keep silence."

When Soeur Marie Mulot, who had no vocation, saw these she began to feel most uneasy. What was afoot? Had they taken leave of their senses? Well, if they wanted to be desert hermits, she would not join them. No, she preferred the flesh pots of Egypt.

"Yes, I was thrown here by my parents, against my will. All this psalm-singing doesn't suit me. I take pleasure in little things. I like paying calls on other abbesses. I like walks outside the enclosure, and I enjoy the food, which of late years has not been too bad. But if we're going back to the primitive Rule, I won't stay. I will ask to leave at once."

She began to notice many things of which she did not approve. The Abbess hardly ate anything at meals now, her habit grew more dirty and disreputable, she always came down to Matins at 4 A.M., however cold the weather. She played less, she was often alone in her cell, unless she were having private confabulations with two or three of her friends, who looked like conspirators.

When Angélique spoke to the Prioress of her wish to reform the Order, Dame Dupont, who was so good a manager and full of good sense, replied: "Oh, this is only a passing enthusiasm, *Madame l'Abbesse*. You're temporarily infatuated with some new idea. And in three months it will all have faded away. But if you try to impose your reform on the Abbey, everything will be topsy-turvy, for you will change your mind later. After all, the nuns are perfectly correct, and I know that I, for one, don't need reform."

And indeed this was true. The unenthusiastic ones, the nuns who were most regular in their habits, most assiduous in their keeping of the Rule, would have been horrified had Angélique suggested that they needed reform.

Angélique and her little group were very amiable to the others, in the hopes of winning them over. This was typical of Angélique, who always exerted her charm for a purpose.

Had she been swept through and through by a continuing inward mystical experience leading her to prayer, she might have been able to win her cause more easily than she did. But at that time, the wily Dame de Jumeauville lent her a book on mental prayer which warned her against illusions, and hinted that they were devised by the Evil One. This made her so frightened that for the rest of her life this idea kept her from attempting to prepare for mystical prayer. Indeed she seemed to lack that trust in God's goodness, that self-abandonment to the kindness of God, which is the great necessity for progress in contemplative prayer.

Although on the one hand repelled by the warnings of the book, on the other hand she was spurred on by an extraordinary dream which she had at that time. She saw a church on the mountain called Les Mollerets overlooking Port-Royal. Around it wound a little path of very green grass. All of a sudden, angels of remarkable beauty appeared and opened the mountain to her. They had wings and were clothed in white of marvellous radiance. She said: "I saw within something ineffable which can compare to nothing I know. For I saw no form, but only a beauty which filled me with admiration and strange rapture. I think that it was God, and I said within myself, 'I do not deserve that which I see. I must return and work and fight before I can claim it.' And then I woke up!"

She continued to wilt and feel ill throughout that winter. Then one day in March 1609, the Prioress, Dame Dupont, who was very devoted to her, asked her to come into a cell with some other nun, as she wanted to speak to her: "*Madame l'Abbesse*, I am grieved to see you looking so ill. I would do anything to restore you to your former high spirits."

And then Angélique opened her heart to her and said she wanted, first to reform herself, and then to draw the other nuns into the primitive observance of the Cistercian Rule. She said: "I think the first thing to do is to pool all our belongings and live in common."

Dame Dupont replied: "I think that's a mistake. The nuns here look after their clothes because they belong to them. If they belonged to the community, they would cease to look after them, and then all our things would fritter away."

"Oh, no," replied Angélique. "They would have to look after the communal possessions as if they were their own."

She won the day.

So, on the Feast of St. Benedict, March 21st, very early in the morning, all the nuns met in the Chapter House, each bringing her private possessions in a sheet. Rosaries, underlinen, spare habit, books, jewels, money, and so on. Angélique received the greatest and the smallest offerings with equal delight. She noticed, however, that Soeur Marie Mulot stood away from the rest. Angélique said nothing, but she realized that this nun had kept everything in her cell. As for old Dame Morel, she brought all except the one important thing—the key to her private garden. She had hidden it in her bosom!

When the poor imbecile, deaf and dumb Soeur Anne-Marie Johannet, understood what was afoot by the comings and goings of the nuns, quickly she went up to her cell and came down again with all her possessions for the central pool. From having been the neatest of all nuns, she now became the most neglected-looking. Angélique and her contemporaries considered that this was admirable!

That morning was one of high elation for Angélique, for she felt that they were all returning to the springtime of the Order, to the early days of Cîteaux and Clairvaux, with golden-haired St. Bernard as their tutelary spirit.

Next came the burning question of the habit, which probed deep down into the fallen nature of these young women. There was something extremely becoming about a snowy-white habit of thin serge. One likes to picture white-habited nuns in choir or garden, or chanting in procession to the cloister.

Many years afterwards, Soeur Angélique de St. Jean, Angélique's niece, had a dream about the beauty of the habit. "I thought I was at Port-Royal of Paris in a place where there was a grid window overlooking the lower gallery, and that I saw all our Paris sisters walking there in procession, all holding flowering branches of crimson roses, the most beautiful in the whole world."

They were all aware of the picturesque. And now Angélique planned a straight habit, like a sack, with a black scapular over the white robe. (In 1623 she put the wimple under the scapular.) There was a leather belt under the scapular, and each nun had a rosary of large wooden beads. For the choir, they continued to wear a white cloak, but this time it was unpleated. In 1647 a red cross was affixed to the scapular, so that it became the habit we now see in Philippe de Champaigne's portraits in the Louvre and in the Château of Versailles.

And then Angélique indulged in a personal eccentricity which was really unnecessary, and which caused a lot of criticism afterwards. She made a habit for herself out of little bits of stuff, sometimes as many as thirty or forty patches. She used to say that those odd pieces were the treasures of nuns. All her life, Angélique never wore a habit especially made for her. It was either too tight or too large, too long or too short, and it was never new.

One or two of her nuns asked for exceptions. The others thought they were monsters. Angélique granted their requests, but the others showed more compassion than envy.

Then there was the problem of the material for those new habits. Angélique ordered a rough serge coming from Nogent. Never before had she been able to find a serge coarse enough. It was heavy material, falling into stiff pleats, yellow as wax, and so greasy that it was almost gluey. St. Teresa of Avila had said that the wearing of wool chemises in summer would have been an act of folly. Not so Angélique. She said that the first Cistercians wore wool next to their skins, and that the present linen shifts were scandalous. What about unbleached holland or coarse canvas? "Oh no," she said, "They become quite supple with wear." And so, she devised the reformed chemises, which were of the same cloth as horse blankets, and so heavy that they were quite a weight to carry about. More than anything else, these chemises destroyed the health of her nuns.

Dame Dupont had said: "*Madame l'Abbesse,* don't you know that thick wool brings lice? I really think we ought to have un-bleached holland for our chemises."

Angélique replied, looking rather harsh: "If we wash the wool chemises often, we won't get lice. Anyway, wool next to the skin, especially in hot weather, is more of a mortification. We belong to a penitential Order. I don't think we should ever complain of any-thing, even under pretext of cleanliness. Too great a regard for cleanliness makes us commit many sins against true mortification."

One has a suspicion that Angélique's disregard for cleanliness had something unhealthy about it. A hawk will tug at its perch when deprived of water. Even a little owl will lie down in a dish of water and splash about to get clean. And human beings are so much higher than owls and hawks. There must be some affinity be-tween unresolved sexual repression and bodily uncleanliness.

Angélique now made a pillow for her bed from a coloured patch-work of many stuffs. She made her nuns use other people's bed-clothes, underclothes and possessions, when changing from one cell to another. If the last occupant of a cell had been dirty, this was a sore trial to the newcomer. Angélique renounced her Abbess's apartment and gave it over to the sick. She herself slept in a room which served as passageway. The door would open and shut twenty or thirty times a night. As a result she had terrible mi-graines.

For long she lay on an old mildewy paillasse which was rotting away under a filthy dirty cover. All this smelt so disgusting that it almost made her retch every time she went to bed. And yet she says that all this filled her with secret joy. Here at last was the poverty of the stable of Bethlehem. (Or so she thought: she could not dis-tinguish between poverty and squalor.)

Angélique had Dame de Jumeauville dismissed to St. Cyr so that no more information would reach her parents.

In those early times, she was very kind to the sick nuns and took especial trouble to console them. They were so glad to see her in the infirmary that her very presence made them feel better. She performed many of the menial and distasteful tasks of the infirmarian. When she bled her nuns, they said she did it with a heart which was worth a hundred times more than the action itself.

Once, in the infirmary, she saw a nun shivering with marsh fever, without enough bedclothes. It would have been more simple and more practical if Angélique had gone to fetch another blanket. But instead, she climbed onto the nun's bed and lay on her feet to keep her warm.

The rest of the community was looking for her everywhere. When at last they found her there, she said with her ordinary cheerfulness that she was serving as bed cover to a poor invalid who didn't have enough blankets.

It was eccentric indeed; on the other hand, it revealed a depth of real and almost passionate tenderness. Angélique's own fever had disappeared on that great feast of St. Benedict, when all the nuns had pooled their resources. But soon she fell ill again, for a beam of wood fell on her head, and her terrible migraines increased so much that at sight of her suffering from them, one of her sisters was dissuaded from becoming a nun for a long time. Angélique lay prostrate, unable to speak or move; she was just an abyss of acute anguish.

Her confessor urged her not to go to bed in her day habit when she was ill.

It may be imagined that during this time of reform, the Cistercian monks who had haunted the Abbey mocked the nuns. Angélique felt it was no use looking to her own Order for support.

At length her parents met a remarkable English priest who had fled from Elizabethan England—Père Archange de Pembroke. His French was very anglicized, most amusingly so, but he was full of good English common sense and extremely aristocratic. In his early days, he had known St. François de Sales, whom he had met through Père Ange de Joyeuse, his intimate friend. Somebody has likened him to an amiable mixture of St. Francis of Assisi and St. François de Sales. His style in his letters to Angélique was clumsy, but he was tender and good to her.

When this Englishman saw the pluck of this twenty-year-old abbess trying to reform her abbey, his heart went out to her:

"Courage, courage, my good little abbess. May Jesus Christ protect you as His beautiful dove in His side opened by the lance."

He would try to temper the impetuosity of her ascetic ardours. He reminded her that she had the responsibility of tender children and "little lambkins." If she overstrained them, the whole sheepfold would die in a day.

4. *THE DAY OF THE SPY-HOLE*

PÈRE ARCHANGE came to Port-Royal des Champs for the first time in October 1609, when Angélique had just established the primitive enclosure again at the cost of grave trouble with her parents. In France, the event is known as *la journée du guichet;* in English, it would be "the day of the spy-hole," referring to the little grilled opening in monastic doors which allows a nun to see who is on the other side, without opening the great door.

Without that day, the reform would have been stillborn. From the heroism of that terrible morning the Port-Royal of history was born. All this made so many demands on Angélique that she never fully recovered her health for the rest of her life.

Only in the seventeenth century, when passions were strong, could such a scene have taken place. It will be recalled that the nuns of Port-Royal did not keep strict enclosure. In the guest room there were no iron bars or curtains. All this, of course, was the occasion of much frivolity and licence, and at Maubuisson it had caused grave moral disorders.

At the clothing of a sister, Angélique had ordered that all the festivities were to take place outside the enclosure. One or two of the nuns grumbled, and one of them was heard to say: "H'm, I'm sure our Abbess wouldn't keep her own parents out."

Angélique heard that and thought it over. Yes, her parents must be kept out. They came when they pleased, without asking permission. And her mother, it will be recalled, had gone through all her private things, papers and letters—an unspeakable thing to do. The

77

Arnaulds just arrived, bringing their children, breaking up the tranquillity and peace of the cloister. No nun could keep silence when they were about, especially as Monsieur Arnauld had a booming barrister's voice and his eldest son, Robert, spoke in high-pitched tones.

Before the fatal day, Angélique had written to Catherine, asking her to prepare the way with her parents and to tell them that from now onwards they could not enter the enclosure. When Madame Arnauld heard this, she sniffed and said she knew her daughter quite well, and that she would never do such a thing. There was no use trying to make her angry by repeating such silly nonsense.

Monsieur Arnauld had announced that he and his wife, Robert, Catherine and Anne-Eugénie would all come on the Friday before the Feast of St. Michael, September 25th, 1609. They would leave home early and reach Port-Royal some time during the morning.

Angélique knew that this crisis would be decisive. Ordinarily, she was a good sleeper, but the night before September 25th she did not sleep at all. At about eleven o'clock on the following morning, when the rest of the community was in the refectory, Angélique was praying in the chapel.

She had already taken all necessary precautions. She had told the extern sisters to give up their keys, she had locked every exit in the convent and all the doors both inside and out. She would have liked to lock up the nuns in the refectory, but thought better of it. She had a band of two or three on whom she could depend for support.

At length she heard the rumbling of wheels in the courtyard. It was the coach containing the five Arnaulds. Her father leapt out and knocked on the great entrance door, expecting as usual to be admitted at once by the lay sister. No one appeared. He lost patience and started hammering at the door very hard with his stick.

At length Angélique came and opened the little wicket grating, six inches square, in the door itself. She could just glimpse her father through the iron bars. He looked very angry indeed.

"What is the meaning of this?" he said. "Open at once."

"Didn't you read my letter, *mon Père?*" she asked in a trembling voice.

"What letter?"

Madame Arnauld then interposed. "Oh, my dear, it was just some nonsensical idea of hers that she must keep the enclosure and we her parents were to be excluded. I thought it not worth while mentioning it."

Monsieur Arnauld refused to argue. He struck the door as hard as he could and started shouting in his theatrical voice.

"Open at once. Do you hear me? Open immediately."

In the short interval when he paused for breath, Angélique besought him to go to the parlour next door so that she could speak to him more conveniently and explain everything. He took no notice, and went on behaving in a threatening way. And then Madame Arnauld started to reproach her daughter.

"You ungrateful wretch!" she cried. And then her brother Robert, in his high-pitched voice:

"You monster, you parasite!"

He used the kind of words he had heard his father declaim against the Jesuits. Then he appealed to all the other nuns.

"How could you allow your Abbess to treat a man like my father in this way? How could you permit us Arnaulds to be flouted like this, you who owe us so much?"

No need to say that all this pandemonium could be heard in the refectory, where the frightened little nuns had long ceased eating. They looked at one another, scared out of their wits; some wept, others prayed. A few, alas, took sides for the Arnaulds against their abbess. The strongest of the partisans was old Dame Morel, who had not yet given up the key of her garden. She cried out:

"It is a shame not to open to Monsieur Arnauld."

And then the charwomen of the Abbey, at that moment in the courtyard, also took sides and began murmuring about the ingratitude of *Madame l'Abbesse.*

According to later memoirs, Angélique profited from a pause in this scene to give vent to her own bitter and long-repressed fury against her parents, and exclaimed:

"Indeed, this is very amusing. They made me a nun at the age of

nine, when I didn't wish to be one, and when I was really too young
to want it. And today when I wish to be a nun, they want me to be
damned by breaking my Rule. I will do nothing of the sort. They
did not consult me when they made me a nun, I will not consult
them, to live as a nun and to save my soul."

At length Monsieur Arnauld understood, for the first time in his
life, that he was defeated by a daughter, and that he would not
cross that enclosure. So he bethought himself of a trick—for, it must
be remembered, he could resort to low cunning. He called out:
"You must give me back Agnès and Claire."

He hoped that, when they opened the door to let them out, he
could break in by force. But Angélique was a match for him, for
she foresaw this. With great presence of mind, she went away from
the door and whispered to one of her trustworthy nuns. She gave
her the key to a door in the church through which her two sisters
could leave unobserved by her father. Indeed, when Monsieur
Arnauld turned round and found Agnès and Claire beside him, he
said: "How did you get here?"

And then Robert started complaining to Agnès about Angélique.
She replied with great gravity, looking like a Spanish Infanta: "My
sister, after all, only did what she had to, and obeyed what is pre-
scribed for her by the Council of Trent."

Her brother then turned round to the company and railed mock-
ingly: "Oh! Now at last we're getting there! Here's yet another who
presumes to cite the Councils and Canons!"

During all this horrid scene, Catherine and Anne-Eugénie remained very quiet. They understood what their sister was enduring at that moment. Seeing that he was defeated, Monsieur
Arnauld ordered the coachman to bring back the horses. Angélique, putting her face as close to the iron grating as she could,
cried out:

"Oh, please, please come and see me for a moment in the parlour
next door, *Monsieur mon père.*"

At length he relented, though Madame Arnauld cried: "I swear
I will never come and see you again."

So he went in alone. To his amazement, he found this guest
parlour, which before had been one room, now divided into two

by a spiked black iron grille and a curtain on the other side. He waited impatiently for Angélique to draw the curtain. At last, he saw her more clearly than at the grating, and noticed how very white she was. And she, too, saw him more clearly. He was pale, as if he were suffering from shock. Again he behaved very craftily.

"Ah, my Angélique, and so you've forgotten all the happy days of your childhood, all we have tried to do for you! You have forgotten all the interest I have taken in your affairs, how I have struggled to get the Bulls from Rome. And now you declare that all is over. I will never see you again! This is the last time you and I will meet. I will never hold you in my arms again. But I have one last request to make."

"Yes?" she said in a whisper.

"I want you to look after yourself, my poor child. Don't ruin your health by indiscreet austerities."

He burst into sobs. Never before had she seen his face streaming with tears. This was too much for her. She fell down in a dead faint.

In desperation Monsieur Arnauld seized the grille and tried to break through, but of course it was too solid. Then he called and called for help. The other Arnaulds—save Madame—rushed into the guest room and mingled their cries with his: but it was of no avail. The nuns still supposed that Monsieur Arnauld was trying to gain admittance to their abbey.

At length the Arnaulds shouted so loud that the nuns understood: "Come at once!" they heard. "Your Abbess is at death's door!"

The nuns flew into the guest room and found Angélique on the ground. Vainly they did all they could to restore her.

"Fetch a burnt feather," said one nun.

"Bring cold water," said another.

When, after a long time, she opened her eyes, she turned to her father and said in a whisper: "May I ask you a favour?"

"Yes, anything," he said.

"Don't go away just now. Stay for today, please, stay."

He promised that he would. They took her away to her cell for a while, to restore her, and then they prepared a bed for her in the parlour, near the grille, so that she could talk in peace with her family. And then, all would have been well had not young Père de Vauclair appeared. He was the Cistercian confessor who had supported the reformers in their projects, and in fact had said that it would be a mortal sin for them to break the enclosure. And now he came when the worst of the trouble was over, probably expecting congratulations. But he was greatly disappointed at his reception. All the repressed anger of the Arnaulds came flooding out onto him. In the hue and cry, Monsieur Arnauld noticed how young he was, and made up his mind to tell the Master General to dismiss him—which indeed he did before long.

As it happened, this was a good thing, for later memoirs say: "Mère Angélique found out by experience that the behaviour of Monsieur de Vauclair, for whom she had so much esteem, did not answer in everything to her former excellent opinion, and that, anyway, he was too young."

He is the first of many of these Cistercian confessors to be severely criticized by the reforming abbess. She had quite a lot of trouble in connection with his dismissal, because he had gained an influence over some of the nuns, and they rebelled when they heard they would lose him.

For nearly a year, Madame Arnauld kept her promise of not coming to Port-Royal. Then on August 4th, the Feast of St. Dominic, she heard a Friar in the Dominican Church declare that there was no obligation to keep imprudent oaths. Her joy was so great that she set off to Port-Royal there and then. Angélique always kept August 4th as a happy anniversary.

Those early days were the springtime of the Order. That first generation of Port-Royal nuns was very different from the second. There was something youthful, sweet and pure about them. But their successors, among whom was Angélique's own niece, the daughter of her brother Robert, were cold, scientific and reasonable, and eventually broke away from the Church. In the words of their Archbishop, M. de Péréfixe, they were "pure as angels and proud as devils."

Père Archange did his best to make Angélique keep the peace with her family. When he came to see her after the uproar, he saw

how unwell she looked as a result of those emotional upsets. He
tried to broaden her outlook.

"You think this is the centre of the universe, this small Port-Royal.
You must try to forget yourself a little. I have just escaped from
England where priests are put to death. They are hanged, drawn
and quartered in the Tower and at Tyburn. I fled to France in
horror when my best friend was executed after having been denounced for hearing Mass. Here in France, you have a Queen who
performs her religious duties. Over in England, the old Queen
persecuted her Catholic subjects. She was a terrible woman. Pluck
up heart, my little Abbess. When you think you are weakening,
remember England, remember the martyrs of early Rome, St.
Agnes, St. Agatha, St. Cecilia, and an infinity of other very young
girls who won their crown with their blood and who deserve to
live for ever with their heavenly Spouse."

His method of direction was perhaps a little over-sweet, and,
indeed, prepared her for the style of St. François de Sales, but he
could be firm when necessary; one of his first bits of advice was:
"Never allow your nuns to speak to a monk, even to monks of my
own Capuchin Order, even if they preach like angels."

Just then, in the courtyard outside the guest room, they heard
the braying of the donkey on which Père Archange had ridden all
the way from Paris. He laughed.

"That is my little ass."

"Do you mean to say you came on that?"

"I never ride on mules and horses. It is against the spirit of St.
Francis."

Afterwards he wrote to her, "God expects something great from
you." He could not but admire her pluck, her kindheartedness to
the lay sisters, and her sincerity, though of course he must have
been aware of her great ignorance and of the fact that she was not
a real contemplative.

When eventually Agnès was allowed to return to Port-Royal,
persuaded to give up the Abbey of St. Cyr and become a Cistercian
with her sister, he helped her too. He admired her immensely and
said so to Angélique. "One day, she will be one of the greatest nuns
of France."

Agnès had all the makings of a contemplative. Père Archange grew concerned about Angélique's influence on her. And indeed he warned Agnès a little against imitating the excessive austerities of her sister.

Père Gallot, whom Père Archange had sent to instruct the nuns, was the director of the Carmelites, and thus he was unable to inspire the anti-mystical Angélique. Père Archange sent them other good priests, so the nuns were taught their catechism, and many were confirmed.

Of course the neglected Cistercians were jealous of all this, and became very rude. Angélique had good cause to complain of them. The Master General, who insisted that the community confessor should always be a Cistercian, sent her one who was stone deaf! Then he sent them another who was their jester and their affliction. He made long speeches at the bedside of a dying nun, and indeed hastened her end with his unending sermons.

A few years later, a confessor called Dom Bomereau said something suspiciously immoral to an innocent nun, Soeur Madeleine Candide. When she asked Angélique about this something which she had not understood, Angélique set a trap for him. He was heard saying foolish things when this nun was folding the linen near the chapel. A good priest overhead through a window and reported all to Angélique. She called for Dom Bomereau and said sternly:

"*Mon Père,* ask pardon from the Lord for the evil which you have committed here."

And he said, "Is this the beautiful hat of roses which you give me for all the services I have done you?"

"I will never endure having you here again. I never want to see you again."

Apart from these perpetual annoyances from members of their own Order, the nuns went on with their reform. Angélique was very anxious to go back to the fasting from meat of the primitive observance. She tried it out on herself to start with. Instead of taking meat three times a week, she had an omelette which she would hide from the others in the refectory by a lamb's tail—an odd thing indeed to have on the table. She hated eggs, for they made her ill. Anyway, she survived and imposed the fasting from meat on the rest of the Order, on all except Soeur Marie Mulot, who complained about everything very loudly. Angélique forced her to apologize publicly before the rest of the community, then dismissed her to the Order of the Paraclete near Amiens, Héloïse's old abbey.

Now at Port-Royal all the nuns did their daily stint of rough work, at the kitchen sink and elsewhere. They used to wash up in turns, instead of leaving it all to the lay sisters, and there is a reference to Angélique making the dormitory fire herself; she must have realized that nuns could not survive in winter at all without some kind of warmth, though one is certain that she herself never went near the fire.

They were very poor in those early days, for now Angélique did not like to accept very much from her father. Thinking that they could not afford linen for their chemises, he sent them some, which however they could not use because it was now against the Rule. When Madame Arnauld gave Angélique some china soup bowls, she would not use them, for she thought she should have earthenware.

However, though she was poorer than ever before, she still gave to beggars, and she was even able to send meat to Père Archange at Meudon. He was so grateful that he called her, not Madame de Port-Royal but "Madame de Coeur Royal." It is easy to picture her in those days, in her early twenties—dishevelled-looking (for she did not change her only habit for weeks at a time and even slept in it), probably crawling with lice, and yet, on fire with enthusiasm. She had put her own house in order, and now, like St. Bernard, she began to attract all the members of her family. They nearly all came to Port-Royal and ended their lives in the Order.

5. *MÈRE ANGÉLIQUE'S SISTERS*

ANGÉLIQUE'S SISTERS were fascinating girls. Agnès would never have been allowed to marry, for she was the plainest of them all, thickset and, as Abbé Bremond says, with the look of a "good Paris bourgeoise." Her face was round, rugged and kindly. It was to atone for these defects of nature that Agnès took trouble with her appearance. This neatness used to annoy Angélique, and she determined to thwart her if ever she came under her power.

As usual, Angélique was critical about the faults of her own sisters. She said: "Agnès was good and punctual but conceited and ambitious beyond what one could conceive. . . . She had a self-esteem opposed to all humiliation and penance, a self-esteem which I found unbearable because God had already converted me. . . . She was particular as to her food, very dainty and neat in her clothes. . . . She was too much attached to the choir."

Agnès happened to be at Port-Royal when she fell seriously ill, probably from severe anaemia. During that long year of illness, Angélique looked after her most admirably. She used to run to the kitchen and make her good meat broths herself. Then she would kneel at Agnès's feet for an hour at a time and beg her to sip a little from a spoon.

But the motives of Angélique's sweetness to her sister were not completely selfless. She wanted her to leave St. Cyr altogether, and be with her at Port-Royal. She caressed her very greatly, she said, in order to wheedle her.

When Monsieur Arnauld saw how depressed Agnès looked,

Angélique went so far as to tell him an untruth to gain her ends. "She is ill because she wants to be with me, *mon Père*." And Agnès was too much afraid of her to contradict. After a while she capitulated.

"All right. I will leave Saint Cyr. I will not be an abbess," she said, "and I will come to you." Angélique was delighted.

Then Agnès's troubles started in earnest. When there was a storm at Port-Royal, the sand and soil used to pour down the hills and fill the narrow valley, so that it took the nuns about a month afterwards to clear up the mess. The ponds, which were at a higher level than the church, flooded into everything, leaving penetrating damp and tenacious mildew. But the physical misery was nothing to the nervous strain. Angélique's eagle eye never missed anything. One day, when Agnès was doing the sacristy work, she spilt a jar of lamp oil down her habit, and a thick, gluey, ill-smelling oil at that. The fastidious Agnès was disgusted. She hurried out to the robing room to ask for a clean habit. Alas, she met her formidable sister in the passage.

"Where are you going? To change your habit? Certainly not. This is a good opportunity for mortification. You are going to keep this habit on, day and night, for six weeks."

"Oh, but, *ma Mère*, this is awful."

"Hold your tongue, that will do," she said. Agnès was forced to obey. For six weeks that unendurable stench remained with her, and it grew more appalling at night, on her wretched straw mattress.

Woman is gifted for detecting little things which will annoy members of her own sex. Angélique observed that Agnès forgot all her troubles and was utterly happy in choir, singing Office, so she deprived her of choir. This caused floods of tears.

"I had her removed from it one day to mortify her. She was then a novice and cried horribly over it. . . . The Superiors carefully thought up devices to humiliate them and mortify them in things for which they were not prepared, lest familiarity should lessen the merit of their ordinary mortifications. . . ."

Those nuns who, in the way of women, took things too literally, went to great lengths to keep the law of silence. For instance, there was one Soeur Isabelle Christine who was sent to a new cell, which the novice mistress must have thought sufficiently furnished, but when the nun got there at night, she found that it was a store-room for faggots. To avoid breaking silence, she slept on her cloak, on these faggots, for several nights before they found out. Then there was Soeur Isabelle Agnès who spent the whole of Lent engaged in kitchen work, without speaking a single word even when it was absolutely necessary. One begins to wonder what the food was like. Angélique, who knew that Agnès was very fastidious about her food, took this opportunity to mortify her and make her eat things she could not endure.

Perhaps the elder sister was prompted by an unconscious jealousy. Had not the Père Archange said to her, "You see, Madame, your sister is only a girl of seventeen, but I presume to tell you that some day she will be one of the greatest nuns in France." Perhaps it is for this reason, in the hopes of catching her out some day, that Angélique treated her like the most insignificant novice. She made her clean out coals and saucepans until her fingers were quite raw. But even here, she could not manage to trip up this exhausted, anaemic young girl. Another time, Angélique accused her of being imperfect, in that she was too much attached to menial work! Agnès would go on, even when her strength was failing. How much angrier Angélique would have been had Agnès stopped work because she was too exhausted to carry on. Angélique blamed her even for her virtues. "I mortified her horribly."

Angélique tells us: "I said to her once, 'My sister, you are not fit for the habit, for if you were to come very late to the choir or the refectory and I ordered you some penance, you would not be able to endure it!' Mère Agnès replied: 'The thing is to avoid being late.'"

Angélique did not care for music; thus it was only owing to Agnès's enthusiasm for choir Office that the singing of the Port-Royal nuns became so greatly renowned. People flocked to hear those Cistercians, whose voices Sainte-Beuve describes as "so sweet, so enrapturing, and specially so clear and distinct."

Far from indulging in feminine trills, they sang with a gravity which caused astonishment and admiration. In the days towards the end, when their brothers and uncles were singing in church on the other side of the grille, if it were a funeral chant, the weeping nuns could sing no more, and the verses were taken up by "*ces Messieurs.*"

But although Agnès and Angélique were associated in their reform of the Order, so that they were compared to two branches of the same candlestick, still Agnès kept her distinct individuality throughout. The Abbé Bremond has said that if Agnès had been at the head of affairs, the later generation of Port-Royal nuns would never have been implicated in Jansenism. She always spoke of the sweet yoke of Christ and of the goodness of God the Father. She was a born writer and her letters delighted the society people whom she met afterwards in Paris. They had a slight preciousness about them which, had she lived in the world, would have secured her success in the blue drawing-room of Madame de Rambouillet. She loved courtesy, and would get quite cross when people spoke of the rusticity of Port-Royal. She said: "There is much affectation in not wishing to aspire to politeness." She grew to love the countryside of Port-Royal des Champs very much, and she speaks of it with delight. "You find a peace there that you find in no other place."

Many people who were frightened of Mère Angélique were drawn to Mère Agnès. Her friendliness was grave like an Infanta's, but it was smiling too. Yet in spite of this she could not endure pious familiarities, which she called "convent foolings." In the self-conscious way of all Arnaulds, she describes herself: "A grave, serious, majestic behaviour which does not, however, exclude gentleness and conciliation, but which has nothing to do with familiarity, which consoles the senses and disperses grace."

She was aware, of course, of the bad impression created by Angélique's abruptness, but she was extremely loyal about it and would try to calm down affronted friends by explaining, "My sister Angélique is like the good angels who frighten at first and reassure afterwards."

Angélique got very tired of one confessor after another. In fact her whole existence oscillated between sudden enthusiasm followed by disillusion and casting off the offending director. But Agnès would assimilate their message, for she was a cloistered contemplative who lived inwardly and loved the things of God. She was not afflicted with the restlessness of her sister.

Angélique was always overactive. She was devoured by an animal activity which made her very difficult to live with. She confesses herself in one of her letters that, even at meals, when she was presiding as Abbess, she used to talk a lot to her neighbours, a thing she would have condemned in anyone but herself. In contrast, one only has to look at Agnès's portrait by Philippe de Champaigne to realize how peaceful she is. True, her closed lips are a little thin, a little spiteful. But somehow or other she creates an atmosphere of the supernatural. She kneels there awaiting the miraculous cure of the artist's daughter, Suzanne de Champaigne.

Abbé Bremond compares the two sisters to Angélique's disadvantage. He says that Angélique drags her nuns along more than she reforms them. "She rules more than she leads. Agnès is less sublime than the other but more luminous, more spiritual. . . . One reveres Mère Angélique, one almost adores her, one trembles before her; one loves Mère Agnès, one gives oneself joyously to her influence. . . . [Mère Agnès] remains the soul of the calm, flowering Port-Royal which so long rejoiced the angels and which did not survive her."

Abbé Bremond saw at once that Angélique's was a sublime and yet weak nature, that she looked at herself too much, was riddled with scruples, was distressed by God's silence. He says that, in spite of her genius, she is not quite healthy, not humble, not simple, in spite of her virtue. And when both sisters came under the influence of St. François de Sales, it was Agnès who profited most. Agnès kept all his advice in her heart until the end of her life. Indeed, she did a thing which her excessively mortified elder sister would never have countenanced: she kept one of his letters on her person always.

Catherine was one of the most lovable of the six Arnauld girls, and the only one who ever married. When she was trying to make up her mind between marriage and the cloister, Isaac Le Maître married someone else. But, wishing to kill off this first wife, he made her go about in a coach on the uneven streets of Paris in pregnancy, and she died in childbirth. He then proposed again to Catherine. The Arnaulds had no idea what a horrible creature he was. Indeed, Madame Arnauld was too much occupied, as ever, in having children. Her nineteenth child was a stillborn boy, and after that the doctor forbade her to have any more children for he said it was too dangerous. Alas, the following year, she bore her twentieth and last child, Antoine, nicknamed Le Grand Arnauld, the one who was to bring Port-Royal to such disrepute and do such a great disservice to his sisters. Odd to think that because Monsieur Arnauld disobeyed a doctor's orders, he brought a dangerous heretic into the world and destroyed Port-Royal.

She was still having children at the same time as her daughter Catherine Le Maître, so that some of the aunts and uncles were younger than their nephews and nieces. For the first three years of her marriage, Catherine lived in the same house with her parents, and all appeared to go well. Isaac was clever enough to be attentive to her in public. In private he was a fiend.

One night, Angélique had a strange dream about Catherine, and her newly married brother, Robert. She saw them both riding on the same horse and coming towards Port-Royal, looking very sad. Afterwards she explained this ominous vision by saying that they came to Port-Royal to seek consolation after they had lost their partners in marriage. And indeed, that is what came to pass.

One day, Madame Arnauld arrived unexpectedly at Port-Royal, looking very much upset. By Papal dispensation she was now allowed to come into certain places within the enclosure. She spoke to Angélique and Agnès in a bare, disagreeable little cell where the rats had eaten away bits of the paper crucifix which Angélique had pinned up on the wall.

Madame Arnauld was so harrowed that she forgot to take out her pomander to ward off unpleasant odours.

"Has anything sad happened at home, *ma mère?*" asked Agnès with concern.

"Oh, yes, something terrible. You know that Catherine was ill and I had brought her home. One night, she became delirious and disclosed the secret of her married life. It appears that all these years Isaac has been appallingly cruel to her, and unfaithful."

"Ah," said Angélique, almost with relish. "That is what happens to those who marry."

Madame Arnauld gave her a chill glance and continued.

"In private, he is ill-tempered, malicious, vindictive, and a heavy gambler. And yet, he appeared so loving. . . . I thought they were happy. He's even thrashed her unmercifully. Your father is now planning a separation. He has hired a detective. As Isaac had no suspicion that Catherine had talked about him, he went to see his mistresses and frequented all sorts of disgusting low haunts. So he's been caught. Your father's reputation stands for something in the law courts, so we will soon get the upper hand. And then poor Catherine and the boys must come to live with us."

"What a pity," said Angélique, "that she didn't become a nun, when she wanted to so much. But that explains my dream." And she told her mother about it.

"But," interrupted Madame Arnauld, "I shouldn't talk to her about it just now. She mustn't be distracted from her duty of bringing up her children. Alas, it looks as if all our daughters will die at Port-Royal. You've already got Claire and Agnès. How is Claire?"

Agnès replied: "Angélique had been urging her to be less fastidious about her food, if she wanted to be a hermit in the desert with her. And what do you think she did? Some of the other little girls urged her to eat a hideous black mushroom, and she was only prevented from doing so because one of our nuns saw her in the garden looking very ill at the prospect. She said she wanted to mortify her greed. She simply worships Angélique and wants to be with her the whole time."

Madame Arnauld said: "She has too ardent a temperament, that child."

Angélique said triumphantly: "What a good thing, then, that we weaned her from the world where she might have lost her soul. But now she loves the things of God so much that the worst punishment I can mete out to her is not to speak to her of Our Lord for some time."

Madame Arnauld interrupted drily: "I hope you let her walk in the garden."

"Quite unnecessary," replied Angélique. "Sometimes I send her out to do some weeding, of course, but there is plenty of exercise inside the house. And if she needs air, she only has to open her window. Walking in the garden is far too agreeable for the senses."

"Remember," said Madame Arnauld, "she has a weak chest; may it fall on your head if she becomes consumptive."

Angélique drew herself up, reforming Cistercian abbess to the fingertips.

"She must obey the Rule, Mamma," she said icily. "She has to forget that I'm her sister; I'm her Superior. In spite of all her youthful devotion, she is often impertinent and answers me back. The other day I had to smack her face."

"Oh, how wicked," cried Madame Arnauld, "how cruel! You must not do that, Angélique."

"She took it quite well. I said to her 'Charity struck you and the Evil One has fled,' and she begged my pardon."

"You mustn't frighten her," said Madame Arnauld. "She's only a child, and if it hadn't been for her smallpox, she wouldn't be here. She would be happily married."

"Ha," said Angélique, "and then she would probably have lost her soul forever."

"How hard you are!" exclaimed her mother. A few tears trickled down her tired face. "I put that plaster on her face to prevent disfigurement by smallpox. And then, when she was at death's door, I thought I should take it off. Alas, that ruined her lovely skin for ever."

"Yes," interposed Agnès, "I shall always remember the first time the poor child saw herself in the looking glass. She covered it with her hand and cried out, 'It's no longer me!' "

"It's no use your being so indifferent to the beauty of your sisters," said Madame Arnauld, turning to Angélique. "You know quite well that you're frightened of smallpox yourself, and God will send it to you as a judgment on your harshness. Why, when poor Agnès had it, you kept her locked up in the attic and would only speak to her from outside. And that, not too often if I remember."

And so ended this acrimonious afternoon. Madame Arnauld returned to Paris, consoling herself for the loss of Claire by the thought that she still had her twenty-three-year-old beautiful Anne-Eugénie unmarried and at home, though pining for the cloister, and also her youngest daughter Madeleine, nicknamed Madelon, who was now eight years old. She was a little beauty, and she knew it. She used to peacock about and enchant her father. He clung to her, and to Anne-Eugénie, for he did not want them to leave home. Madame Arnauld devoutly hoped that the two girls would not see their sister Angélique too often. She was afraid of the attraction of Port-Royal, and of the forceful personality of her daughter, who even in her nursery days, as she recalled, had been able to win Simon's entire allegiance. Did she cast spells on her brothers and sisters?

In spite of her twenty childbearings, Madame Arnauld's nursery was nearly empty, only the three-year-old Antoine in it now. The second Simon was away in the army, and Henri, the future Bishop of Angers, was engaged in his ecclesiastical studies. She now had no children to spare.

She wished that she had been allowed to see Claire. The last time, she thought she had never seen so untidy a little nun, and her habit was filthy dirty. Angélique forced her to wash dishes and scour heavy iron pans. Even in winter, she was made to clean out the chicken houses.

Madame Arnauld decided to speak of all this to Anne-Eugénie, who was a fastidious great lady, who looked after her hands with scented unguents. It might dissuade her. She had been talking of Port-Royal lately. Anne-Eugénie enjoyed the world's pleasures, such as seeing a ballet performed by princesses, or going to a play. She had even taken pleasure in all the pomp and splendour of Henri Quatre's funeral.

While their mother was away Anne-Eugénie and Catherine, who had just risen from her sickbed, were both crouching over the fire and speaking in whispers. They did not want to be overheard by

Monsieur Arnauld in the next room. Twenty-five-year-old Catherine had dark hair, and she had a fine line of down on her upper
lip, which can be clearly seen in a portrait in the museum of Port-
Royal des Champs. She looked fragile and broken-down. And yet,
she was less distraught than before. Oh, the relief of parting from
her terrible husband!

Anne-Eugénie, in spite of having had the smallpox four years
before, still retained her beauty. On her lap was a book.

"What is it you're so absorbed in?" said Catherine.

"St. Jerome's letters on Virginity."

"H'm," smiled her sister. "A great change from L' Astrée,[1] which
captivated you before. How horrified Angélique was when she
heard that you continued to read that pastoral in a thunderstorm,
regardless of God's wrath."

"When I had smallpox, I was tormented by religious doubts, and
I promised God that if I recovered I would choose between the
Protestant and Catholic religions and devote myself to Him."

Catherine exclaimed, "Why, you're not going to join Angélique,
are you? That would break Mother's heart. Then Madelon will be
the only girl left."

Anne-Eugénie hesitated a moment, then drawing closer to her
sister's armchair, she said: "I really must speak to you. And then,
I will have to slip away to Port-Royal and tell Angélique. Something very extraordinary happened to me on her birthday. I believe I received a call to be a nun. It happened in our family chapel
in church."

"Oh," cried her sister. "It's all because you've seen me so unhappy. It's put you off the married state."

"Not quite. You remember, I was very much in love last year,
and I took a long time to recover from the blow when the negotiations came to nothing, on a small question of the dowry. No, please
don't believe it's entirely because of you, nor even because I've
been crossed in love. It is truly because of what happened on September the 8th this year."

"Do tell me," said Catherine.

"I was in our chapel of St. Laurence for Vespers, and I was read-

[1] By Honoré d'Urfé (1577-1625).

ing these letters of St. Jerome on Virginity when, all of a sudden, I felt profoundly absorbed and quiet in my soul. I was, as it were, transported beyond myself and brought into the presence of Jesus Christ. I threw myself at His feet. He drew near me and put a ring on my finger. I shall never forget that hour as long as I live. Mamma couldn't think what ailed me, but I couldn't speak to her about it then. When at length Mamma knew, she said to a priest, 'How could Anne-Eugénie ever be obedient, for she finds it very difficult to be obedient to her father and myself?' I told Papa, and he objected because he didn't want to lose another girl. On the advice of Père Archange, just to put myself to the test, I decided to stay a year in the world. So I've been out to balls and parties and I've called at all the great houses with Mamma as usual. I even tried to pass it off that I was enjoying myself immensely, but in my heart I've been resolved. All the beauty of the world paled before the dawn, the celestial dawn rising before my eyes. I remember one day, at a ballet performed by the princesses, I spent my time comparing what I saw with the least of the joys which I imagined in Paradise."

"I think," said Catherine, "that if you told all that to Angélique, she would mock you. She thinks any mystical experience is connected with the Evil One, so take care."

"I'll convince her about this one," cried Anne-Eugénie.

And convince her she did. And her parents too. At first her father was brokenhearted. He had feared this all along. How was it that Angélique, the only child he had ever disliked, should now steal away all his other children? He said to Anne-Eugénie:

"You realize you will have to do rough household jobs at Port-Royal, and you know how you hate even the light tasks here at home."

In the Arnauld household, all the girls had to do their share of domestic duties, because of their mother's frequent confinements. Anne-Eugénie had always hated housework, for she found it humiliating. She had been ambitious, elegant, beautifully dressed. She was too proud to complain about the housework to her parents, but she told Angélique.

And so, on Friday, October 7th, 1616, a year later, Anne-Eugénie left the Paris house very early one morning with both her parents.

The night before, her mother had taken her apart and given her a little leather casket, studded with nails.

"I've put a few necessities in here for you. I hope Angélique will let you keep them. There is nothing luxurious. Look, powder against insects. You might have to sprinkle it on the floor or the bedclothes for the first few nights."

Anne-Eugénie smiled.

"And then, here are a few extra handkerchiefs because you catch cold so easily, and a pair of nail scissors and a knife. And here is a mixture for your cough. And these, in the corner, are herbs for enriching the blood. I hope you won't get pale, like Claire. And here is some aromatic vinegar, also to sprinkle on the floor."

Then she went to her great oak chest and took out a large, heavy cloak.

"And this is for you to put on in winter. I don't like to feel that you are starting your novitiate in October. I'm sure Angélique can't forbid you to wear this. Anyway, it will hide all your worldly things until you are clothed with the habit next year."

Before they left home the Arnaulds went to hear the nine o'clock Mass at St. Merri. During the Mass Anne-Eugénie heard the words: "Take my yoke upon you, for my yoke is sweet." This echoed sweetly, as if it were spoken to her personally. She turned to her relations, smiling, as if to make them notice the text.

When they reached Port-Royal, her father slipped away because he was too greatly moved. As Anne-Eugénie entered the enclosure —always a terrible moment—she began to sob. When her mother and sisters left, they told her father this, and he returned in order to bring her back. But she held firm and Monsieur Arnauld went dolefully back to Paris.

"Humph," muttered Angélique, "they didn't make such a fuss when *I* left home."

All that long day, Anne-Eugénie was agitated and tempted. At length she went up to her cell. Her bed was made of rough branches plaited together. She looked for her leather dressing-case. It had gone. Angélique had been there before her. The Abbess had laughed to herself as she turned over its contents, and she ordered a lay sister to take it away. Anne-Eugénie never saw it again. So, that night, she spread her only handkerchief on a rough-hewn little table to prepare herself for the night. (Agnès said that at first she was surprised by several things. No wonder.)

In 1650, thirty-four years afterwards, when so many of the early nuns were ordered by their Superiors to write down their early recollections, Anne-Eugénie, who had then become Soeur Anne-Eugénie de l'Incarnation, composed a charming little masterpiece —the story of her novitiate. The cloak her mother had given her, with its collar cut on the cross, became a convent heirloom which was given to postulants. Anne-Eugénie spoke of her soul's desolation directly she had entered the cloister. All her great spiritual joys left her. When she told this to her sister Agnès, she consoled her and said it was not surprising, for, having left all worldly pleasures, she was not yet consoled by the Lord. During that first year, Père Gallot advised her to read the life of St. Teresa written by herself, newly translated into French, and it helped her.

She wrote: "In summer, in the morning, we weeded the garden, in great silence and fervour. These dwellings seemed to me gloomy and threatening, because they were in a deep valley, but, looking up sometimes at the sky above the dormitory, I used to imagine that here it was more serene than elsewhere. All things consoled me, and I remember that once, being extremely depressed, I was quite delighted just by glancing up at the stars, and another time by hearing our three church bells making sweet harmony.

"The first time that I went to the refectory to which the Sisters went in those days with their church habits, I found all this so uplifting, that, as I heard them chant the Benedicite, and say grace, which they completed in procession in the choir, it reminded me of Paradise. . . . During my novitiate a lay sister died. Considering all the ceremonies which took place at her burial, and at the same time, remembering those I had seen for Henri IV, I thought the nun's burial far more beautiful.

"Since my profession I remained in so great a state of joy at being a nun that, on one occasion, I danced when I was alone, and whenever I saw a nun looking depressed or sad, I thought that she only had to look at her black veil to stop being sad."

Père Suffren, a Jesuit who had known Anne-Eugénie in the world, and was always in a great hurry, came to call on her once, and she had to rush out of the scullery in her black apron, a knife hanging from her belt and her hands black from cleaning saucepans and raking out ashes. He said to her playfully, "Don't you want some more pomade for your hands?" She replied: "Dish water is far better, and I no longer need anything else."

Indeed, Anne-Eugénie derived more joy from these occupations than from all her past Paris amusements. She endured the "dark night of the soul" for about a year, a great deal through excessive fear of God's judgments. This trial ended on October 22nd, 1617, which was a Sunday. She wrote: "Having received Holy Communion at the first Mass, and with half-an-hour to spare for myself, I stayed in church to say my prayers, during which time I was much absorbed. This grace of God changed me a great deal, took away all my griefs and bad humours, and filled me with such great joy that it even affected my body, with the result that, although I was only used to going to Matins for three days on end, because we never returned to bed afterwards, I went to Matins for seventeen nights without any difficulty, and I had no more trouble with anything, even when I was reproved for my faults."

Anne-Eugénie, like her sister Agnès, became one of Angélique's most active lieutenants. There is something deliciously springlike about that group of young nuns in the early days before dark troubles fell upon the Order. Amongst the young girls who came to the place at that time was Marie Suireau. Her portrait in oils can be seen in the museum at Versailles, in her beautiful Port-Royal habit. She has a self-willed little mouth and strangely drooping eyelids. Later she became Mère Marie des Anges, reforming Abbess of Maubuisson and Lys, and then Abbess of Port-Royal of Paris.

Anne-Eugénie was to see much of her, for eventually Angélique ordered Marie Suireau and Anne-Eugénie to reform the Abbey of Lys—a thankless task. They were both ill-treated and lost any health they ever had.

Marie Suireau had come to Port-Royal des Champs at the age of sixteen. On the 12th of April, 1615, Angélique had seen a cart of four young girls arrive from Chartres. She looked at the last of the four girls hiding behind the others, and knew instinctively that this was the only one who would remain. There was such devotion, sweetness and humility on her face.

She was the daughter of a poor lawyer of Chartres who was not at all ambitious for the things of this world but only wished to train his two daughters in mortification. He did so by strange means. He would make them take horrid medicines, and this without a murmur. One suspects that the terrible internal afflictions which assailed Marie for the rest of her days were due to this.

Angélique, who was so critical of her nuns, never criticized Marie. In fact, she loved her throughout her life. This young thing imagined she had no spiritual gifts, but she had the peace and simplicity which Angélique so greatly admired. As the younger child she had been particularly devoted to her mother. They used to spin together in their poor little house near the cathedral, and they cheered each other by singing spiritual canticles, especially the one from St. Augustine which begins: "O clear stream of immortality." The songs they sang filled them with a love for their Celestial City, whose sweetness helped them to despise all other joys.

At Port-Royal somebody who saw Marie in the garden turned to Angélique and said: "That young nun will be outstanding."

In spite of her sweetness and her peaceable nature, her natural inclinations, it appears, were ardent and lively. Her good health, of course, began to disappear, just like everybody else's. She had attacks of nose bleeding for ten days on end, and had to lie in a sheet dipped in vinegar. In the end, her mother joined her and became an extern sister. But alas, that was just when her daughter had left for Lys. Afterwards, she attempted to reform Maubuisson.

Although her health was so bad that she could only stay up one day in two and had a nun especially to look after her, she had a gift for persuasion, she possessed that "inflexible sweetness" which helped her to lead some of the bad nuns at the abbey of Maubuisson.

The time was not far off when Angélique would be glad of this kernel of good nuns in the community—Agnès, Anne-Eugénie, Marie Suireau, Marie-Claire—for she was ordered to leave Port-Royal.

6. *THE IMMORAL DAME D'ESTRÉES*

A SHORT time after Anne-Eugénie had entered, at the end of 1616, Angélique received a most unexpected guest in the parlour, Angélique d'Estrées, Abbess of Maubuisson. She had not seen her for fourteen years, since the day Angélique was installed as Abbess of Port-Royal des Champs, and Dame d'Estrées had come to the festivities accompanied by two other not very commendable abbesses.

Thought Madame de Port-Royal to herself: "I wonder what brings you. I'm sure you haven't come here today to talk of holy things."

But surprisingly enough, the aging abbess, who looked as bold and as fleshy as ever, *had* come to talk about holy things. She was anxious to reform her abbey. She wasn't very happy about the way things had been going lately.

Angélique fell straight into the trap, for she said she would gladly try and help her. Would she like her to go to Maubuisson for a time? The nuns there had been her friends, and it might be easier for them to accept her, in a reform. But at this point, Angélique d'Estrées quickly changed the subject.

Madame de Port-Royal offered her old abbess some refreshment.

Angélique d'Estrées was just going to say "hot wine and sausages," but changed her mind: "Er—I should love a little hot milk, or perhaps a coddled egg, if you have some. But how is it you don't live in your Abbess's apartments any more?"

"I've given them over to the sick. You know our infirmary here is very damp."

"But it's not at all becoming," said Angélique d'Estrées, "that you should live in such squalor, my dear child. You have a certain position to keep up. And an abbess has a fire in her room. I must confess this parlour is very cold. I think if I stay much longer I will catch a chill."

Angélique clapped her hands and ordered a lay sister to make up a fire at once.

This visit really surprised her. When Dame d'Estrées had left, she stared at the coach until it was out of sight. "There is more below the surface," she thought, "that I cannot understand." She felt vaguely uneasy, and wondered whether she would ever see Dame d'Estrées again. She was soon to be enlightened.

The old Master General whom Angélique had disliked so much was succeeded by somebody excellent, called Dom Boucherat. He was not the man to overlook the loose behaviour of the great Abbess of Maubuisson, and he had heard many stories about the place. Also Louis XIII, unlike his father, Henri IV, who had had good cause to love the Abbey of Maubuisson, was not the kind of king to stand for immoral behaviour in religious houses. He had himself renounced the woman he loved when she became a Visitation nun.

Through her court connections, tales of the King's displeasure had reached the ears of Angélique d'Estrées. So she thought it prudent to throw dust in Madame de Port-Royal's eyes. Perhaps if rumours of her intended reform reached the ears of Louis XIII, she would be left alone (for she still loved pleasure just as much as in her young days). Twice Dom Boucherat had sent monks from Cîteaux to get information about the state of things at Maubuisson, but they had been imprisoned and beaten. The last one to be sent reappeared at Cîteaux several weeks later with the following story. He looked a wreck:

"Yes, she flung me and my companions into prison in one of the Abbey towers. For four days we had nothing else but bread and water. And every morning, by her order, her steward came to thrash me with belts. Look at the marks on my arms and legs."

"Oh, my poor brother! You will have to go to the infirmary. How did you manage to escape?"

"I climbed up through the window, or I don't think I'd have come out alive. She's a terrible woman, quite terrible—a human fiend."

"That settles it," said Dom Boucherat, "I've made up my mind. She will have to leave. First of all, I'll see that there will be no trouble from her family and relations, for they are powerful. And then with the greatest secrecy, I will engage the Paris Provost and his guard for protection. First, we will hide in Pontoise. I'll try to move her quietly, and if that doesn't succeed, I'll have to summon the guard. We'll break open the doors, and I'll have her taken to a home for repentant prostitutes. I think I'll choose the Filles Pénitentes de Saint Magloire in the rue Saint Denis. It would do her good to spend the rest of her days under lock and key. The only thing I'm afraid of is that she might start a lawsuit."

"*Père Abbé*," said the monk, "you must give instructions to the nuns of Saint Magloire that she is to be given no chance of escaping. I know what they do, these fallen women. They take the opportunity for a walk in the garden, and they climb over the walls before you can say *Ave Marie*."

"And then," added Dom Boucherat, "there is the trouble of her successor. I don't know whom to send to Maubuisson in her stead. The nuns will make a terrible uproar."

So, early in February of 1618, Dom Boucherat left Paris with the written consent of Parliament, accompanied by the Provost and a good company of armed men. These waited at Pontoise, while Dom Boucherat went alone to Maubuisson. The cronies of the Abbess knew there would be trouble directly they saw his face. He looked very angry indeed. They slipped up to her to warn her not to move.

"I want to see the Abbess immediately," he said.

The Prioress came up to him and said, "I'm sorry, Dom Boucherat, but you cannot see our Mother Abbess. She is very ill in bed. She's just been bled and it would be very unwise to move her now."

"By Saint Martin's bones," cried the Abbess to her crony, Dame de la Serre, "I don't relish the idea of prison. Let him try." And she resolutely refused to see him.

By the 4th of February he lost patience and dispatched a messenger to Pontoise. On the 5th of February, before dawn, the Provost and his men were admitted by Dom Boucherat. He himself opened the door into the courtyard. But, alas, whilst he had gone out to the courtyard, the watchful Dame de la Serre, or some other nun, had locked all the inner doors. He returned with the guard to find himself locked out. This was really too much. The Provost ordered his men to cut down a young tree or two, and with the trunks they started to ram the door. It took a long time and the noise was dreadful. They kept seeing startled nuns peeping at them from the windows.

The Abbess, in bed, roared with laughter: "Let them try!" she cried.

At length the men found ladders and climbed up over the inner walls. Soon the whole army of them was let loose in the Abbey.

Dom Boucherat, his hunting instinct up, ran up to the Abbess's suite, and, without troubling to knock, went to her bedchamber, a very luxurious apartment. The bed, the sumptuous, glorious bed with its linen sheets and silken hangings, was empty. She had escaped.

He and the Provost's men spent a fruitless day searching for her everywhere. The nuns, it can be imagined, were not very helpful. He put some men outside the enclosure, to watch the exits, and others in the tower so that they could keep a lookout on the park. No, she must be inside.

Towards evening they heard a suspicious sneezing coming from a nun's cell. They broke open the door. The nun in question swore that the Abbess was not in her cell. But there she was, half naked, shivering with cold, cowering in a corner.

The Abbot had her thrown onto a mattress just as she was. Four strong men carried her screaming into a coach, and it is in that condition that she was brought to the Filles Pénitentes.

"And now," thought the Master General, "the question of her successor."

When the Provost's men had left and the place was quieter, he convened all the nuns to the Chapter House and proposed three abbesses for them to choose from. The third was Angélique of Port-Royal. Many of them had loved her as a child at Maubuisson, but since then, they had heard about her severe reform, and they were frightened, we are told, "of falling into the hands of the tyrannical monster of a horrid and savage reform." The Master General, having already spoken about all this to Monsieur Arnauld, who agreed, sent his order to Port-Royal that Angélique was to leave at once for Maubuisson.

From the start, she knew it would be a thankless task. What was the use of trying to reform nuns who had no wish to be reformed? They had all grown old in their sins and evil habits. Besides, it was almost unfair on them. They had come into the Order, which they looked on as a kind of club, on the understanding that they were to obey the existing Rule, which, unreformed though it was, could not be enforced. All she could now hope for was, by example and gentle persuasion, to make them keep some sort of outward decorum. She knew she could not do this alone, so she decided to take three other nuns with her, among them her devoted sister Claire, who would have been brokenhearted to be left behind.

Then Angélique broke the news to her nuns. They were dismayed. She left on the 19th of February, the day after her sister Anne-Eugénie's profession.

All the nuns were in floods of tears. Alone, Anne-Eugénie was dry-eyed. When they expressed astonishment, she said: "God gave me too many graces yesterday for me to cry today."

As Sainte-Beuve has said: "Her human grief was lost in the radiant exultation of the bride of Christ."

And when all the others were almost dying of sorrow, she said she was very near to dancing with enchantment. Her profession day had made such a profound impression on Anne-Eugénie that, on her deathbed, she still derived consolation from the sermon she had heard, and which she still remembered thirty-five years later.

7. *MÈRE ANGÉLIQUE TRIES TO REFORM MAUBUISSON*

ON THE way to Maubuisson, Angélique went to stay a day or two with her parents. This is her own account of the visit:

"When I went to Maubuisson . . . in 1618, I passed through Paris and went to lodge at my father's. There I found my little sister, Madelon, who was very worldly and who acted the beauty, as indeed she was. As soon as I saw her, I was upset and I said to her, 'What's all this, my little sister Madelon? Don't you want to become a nun . . . ?' To which she replied impudently, 'Oh, no, my sister. I haven't the least desire to be one.' 'Then what will you become, my child?' 'My sister, I want to get married.' To which I replied, 'What makes you desire to be married?' She said to me: 'Nothing else than the affection I have for little children. I love them with all my heart. I never get tired of kissing and holding my little nephews . . . and that is what makes me want to have some.' It is true that this simplicity of a small ten-year-old girl who did not know the meaning of virginity and marriage . . . made me laugh a little to begin with. But afterwards I felt grief to see her so worldly and so far from giving herself to God."

This is the first passage to show up Angélique becoming a real Jansenist, a lineal descendant of the Albigensian heretics who thought that holy matrimony was evil in itself.

It must have been strange for Angélique to return home, when she had thought she was going to spend the rest of her life at Port-Royal. She was now twenty-seven and a half, at the height of her powers. Ill-health had not yet fully undermined her, apart from terrible migraines. But she knew she was going to a place which would use up all her remaining strength.

As for Soeur Marie-Claire, Angélique had pointed out to her the bed in the infirmary of Port-Royal to which she would retire when she returned from Maubuisson. Indeed, it was at Maubuisson that Marie-Claire lost her health completely. Ever afterwards she had a high temperature every afternoon, and she finally died of consumption.

On February the 24th, Angélique arrived at Maubuisson. As the coach approached Pontoise, she said to the coachman: "I want you to stop at the Carmelite Convent."

This Order, newly arrived from Spain, had always greatly intrigued Angélique, but in her usual way she never ceased criticizing it. She was completely blind to its magnificence, never realized how much it attracted the allegiance of some of France's most spiritual men and women. All she saw was that the convent in the rue St. Jacques in Paris had wonderful paintings on its walls, quite forgetting, of course, that those were all gifts from friends and offered to the glory of God. Angélique criticized little things like nuns buying pumpkins when they were expensive in the market. Madame Acarie, the mystic who had helped to bring the Carmelites from Spain and who was now a humble lay sister at Pontoise, had fallen ill the day before, so Angélique missed her by a day.

After her death, Angélique went to visit her tomb, and she, who was never impressed by supernatural phenomena, could not help noticing the sweet smell which arose from it. And Agnès, afterwards, although she had no sense of smell, noticed it too.

Eventually, they drove to the Abbey of Maubuisson—Mère Angélique, her sister Claire, the Master General Dom Boucherat and two other nuns of Port-Royal des Champs, Dame de la Croix and Soeur Isabelle de Châteauneuf, who both soon died as a result of the hardships and strain they endured in this rich abbey. Angélique looked resigned and apprehensive. She gave her last instructions to her three nuns, whilst Dom Boucherat nodded approvingly.

"Remember, we are to be their servants. We musn't make them

feel small. We mustn't put them to shame. We've got to caress them and be very agreeable, in order to win them to some kind of obedience to the Rule. And remember, older nuns love endearing little epithets. I must be as kind as I can to the nuns who were good to me when I was a child. They use endearments among themselves. I know it's against all our traditions, but it will help us to influence them in the end."

"We're almost here," exclaimed Dom Boucherat, "I must give you a special blessing."

The great door was opened to them by the porter, and they drove down the wide alley leading to the church. As it was Vesper time, they knew that the twenty-two nuns would probably be in choir, so they came in quietly and knelt down. The nuns were screaming the Office at each other. One had lost her temper and nudged a nun next to her, another nun threw down her Office book, and yet another pulled her neighbour's veil awry. It was not the singing of angels, obeying the example of the great St. Bernard; it was the cacophony of evil spirits.

"Good gracious," thought Angélique, "to think that I will have to drown that noise with my feeble little choir of four. I don't think we'll ever be able to do it. I shall have to get in some more nuns and train them to sing Office properly."

She remembered, from the old days, that all these old nuns thought that they sang Office beautifully. She was sure she could never induce them to come to choir practice, and they would object if other nuns took the lead. Angélique decided there and then that the band of new nuns must be lodged in separate quarters and eat in separate refectories. But alas, they would all have to meet in the same church. The old nuns sang on in discordant squawks. It was difficult to know whether they were singing or quarrelling. She made up her mind she would never show them how distressed she was by their singing. She knew they were very sensitive and would easily take umbrage, imagining they were being despised. Eventually reformers suffered, physically, and got quite hoarse, trying to cover up the performance of the die-hards, by their own chanting.

After Vespers, the ancients of Maubuisson assembled at the door to receive Dom Boucherat and the new nuns. At first they greeted them with respect, but somewhat frigidly. For days before, they had entertained each other with rumours about the horrors of Port-Royal and of what an ogre this Angélique Arnauld had become, and they trembled. The older nuns, who had looked after her when she was a child, all exclaimed: "To think we had nurtured a viper in our bosoms!"

But when they actually saw her, when they saw her warm, affectionate greeting and heard her cordial endearments, they began to feel much less apprehensive. When she caught sight of Dame Desmarest she embraced her and said to her in a gay voice: "Good day, my great friend" (for she remembered she had called her this as a child, and that almost all the nuns had such alliances of friendship amongst themselves). They were delighted with this frankness and cheerfulness. (All this is described by Angélique's great-niece, Mère Angélique de St. Jean Arnauld, Robert's daughter.)

"And where is Dame Le Vasseur?" she said, recalling the nun who had first shown her around Maubuisson when she was a little girl.

A blind old nun was brought up from the back. She was trying to grope her way towards Angélique on two sticks.

"Here I am, my dear," she said. "I am quite blind."

"Oh, poor thing. I will look after you," exclaimed Angélique, embracing her. "I have never forgotten how kind you were to me as my mistress."

And indeed, all during Lent, Angélique went to see her each evening, taking her supper with her, which consisted of lay sisters' coarse bread (for she would not eat white bread), with seven or eight chicory leaves, quite raw without oil or seasoning, served in a hollow in the bread. The old nun, who was a little neglected, grew to look forward immensely to these evening visits from her old pupil, and they helped her to bear her affliction.

Two or three of the aristocratic ancients who wore beautiful habits of very thin stuff, and quite transparent head veils, looked with distaste at Angélique's terrible habit of coarse *"serge de Nogent."* Angélique saw their glances, and said: "Patches are the jewels of nuns."

Dame d'Estrées' old confederate, mannish, tall Dame de la Serre, who was always remarkable for vanity and singularity of dress, and who was wholly unreconciled to reform, looked at her new Superior with haughty, almost artful glances, and then said aloud: "But you are Abbess now, *ma Mère*. You should look much more comely than any of us. After all, the habit of Saint Bernard is meant to be becoming."

Angélique quelled her with a look. She foresaw that she was going to have great trouble with this Dame de la Serre—as indeed she did, for she was keeping up a secret correspondence with Dame d'Estrées in Paris. The Master General also sensed disturbances, so in order to lighten the tension he suggested that the new Abbess should be shown her apartments.

Angélique was brought to the suite of rooms especially prepared for her in Angélique d'Estrées' sumptuous building. True, all the fine hangings and furniture, and the bed which had belonged to the Abbess, had been returned to her, and her four so-called ladies-in-waiting had left. But even so, the place was very comfortable, with a cheerful fire crackling in the immense hearth. The bed had a good mattress and was surrounded by clean hangings. There were earthenware bowls for washing, a wooden writing table and an ink well, and some newly sharpened quills. There was even a carpet on the stone floor, and the windows were clean and well-curtained. There were several holy pictures hanging on the walls, a chair or two, a *prie-dieu* with its red cushion.

A lay sister came up and said meekly, "May I have your trunk, *Madame l'Abbesse?*"

Angélique opened her cloak and disclosed a bundle, made out of a large handkerchief into which she had packed the bare necessities, which, one can be assured, did not include soap balls, tooth brush or comb. Angélique looked round her cell and its adjoining room with distaste, remembering all she had learned there. The lay sister began to wonder whether she had forgotten anything in its preparation and asked: "Is everything to your liking, *Madame l'Abbesse?*"

Angélique replied, "It would be very imperfect of me, if I took this place. Cleanliness is held by most to be a virtue, but it is only a fleshly virtue, a real vice before the Lord, for it is opposed to the

poverty in which Our Lord lived, in order to expiate our vanities.
Don't you remember, He was born in the straw of a stable?"

The lay sister began to quail. Angélique continued: "Devotion
is the pearl of the Gospel which you only acquire when you sell
everything you possess. Now at Port-Royal, when a girl enters my
novitiate I make her practise the virtue of holy poverty even at the
expense of cleanliness, for cleanliness is usually the pretext she
takes for dispensing herself from poverty. In private one should
desire always the worst objects and the less clean ones. No, this
room will become the infirmary." Then she turned to the lay sister
and said, authoritatively, "Let me see where *you* sleep."

The lay sister exclaimed: "Oh, but it's not a fit place for you to
see, *ma Mère l'Abbesse.*"

Angélique imperiously repeated, "Take me to your cell, instantly."

"*Ma Mère*, it isn't even a cell. You'll be horrified."

However, she led the way into the main house, where they
climbed up a flight of rickety stairs until they reached the attics.
The lay sister's little hovel was close to a staircase in frequent use.
It was unhealthy, because it was immediately under the roof and
near an ill-smelling drainpipe through which lizards and toads
came in. It was almost pitch dark, and the stench was unendurable.
The filthy bed was not fit for an animal. It was dreadful to think
that the lay sister had slept in such a place.

Angélique looked around her with great pleasure. She said: "I
will have this cell. I will get you somewhere else for yourself."

The lay sister began to protest, but again was quelled by the
imperiousness of Angélique.

"I would not change this place for the whole world. It will be
my only consolation. I know that directly I'm in here I will imagine
myself in the grotto of Bethlehem in which Jesus Christ was the
only light."

She grew to love this dark place just as St. Bernard had loved his
nook at the top of the stairs at Clairvaux when he was Abbot. But,
as she wanted to be austere in all things, she renounced even the
spiritual delight of privacy and, after a while, slept with a Soeur
Augustine de St. Paul, who was very rude to her.

The lay sister took away her cheap little lamp, which had only cost a few pence, a lamp which the community had deemed sufficient for her; it smoked, for the oil was not pure nut oil but mixed, and gave forth a terrible smell, and the wick always seemed to be uneven.

"Where are you going?" said Angélique.

"I'm going to give you a proper wax candle in a lantern."

"No, no, I'll have that lamp," she said. "Put it on the floor."

She kept that lamp for twenty years, although it was a great nuisance to her always.

It was indeed ostentatious and unnecessary for Angélique to perform these conspicuous penances. They used to fill the nuns with despair, for they knew they were inimitable. It would have been far more holy if her penances had been hidden, and if she had lived in the normal way of Benedictine abbesses. She could always, unbeknown to all, have slept on the floor after she had locked her door, and she could have put out her fire when she was alone. But no. Everything was obvious. One feels this was a great imperfection which helped to bring others to despair. The Psalmist says: "God giveth sleep to his beloved." She had indeed a great need of sleep, in her onerous and thankless task, and it was at Maubuisson that she began to lose her good health by losing sleep and disobeying all the laws of nature. Before long, very soon after leaving the Abbey, she had cardiac asthma, digestive trouble, stomach ulcers, and diabetes, which caused her to swell gradually and become shapeless. And then she had terrible attacks of kidney trouble through stone, and consequent migraines. She took so little advantage of the few hours of rest which the reformed Rule allowed, that she must always have been in a state of despairing and hopeless exhaustion. For example, when she went to reform the Abbey of Poissy, she would talk with the Superior until eleven o'clock at night, although they had to rise three hours later.

In winter Angélique only ate an egg yolk for her evening meal, and then it was not very fresh, and as she hated eggs anyway it must have been a real penance for her to swallow this mess. Later, St. François de Sales was to say to her:

"To eat little, to work much, to have many troubles on your mind, and to refuse to give your body sleep, is like wanting to drag a lot of hard work from an exhausted horse without allowing him to refresh himself."

Unlike her sister Agnès, who was outwardly restrained in her endearments, Angélique had a kind of passionate tenderness about her. It served its purpose. The abbesses she used to visit, to reform, would embrace her and exclaim to her nuns, "How happy you are to have so good a Mother!" Other nuns would repeat, "What an admirable Abbess you have! What a mind. What strength of persuasion."

And here at Maubuisson, Angélique used all her powers of charm and persuasion. Sometimes she would draw a tear from the older, more sentimental nuns, but their good resolutions did not last. Directly they had left her, they discussed it all and encouraged one another in their old ways.

Quite soon, Angélique began to see it was no good. She knew she would never establish a solid inward reform, whatever she might impose on outward appearances. Old nuns were forever wrangling, forever slipping in to her to complain. They were ultra-sensitive. They thought they were being shown up by the behaviour of the young. One day, Angélique realized how many enemies she had amongst the monks, who of course detested this reform which would affect their way of life and deprive them of their good meals.

She had drawn up a plan of reform and submitted it to the Master General. He approved it and returned it by his secretary. After it had been read aloud in the Chapter House, the secretary was left alone for a moment with some of the older nuns. He said in a whisper, that as this plan had been composed by Mère Angélique, they could look upon it as coming from her and accordingly do what they pleased about it. The confessor of the community, also a Cistercian, the ignorant Dom Sabbatier, was against her. "Yes," he murmured, "please yourselves."

One day before a great feast, Angélique saw the old nuns preparing to go to confession in the chapel. In turns, they were handing each other an enormous book. She went up to them and said: "May

I know, if you please, what is this book that you are all chattering about so loudly?"

Dame de la Serre exclaimed in her loud voice: "Oh, it's our confession book."

"When you have all made your confessions, will you please come up to me in the Chapter House? I want to speak to you."

Angélique was shocked to find that for years they had never made their confessions properly. The priest used to ask them questions to which they answered Yes or No. Their ignorance of their first duties, and even of the elements of Christianity, was amazing.

"But I can't understand how Dom Sabbatier would give you absolution if you didn't know how to confess properly. Now I want to know what is in this book."

"Ah, well you see, *ma Mère*," said Dame de la Serre, "we knew that Dom Sabbatier was a bit cross with the way we didn't know how to confess, so we composed three kinds of confession between us."

Two or three of the nuns sniggered.

"One for great feasts, one for Sundays and one for work days. We wrote them all out in this big book, and we lend it to one another in turns."

"In other words," interrupted Angélique, "you all confess to exactly the same misdeeds, even though you may not have committed them. But this is dreadful! I will have to get in some good priest to teach you how to confess your sins properly." She glanced at the book, and could not help smiling at the childishness of some of these confessions, which of course never probed to the roots of their troubles. She looked up and said, "I see that your confessions do not include some of the things I have noticed here. The use of beautiful headdresses and scents. And I happen to know that many of you have long tresses which you brush every night. And of course, breakings of the Rule connected with enclosure. And you all have private property and serve picnics in green arbours in hot weather, regardless of your poor fellow nuns here who have no dowries and who are sometimes starving. You confess to tiny little sins which really are quite unimportant, and you forget the law of charity to your neighbour. You break silence all the time. My poor dear sisters, you must really try not to talk so much in the cloisters. It disturbs the young ones. It is an ill example. Try and please me a little more in one or two things. Let us try, first of all, about talking in the cloister."

Dame de la Serre's eyes blazed. She said in her loud tones: "*Madame l'Abbesse,* when we entered this house, it was for the un-reformed Rule. We never wished to adopt the Rule such as it was practised at Port-Royal des Champs." There was a disdainful tone in her voice.

Now if one of Angélique's own nuns had spoken to her like that, she would probably have boxed her ears, but she controlled her temper and quietly walked out of the Chapter House.

When she had left, all the nuns chattered like starlings. And then Dame Desmarest who, being reliable, had been appointed portress, exclaimed: "I like to peep at Sister Claire when she is at her prayers. She really looks like an angel. And then, she's so sweet to me. These new nuns behave to us as if they were our lay sisters. They wait on us with great care and charity, and I must confess I am edified by their spirit of peace and humility."

"Ho!" exclaimed Dame du Meng, "it is only to win you over. And when you've fallen into the trap, you wait and see how uncomfortable your life will be made, *ma mère.* There'll be hair shirts and iron chains, and no one's going to light a fire and we'll have hardly anything to eat. She'll starve us to death. I feel sure she's going to recruit some new nuns. Very often, you know, I see the post as it comes through—I'm sure there are many applications."

After a while, by sheer sweetness and patience, Angélique was able to persuade them to keep inside the enclosure. She forbade the admission of seculars, and she built iron grilles for the parlours, dividing them in two, and the mesh was so strong and close, that nobody could slip his hands through or pass little notes. She left the older nuns undisturbed in the enjoyment of any privileges which were consistent with decency; she allowed them to keep their titles, their mundane attire; but she simply would not have them gallop-ing along the high road with the monks of St. Martin. Very soon the local gentry, who had been entertained with lavish picnics and

theatrical performances at Maubuisson, began to complain that
Angélique had the evil eye.

The chanting was as bad as ever. Angélique injured her health,
at that time, more by constraining her impatience in choir than by
her austerities.

It was from those days at Maubuisson that she got such a poor
idea of her own sex. She talked of nuns as imbeciles, and said that
their pet sins were jealousy and ingratitude. All this she must have
gleaned from the ancients of the Abbey. After a while she began to
regret more than ever that she had been elected Abbess.

She was as anti-mystical as ever. Her voice was still harsh, she
talked too quickly and too loud, she did everything in a hurried
manner. In fact she was completely uncontemplative. If she had to
leave her abbey for one or two days, either to go to Pontoise or to
reform some other abbey of the Order, she was so afraid of what
her nuns would do in her absence, that she would never say she
was going away. She left the place in the hands of the Prioress and
slipped away before dawn, unheard, when everybody was asleep.

Since the older nuns were deprived of their pleasures, they had
more time in which to complain about their Abbess behind her
back. Angélique became apprehensive, as if she were living on the
brink of a smouldering volcano. Something told her, some instinct,
to beware of Dame de la Serre. She had heard rumours of her
friendship with Dame d'Estrées and how furious she had been at
that Abbess's departure. A great deal of the housework was done
by the younger nuns whom Angélique had brought. They did the
laundry too, and the gardening—at least, the weeding. Angélique
used to light fires, sweep the cloisters, help to wash up: all really
very unsuitable and unnecessary, because the lay sisters were there
for that, and Angélique could have employed her time in trying
to learn how to pray, and in teaching her nuns the elements of
Christianity. She never seemed to get to the heart of the matter,
and that is perhaps the reason why she was not successful at
Maubuisson. Some of the old aristocrats secretly despised her for
belonging to the middle classes. Her father was only a barrister,
whereas their papas had been soldiers and courtiers with high-
sounding titles and ancient châteaux.

Angélique had two consolations. Her mother's lady's maid came to her and told her that she wanted to be a nun. Angélique reflected for a moment or two and then said that if the maid would pray especially that her little sister, Madelon Arnauld, should join her, she would do all she could to help her. The lady's maid looked very much upset. She knew what Madame Arnauld thought of her daughter's malevolent attraction. Angélique, who was used to reading faces, exclaimed:

"I know what you think! But you see, I'm trying to build up a community within a community here. Madelon will be quite all right."

The lady's maid interrupted. "But *Madame l'Abbesse,* I saw you carrying the linen and laundry up to the attic. I saw you hoeing the garden. True, you did it with such an appearance of joy, that it seemed the greatest pleasure in the world. They tell me that things go smoothly since you've been here. And all the old nuns, who are very hard to please, are served, according to your orders, with great care. But I can't see your frivolous little sister Madelon behaving like this and being happy here. And I know Madame Arnauld would be worried for her health."

Angélique exclaimed impatiently, "Please don't be anxious about my sister. I will take great care of her. I don't want her to lose her soul in the world."

The lady's maid interrupted: "But I know she wants to marry. She loves children so much. You should see her with her nephews."

"How terrible!" exclaimed Angélique.

Gradually Angélique began to lose hope about the nuns under her charge, with their quarrels, their human ambitions, and above all their curiosity. Angélique said, "A nun never needs to know what is happening outside the enclosure, even about her own Order." Yes, Madelon would be as pliable as wax, she would be able to make of her all she wished, and with her begin a nucleus of good nuns. A poor young girl from Paris had called the other day. She was infirm and her voice was not very strong. She wished to enter the Order, but the older nuns would not have her. Angélique felt she must be backed by her own sisters, to do as she wished.

Angélique was greatly consoled about that time because her sister Anne-Eugénie, who had fallen very anaemic at Port-Royal, came to Maubuisson for a change of air. Even the older nuns admired her. She was so beautiful, so austere, so aloof. She was withdrawn into a life of prayer—a living example. With her ever increasing infirmities, Anne-Eugénie ceased to walk upright as in the old days, but held her head a little bowed. She was indeed a king's daughter, "all glorious within," she who had disdained to marry even the greatest of earthly princes.

Even her sister Angélique, who so much despised mystical experience, spoke with awe of that first vision of her sister's. She was almost envious, for Angélique herself was for ever spiritually unconsoled. Perhaps that was half the trouble: her dark nights seemed to last a lifetime.

There was no special trait in the prayer of the nuns of Port-Royal under Angélique's régime. Perhaps they were characterized mostly by abandonment to the Holy Spirit. They had no precise spiritual physiognomy. They were nebulous because they had had so many different confessors, and because in the way of prayer herself, Angélique, unlike St. Teresa, had no very great devotion to the person of Christ. (She thought she had.) She was imbued with a great sense of the presence of God. She wrote to a Soeur Suzanne: "The immensity of God is infinite. For this reason, we must not shut Him up in a choir or in a solitude. His grandeur is so marvellous that He increases the stature of everything which draws near to Him. He is so intimately close to the souls who desire Him that He remains in them even in the midst of their distractions and troubles, and even before they call upon Him, He says to them 'Here I am.' "

To nuns in Poland, she wrote many years afterwards: "Our Lord has only showed His glory on the one occasion on Thabor. He lived as a poor man." That short sentence epitomizes all she thinks of religious duty; no mystical flights, no ecstasies, but simply this exaggerated and lopsided love for poverty. She was never open-hearted about receiving help from other religious Orders. She haunted the Carmelites of Pontoise. It is known that she went to see them, both in the March and September of 1620, but she never seems to have gleaned anything from them, though they were very remarkable nuns. The famous lay sister who had helped to bring the Carmelites to France, Madame Acarie, had died on April 18th of the year that Angélique had come to Maubuisson. It is at the Carmel of Pontoise that Angélique had the great privilege of meeting the nun who had been the companion of St. Teresa on her journeys and who became the Venerable Anne de St. Barthélemy. She had been at Pontoise seven or eight months after the foundation of 1618. She eventually went to Flanders. Angélique tells us herself, "I had written in the old days to Mère Anne de St. Barthélemy, who was then Superior of the Carmelites in Flanders, to ask to be a lay sister in one of their monasteries, and I received an answer." She never told us the answer.

Angélique spoke to the Carmelites of her own private troubles at Maubuisson. She said how awkward it was to be under the jurisdiction of the unsatisfactory Cistercian monks.

"Ah, yes," exclaimed the Prioress, "we would have had that trouble too if we had brought our Carmelite monks from Spain. I advise you to put yourself under the jurisdiction of the Archbishop of Paris."

(It is a fact that the talks which Angélique had with the Carmelites at Pontoise influenced her to break with the Cistercians completely and eventually to put her abbey under the jurisdiction of the Archbishop.)

The Prioress said: "Mère Madeleine de St. Joseph is a remarkable person. You really must go and see her when you are in Paris. I'm sure she will welcome you, for we have often told her about you."

Indeed, Mère Madeleine de St. Joseph is said to have affirmed that, if she had lost her cause at Rome against the Carmelite monks, she would have left her Order and joined Mère Angélique at Port-Royal. She was greatly revered in France, and Angélique had the great privilege, a few years afterwards, of spending a whole day with her, from six in the morning until two in the afternoon at the end of the month of May. Mère Madeleine was the very best type of French nun, and that means something very magnificent indeed.

It has been said of her that she was a fire hidden beneath the ashes. Anne de St. Barthélemy, who was Prioress in succession to her, thought she was an angel, and proposed her to the others for imitation. She and some other nun wrote to say that to receive her into the Order, they would cheerfully have undertaken the journey from Spain to France. They said that even as a novice she was eminently qualified to make a very accomplished prioress, and that she bore a great resemblance to their Foundress, Mother Teresa, being the lawful heiress of her spirit.

But hardly any of this impinged on Angélique. By her blindness she missed taking part in the most thrilling religious renaissance in France—the coming of the Carmelites from Spain.

The Carmelite Order was very austere, and only people of terrific pluck could bear the penitential Rule. Few people realize that the spiritual side of the Rule of the Visitation Order was inspired by the Carmelite ideal. Visitandines made up for lack of austerities by a severe spirit of inward mortification. The founders, St. François de Sales and Ste. Jeanne de Chantal, took pity on women whose flesh was not strong enough to bear camel hair cloth, or whose digestions were not strong enough to digest roots. And so, they founded an Order in which women of poor health could take refuge.

Very soon began Angélique's own connection with St. François and Ste. Jeanne de Chantal. She did not realize how greatly these two admired the Carmelites and how Ste. Jeanne de Chantal had been for long months at the feet of the Dijon Carmelites, trying to learn their spirit of contemplative prayer.

8. MONSEIGNEUR DE GENÈVE AND MÈRE DE CHANTAL COME TO THE ABBEY OF MAUBUISSON

AFTER A YEAR at Maubuisson, Angélique met St. François de Sales, then the Bishop of Geneva.[1] He was fifty-one, and had come to Paris because Mère de Chantal was founding a Visitation convent in Monseigneur Zamet's stables. She had undergone such hardships through illness and poverty that neither she nor her nuns possessed a change of linen.

Angélique had heard about him, and longed to meet him. She was providentially helped, for the father of one of her novices, the unsatisfactory Soeur de Bonneuil, had asked Monseigneur de Genève to confirm his daughter. He was in an important position, being the usher of the Corps Diplomatique.

Soeur de Bonneuil spoke enthusiastically about the Bishop to Angélique: "He attacked the Calvinists of Thonon in an unusual way. In his badly lit, cold little room, he read Protestant authors in order to find out their objections and answer them by delving deep into the Bible, the Fathers of the Church and the Catholic theologians. Then he wrote hundreds of short tracts which he addressed very politely to 'Messieurs de Thonon.' Every night he would slip these under the doors of houses in the town and the outskirts. He has converted hundreds from heresy. He is so beloved in his dio-

[1] He was consecrated in 1602. Monseigneur is the common title of Bishops in France.

125

cese that the boatmen of the Lake of Annecy call him Father, not
Monseigneur."

So, on April 5th, 1619, Monseigneur de Genève came to Maubuisson for the day, an event which occasioned much jealous grumbling among the Cistercian monks.

The gentleness of Monseigneur de Genève did not come to him
naturally. His family was renowned for fiery tempers. But he had
achieved tranquillity. He had the high colour of a man who lives a
great deal out of doors, his hair was a blend of chestnut and red,
he had regular features which looked as if they were carved out of
wood, and his face was full of rustic dignity. That startling, glowing beauty of his had caused him many troubles, as he once confessed to Mère de Chantal. He was a very good listener. His manner was majestic and serious, though his talk was always sprinkled
with cordial expressions. He used to say about himself, "I am
completely human." He had no use for people with hard hearts. He
gave you the impression that you were the only person of importance. Time was of no account, precious though it was to a man as
overworked as he.

Before meeting Angélique he had heard a great deal about this
young reforming abbess, for of course all Paris was talking about
her—the court, the clergy and the religious orders. It was not the
first time that Monseigneur de Genève had met a reforming abbess,
for he had guided the beautiful Abbess of Montmatre, during very
difficult days, when she had risked being poisoned by her own
nuns. He had told her to be gentle with the old, unreformed nuns:
"They can't get used to new things so easily. They are not so
supple, for the nerves of their minds, just like those of their bodies,
have already contracted." As he looked at Angélique he thought
that he would probably give her the same advice, if she asked for
it.

To Angélique's surprise, he enquired whether he and his chaplain might walk in the garden with her and meet two or three of her
nuns. "And then we will all get acquainted," he said with his
charming smile. Angélique replied:

"Monseigneur, I hope you will come again very soon, and stay for a long time."

"I will do anything you ask me, *Madame l'Abbesse*," he replied, still with that grave, quiet courtliness.

He walked slowly in the garden and noticed, rather sadly, that there were very few flowers. He said, "Could I go to your farm? You see"—again with a smile—"I am a true rustic. I was born and bred in the country. I spent all my young days barefoot with my brothers and little friends, leaping about in mountain streams and on rocks, watching the farmers and talking to them about their crops, and hearing their talk with my father in the great kitchen of our château."

Angélique began to feel envious. What a childhood he must have had! And to think she had never seen a real mountain. She found it hard to walk as slowly and as deliberately as he did. He paused every so often to admire a tree, a bird or an insect. His eyes were full of wonder. Together they walked towards the Abbey farm.

The farmer's wife was suckling her baby near the sunlit barn. And then took place the miracle which was always occasioned by the saint's presence. The baby left his mother's breast directly he heard the footstep of Monseigneur de Genève, and champed with his little feet and struggled and cried. The chaplain went up to the woman and said, "Bring your child to be blessed by Monseigneur."

When Monseigneur put his hand on the child's brow and blessed him, and when he had caressed his little cheek, the baby calmed down and started to coo. The chaplain smiled and said: "You see, Monseigneur, it happens at Maubuisson, just as in your own diocese."

No wonder that, many years afterwards, Angélique told her nephew, Antoine Le Maître: "I put my heart into his hands without reserve."

After the nuns had knelt to kiss his ring and receive his blessing Angélique, who had not asked for any help for herself, repeated: "Monseigneur, I hope you will come again and stay a long time."

"Yes, that would give me very great joy," he said. "I will be in Paris on the first of May, because Mère de Chantal is founding a house of our Visitation. If you are in Paris on that afternoon, I hope you will come too."

When he was alone with her for a moment before going to his coach, he said that he found the reform of Port-Royal austere. "My daughter, it would be better, not to catch such big fish, but to take a greater quantity."

Angélique replied: "If I had had to make a Rule, I believe I would have made it more lenient, but finding myself in an austere Order, I thought it my duty to keep its Rule as much as possible."

"I agree," he said.

When he had left, she turned to her sisters and said: "God is truly and visibly present in this holy bishop."

She began writing to him, and he, who had made it a rule always to answer every letter, answered all hers, although he was working himself to death. (He died of overwork in his early fifties.) She was consoled by the affection of these letters, not realizing that this did not necessarily imply favouritism. He was often stern with those he loved best.

In mid-July he visited Agnès at Port-Royal des Champs. Ever afterwards he spoke of the place as "*mes chers délices.*" And then on August 25th, although suffering from dysentery, he came to spend ten days at Maubuisson. He was accompanied by his brother, the Bishop of Belley.

Angélique had planned to make a general confession to him. With Marie-Claire, she retreated to a parlour which she had turned into an oratory, and she dined off two eggs.

The saint felt so ill that he went upstairs to his room to rest for a time, whilst Angélique entertained his brother. He asked to see the famous Maubuisson relics, so all the nuns were summoned to venerate them too. Afterwards he said to Angélique:

"Who was that nun, *Madame l'Abbesse,* rather tall and commanding, in a well-cut habit?"

"Oh," said Angélique, "that was Dame de la Serre, a great friend of the last Abbess, Dame d'Estrées."

"Alas," he said, "she is both haughty and sly. I am afraid she is not in sympathy with your reform."

"Far from it," sighed Angélique.

"Would you like me to speak to her?"

"Perhaps," said Angélique, rather dubiously. "I myself have been unable to do anything with her."

He said: "You don't think she is corresponding with her old Abbess, do you? We've all felt very uneasy in Paris, since she escaped from prison last February."

"I hope not," said Angélique. "I always read the letters that go out."

The Bishop of Belley did not say that his brother, Monseigneur de Genève, at the sight of Angélique's untidy habit, would have echoed Socrates, who, glancing at some other philosopher whose clothes were all holes, exclaimed: "Through these holes, I see thy vanity!"

And indeed, if Angélique had imagined that St. François would find nothing to criticize in her, the reforming abbess whose reputation had spread even to Rome, she was greatly mistaken. He even reproved her for an unnecessary glance out of a window. He said she must really walk and talk more slowly. But he appreciated her good qualities—her strength and independence, her sincerity, lack of affectation and her kind heart. He called her "*un coeur extraordinaire.*" He disliked effeminate souls. Very cleverly the saint probed to the root of her trouble: he said that she must have half an hour's prayer a day. It seems odd that she should have needed this advice at all.

Strange though it may seem, Angélique's reputation in Paris was higher than that of Mère de Chantal, who had not begun reforming so young. Monseigneur de Genève regretted that his lips were sealed and that he could not tell Angélique how Mère de Chantal had been fashioned by her fidelity to prayer, arising at five each morning, even in winter, making her fire herself, in order to have an hour's mental prayer before she started her household duties.

He advised Angélique to read his *Treatise on the Love of God,* for he had written it after noting all the beauties of the great souls entrusted to him, of Mère de Chantal and the early Sisters of the Annecy Visitation. What a pity that Angélique was so cramped by fear of illusion.

Angélique began to long to enter this new Order. She felt that her vows were null and void and that she would easily get a dispensation from the Pope to leave the Cistercians. But she did not speak to Monseigneur about it that August.

Observing that Angélique was a little too brusque with some of her more tiresome nuns, he advised her to caress them. "Oh yes, I mean what I say, my daughter. I am not joking. When a nun is ill or afflicted or even a little melancholic, kindness will do her so much good. I know a Superior who is so kind when she upbraids, that they speak about 'her punishing love.' Even her severities are tempered by the attentions of a true mother. I don't want your devotion to be temperamental, muddle-headed, melancholic, tiresome, fretful, but I want it to be sweet, gentle and peaceful."

He deplored her tendency to sarcasm and irony, and her condemnation of the world—that world she knew so little. He himself greatly appreciated the beautiful things of the world—buildings, painting, music, hunting, birds, all the flowers of garden and field —and he used them all as mystical staircases to rise up to God. She was so pessimistic: she seemed to think that worldly things were wholly evil. What kind of upbringing had she had?

He was soon to have an opportunity to see, for he received an invitation from the Arnaulds to stay with them at Andilly. But before he left Maubuisson, he offered, ill though he was, to consecrate the high altar. He preached to those unworthy nuns for an hour and a half, looking like an angel, explaining point by point all the meaning of the consecration ceremonies.

When the ten days were over, he bade good-bye to Angélique. Alas, the letters between Maubuisson and Savoie took six weeks. She was never to see him again.

When he had left, Angélique wrote and implored him to admit her to the Visitation. As he said himself, he "dodged" the issue. He said kind things to her, but underneath he remained implacable. One is not surprised. How greatly this tormented abbess would have disturbed the peace of his newborn dovecot! To soften his refusal, he made out that he did not want to steal her from Port-Royal. "I think I can assure you, on God's behalf, that He will use you for important things and in an extraordinary fashion."

To another, he wrote: "I would not have deflected from her just vocation the most excellent creature in the world, even if she were to become a canonized saint at the Visitation."

Mère de Chantal, writing to him enthusiastically about Angélique's vocation, sought his advice before taking any steps. He eluded the whole question by submitting the decision to Rome. Rome refused permission. So it all came to nothing.

It wanted but a few years to the birth of St. Margaret Mary Alacoque, who founded the great Catholic devotion to the Sacred Heart of our Lord, in the Visitation Convent of Paray-le-Monial in Burgundy. Indeed, in the year of Angélique's death, 1661, St. Margaret Mary was already being trained in bitter suffering. By the time that the Port-Royal nuns had fallen into heresy and were condemned by Rome, the devotion was being firmly established throughout France.

Angélique's nuns deviated so far from the true spirit of St. Bernard, that at the end, one can really say they were no longer true Cistercians. A marked antipathy grew up between the nuns of Port-Royal and those of the Visitation. And yet, it was the Visitandines whom the Archbishop of Paris sent to Port-Royal to try and wean it from heresy. Ever afterwards, Jansenists entertained a particular dislike for the devotion to the Sacred Heart; indeed they would never attend a High Mass on that feast day. How regrettable, after the friendship between the reforming Abbess and the Foundress.

Monseigneur de Genève had always disapproved of great physical austerities. He preferred the much more penetrating mortification of the spirit. In this, he was wise. Angélique would load herself with hair shirts and chains, scourge herself to blood, but she never learned true gentleness or self-control.

9. *THE ABBESS ESCAPES FROM THE PENITENTS' HOME*

THOUGH THE Cistercian monks lay low when Monseigneur de Genève was at Maubuisson, yet directly he had gone, Angélique had a great deal of trouble with their envies and jealousies. Also she began to feel suspicious about Dame de la Serre. It is so easy to sense trouble when nuns live together in community.

Angélique kept a strict watch on the posts at that time. But how was she to know that Dame de la Serre had outsiders to help her —stewards and farm servants who would pick up letters dropped from a window at night? Angélique knew that a few of the nuns were rather frightened of her, and she wished that some incident would bring things to a head, to reveal which nuns were on her side.

Dame de la Serre waited until Monseigneur de Genève had gone. Then she had wax impressions made of all the keys and posted them secretly to her old friend, Dame d'Estrées, who had escaped on the 10th of February from the Couvent des filles repentantes de St. Magloire, in the rue St. Denis. What an escape!

One fine afternoon, when Dame d'Estrées in her drab penitent's robe was walking with all the other repentant prostitutes in the garden, she slipped behind a bush when the supervising nun's back was turned. While the disconsolate crocodile swarmed into the prison, she let down a rope ladder over the wall at a spot arranged beforehand. Her brother the Comte de Sanzai and his armed friends were on the other side with a coach and some swift horses. She scrambled down the ladder. She rushed into the coach. The coachman cracked his whip and they dashed off through the Paris streets at breakneck speed.

She went into hiding in her brother's house and made her plans. Several months later, at midnight on September 10th, she had a bath—a thing she had been most particular about during her days at Maubuisson. She put on her beautiful Cistercian habit and a becoming headdress. She ate a good meal—her appetite was always hearty. She and her band must have left Paris at about 3:30 in the morning, before the sun had risen, in order to reach Maubuisson just before Terce, which is usually said at 7:45, before the conventual High Mass. It is Angélique Arnauld who gave a spirited description of these events to her nephew, Antoine Le Maître, and he, in his usual fashion, scribbled it all down directly after the interview.

The porter, a good man who was loyal to Angélique Arnauld, must have been surprised when he heard the command to open. When he saw the deposed Abbess appear with a lot of armed gentlemen, he did his best to prevent them from entering the enclosure. But alas, he had to do with unscrupulous ruffians who stopped at nothing. When he was beaten up, he gave a piercing cry. Dame d'Estrées and her accomplices threatened to throw him into the pond unless he hushed. They left him for dead. (There is a theory that the porter may have gone round by the farm and kitchen gardens, over to the Abbey, to warn Angélique Arnauld, so that when her old Abbess appeared at the church door, she was not taken by surprise.)

He lay for some time, his wounds bleeding; then he realized that he must creep quietly and unobtrusively into his lodge to bind up his wounds, have a good drink of hot wine, and then slip out to the high road to Paris. There, he would get in touch with Angélique's brother, Henri, Bishop of Angers. He was the only member of her family in Paris at the time, for her parents and relations were at Andilly.

Had it not been for his speedy action, the coup of Dame d'Estrées might have been successful and Angélique Arnauld would have been thrown out. As it happened, it was very impru-

dent of Dame d'Estrées to use armed force when she was in the
middle of a lawsuit for the restitution of her old Abbey. Had she
waited, she might have had the letter of the law on her side.

In order not to warn the community of their arrival, the conspirators put the horses and coach in the coach house at the right
of the entrance. Then they passed by the confessor's house. Dom
Sabbatier was on their side. By then the sun had risen.

They crept stealthily towards the church and made for the door
between two woodpiles, near the Abbess' garden. Dame d'Estrées
had taken great pleasure in her garden, but now it was completely
neglected, as the new Abbess did not care for flowers. Dame
d'Estrées' face flushed with anger that her old pupil, to whom she
had been so kind, should have ousted her from her rightful position in which she had been installed by the King himself. Yes, she
had had some good times here. She glanced towards the windmill
on the bank of the ancient pond, and recalled picnics with local
gentry. Oh, those men would be glad to see her return!

What wouldn't she do after turning out Angélique Arnauld, her
two sisters and the two other nuns from Port-Royal des Champs!
She'd also heard rumours that the Arnauld women had recruited
poor novices without a dowry. Yes, she would throw out those
paupers, if they weren't to her liking. She would close the door to
ecclesiastics like Monseigneur de Genève, and give a good reward
to Dom Sabbatier and Dame de la Serre, who had been so loyal
to her. She would bring back her children to live in her turret, and
the good old times would start all over again. She knew she would
be backed up by the local gentry, who had always regretted her
hurried departure; with their help, she would know how to deal
with any guards the Master General might send. She was quite
ruthless and would shoot at sight.

Dame d'Estrées knew that it was almost time for Terce and
Sext, and went to wait by the church entrance. The tall figure of
Dame de la Serre lurched out of the woodpile by the door; she was
holding the key. Embracing her old Abbess, she whispered: "Be
careful, the Arnauld is in the confessional near the door. You'll fall
straight into her arms."

Dame d'Estrées seized the key. As she turned it in the well-oiled lock, a flood of memories overcame her—her sister Gabrielle, all the ceremonies at which she had presided, all the Abbey treasures which had delighted her eyes. She supposed that middle-class Angélique Arnauld had not taken care of them. Dame d'Estrées had even heard it rumoured that she would never use the crystal and gold crosier, but had had a plain oak one made for her. What a tragic comedy began on that 10th of September!

"You remain outside," said Dame d'Estrées to her band in her imperious way.

She turned the key, and there was Dame de la Serre again, waiting for her behind the door, just as the nuns were filing into choir. Angélique Arnauld, just emerging from a confessional, did not look very surprised when she saw her, but one can imagine that the nuns coming into choir were amazed at the sounds of altercation which followed. Anne-Eugénie and Marie-Claire felt very apprehensive when they realized who had returned, but Anne-Eugénie, for one, was always very calm, and started to pray for her sister. "And to think," reflected Angélique Arnauld, "that d'Estrées actually came to Port-Royal, to hoodwink me into believing that she wanted to reform her Abbey! Oh, that was a sly one." The two women confronted one another.

Dame d'Estrées began—aristocratic to the finger-tips: "Madame, I am come here to thank you for the care which you have taken of my abbey during my absence, and to ask you to go back to your own, and to leave me to rule mine."

Angélique Arnauld replied—true descendant of barristers: "Madame, I would do it very willingly if I could, but you know that it is the reverend Abbot of Cîteaux, our Superior, who has ordered me to come and rule this house, and, that having come here under obedience, I cannot leave it except under the same obedience."

Dame d'Estrées replied, "I am the Abbess and I'm going to take your place."

"Madame, you are no longer the Abbess, having been deposed."

"I have given notice of Appeal."

Angélique Arnauld replied, "Your appeal has not been granted. The sentence of deposition pronounced against you remains with regard to me. . . . I have been established in this house by the authority of the Abbot of Cîteaux and the King. That is why you must not object if I take the Abbess's place here."

And she went quietly to the choir and sat down on her monumental chair. All the listening nuns quivered with excitement.

"What impertinence! What impudence!" yelled Dame d'Estrées. "My pupil to take my place! Oh, I'll have you turned out!" Her yells were drowned by the chant.

After the office of Terce, and before High Mass, Angélique Arnauld told her nuns that she wished to speak to them alone, and they left the church. She said to them quite quietly: "We must all receive Holy Communion at this Mass, to implore the Holy Spirit's help in the storm which is about to rise."

Almost all were prepared to obey, for it was a Feast of the Cistercian Order, so that about thirty of them received Holy Communion. Then Angélique Arnauld went to attend to Dame d'Estrées, who had been trying to secure the allegiance of the Portress and the Cellaress. But they refused to give up their keys to her. So, in a terrible fury, she turned on Angélique Arnauld and, shouted:

"Show me at once to my suite of rooms."

She expected to find it just as she had left it, and great was her surprise to find it in a filthy condition, with six ailing nuns who had just taken a purge lying on mattresses on the floor. She turned on Angélique Arnauld:

"What is this disgusting mess?"

"We were not prepared for your coming," she replied, with a sarcastic smile and a lift of the sardonic eyebrows. And with that she left her, dashing to the archives to secure some important title deeds. She knew that the unscrupulous Dame d'Estrées would lay hands on anything to serve her purpose; in fact, she realized that the deposed Abbess was a thoroughly dishonest woman. Then she went to the kitchen and ordered a good meal to be served privately to Dame d'Estrées. All the time, she was feeling anxious in case the porter had been unable to reach Paris. She calculated that he should be there by midday, and only hoped that he would find her brother without delay.

Then she went to the refectory for her first meal of the day. She advised all the nuns to eat well, in order to keep up their strength, for they would have much to try them. Indeed, Angélique Arnauld realized by then that Dame d'Estrées was determined to drive her out of the Abbey. Of all this, she recounted:

"But I was very much astonished; after she [that is, Angélique d'Estrées] had spoken to Père Sabbatier, that monk, our confessor, came to tell me after dinner that I ought to retire and cede to force. I answered that I would do nothing of the kind and that I could not indeed do so in all conscience. The confessor looked ominous and said, 'Well, I am afraid you will have to be prepared for the worst. She is accompanied by armed men who will stop at nothing. You will all be hurt in the conflict.' I replied, 'I will not leave the enclosure except by force.' In the meantime Dame d'Estrées had been going from one nun to another, trying fruitlessly to win the young ones to her allegiance, but being more successful with three of the old ones."

During all that time the Comte de Sanzai and the four armed gentlemen were hiding in the woodpile near the church door. Then Dame d'Estrées was very clever: she said in honeyed tones to Angélique: "Come and discuss all this with me in church."

Angélique fell straight into the snare and replied: "Let us go, Madame, we could not choose a more suitable place."

All the nuns followed them.

In the choir, Anne-Eugénie, as if this were quite an ordinary day, was praying quietly in her stall, completely detached from the turmoil. What was her horrified dismay when she saw the confessor come in! (The Comte de Sanzai and the four armed gentlemen had left the woodpile and were hovering outside.) Advancing towards Angélique, Dame d'Estrées and the confessor exhorted her to yield to force and go at once, in order to prevent the further harm which might befall her nuns if she had to be taken away violently. Then one of the men who had remained outside fired a pistol, hoping to frighten Angélique's nuns, but they were far too self-controlled to mind. Angélique was the least surprised of all, and she exclaimed, "I am not at all upset, and again I repeat that I will not leave unless I am made to do so by force. Only in that case could I be excused before the Lord."

"All right," cried Dame d'Estrées. "You asked for it. You said you would only go by force, and by force you will go."

And, her face red with fury, she seized Angélique by the belt and pulled her towards the big door. Angélique Arnauld's nuns then rushed out of their choir stalls and held their Abbess back by her belt, until she began to fear that she would be suffocated in the struggle. Dame d'Estrées clutched at Angélique's veil and tore it off. At that, a loyal nun lost her temper; she rushed to Dame d'Estrées, tore off her veil and threw it to the ground. Dame d'Estrées cried out:

"Help, help, brother, they're killing me!"

At that point, Dame de la Serre opened the door with a flourish, and the other men rushed in with swords and pistols. Angélique Arnauld was being dragged back and forth between Dame d'Estrées and her novices. At length the men and Dame d'Estrées managed to pull her into the poultry yard.

Jean Racine gives a significant little detail: "A pistol was held to her chest there in the poultry yard. She saw a coach all prepared to take her away."

Angélique Arnauld said, in her very interesting report: "My sisters, who were lambs, became lions. They could not endure to see me being molested, and one of them, a tall nun called Anne de St. Thècle, the daughter of a gentleman, came towards her [Dame d'Estrées] and said, 'What, wretch that you are, you have the effrontery to take away Madame de Port-Royal's veil. Oh, I know you, I know who you are.' And as she said this, in the presence of these men who had naked swords in their hands, she tore off her [Dame d'Estrées'] veil from her head and let it fly to a distance of six paces.

"Dame d'Estrées, seeing me resolved not to go out, ordered these gentlemen to make me leave by force, which they did, taking me by the arm. I did not resist, for I was very glad to go away and retire with my nuns from a place in which men like these could be found, from whom I had everything to fear. However, the design of Dame d'Estrées was not that they (the nuns) should follow me. She feared that scandal. This is why she made me get into a coach. But as soon as I was in it, nine or ten of my nuns climbed in too.

Three scrambled up onto the coachman's seat, three on the back
and the others clung onto the wheels. Dame d'Estrées told the
coachman to whip up the horses, but he replied that he daren't,
because, if he did, he would kill several of the nuns. Immediately
I threw myself out of the coach with the sisters."

Dame d'Estrées posted a man at the door of the enclosure to prevent the other nuns from leaving. The strong nun got hold of him
and squashed him behind the door, and another very hefty nun
pushed the door against him. Then she threw Dame d'Estrées to
the ground and sat on her. What a picture!

"You fool!" cried Dame d'Estrées to the coachman. "I'll have you
horsewhipped for this. Didn't I tell you to ride on?"

"But I couldn't," said the poor man. "I would only have killed
the nuns and then been thrown into prison or sent to the galleys
for life, for murder."

"I'll have you murdered," she said, grinding her teeth at him.

The door was now open onto the high road to Pontoise. Angélique left on foot with thirty-five nuns. Directly they were out of
earshot, she stopped the procession and said, "You must all take
some cordial waters, because there's the plague at Pontoise." And
she took some out of her pocket. She had thought of everything.
Her sister Marie-Claire looked very ill; she was suffering from a
bad attack of dysentery. But Anne-Eugénie was as peaceful as ever,
telling her beads. Angélique said to a postulant in lay-clothes:
"Take off your green underskirt."

Angélique tore it up into veils for the nuns whose veils had been
destroyed in the skirmish. Then they formed up in a procession,
two by two, and walked quietly to Pontoise. On their way, they
were met by the Lieutenant of Pontoise, riding towards Maubuisson. Being Dame d'Estrées' liegeman, he made fun of them, for he
imagined that Dame d'Estrées was already safely established.

"Aha," he cried, "I knew you wouldn't stay there long! Usurpers!
hypocrites! Now try and find somebody to look after you, or go
back to your horrible Port-Royal in the swamp and don't trouble
us here any more."

Angélique took no notice. She thought: "Soon, soon, we'll get
help from Paris." Oh, if only she could be quite sure that the porter

had got there! If no help had come by the following evening, she would have to go to Paris herself.

As they walked through the narrow, tortuous street of little mediaeval Pontoise, people rushed to their doorways and windows, crying out:

"Here are the daughters of the good Madame de Port-Royal! They have left the Devil in the Abbey—they have really left the plague there—that infamous one, that lost one who has driven them out."

Angélique says in her report:

"I resolved directly to go into the first church I found, which belonged to the Jesuits, who came to receive us with outward proofs of civility and respect. After we had prayed in there, we came out again, and M. du Val, a doctor from the Sorbonne whom I knew very well, came to find me, and he told me that all the nuns of Pontoise were offering me their houses.[1] I said to him that in order to act with prudence, I must not accept their offers, and that I had to retire into a private house in which people could say that the Maubuisson nuns could be found. At once, Monsieur the Vicar General, a wise ecclesiastic, offered me his own, and I accepted. He retired into another, and in this way we lodged in an official dwelling, which we did all the more willingly, as it was a Church house."

Angélique arranged a chapel. Her nuns were glad to be all together. Marie-Claire was put to bed. The inhabitants of Pontoise, including the religious orders, offered them beds, china and alms. Angélique was delighted to accept alms, for it was a joy to her to be poor.

When she was counting her flock, she said that she wondered what had happened to a lay sister: "I remember. She was working today in the cellar. She can't have heard the noise, and may have turned up after we'd left."

"Here I am, *ma Mère*," said the sister in question, suddenly ap-

[1] (That is to say, the Ursulines, the principal hospital called the Hôtel-Dieu, the Carmelites.)

pearing at the door. "And here is a *pistole* which I found on the window sill before I left. I thought it might be useful to you."

Angélique received her with joy. They all began to live a fully cloistered life, keeping the monastic silence and the hours of prayer, and chanting all the Offices. They were as celestial as angels. The townsfolk came to hear Vespers. They had never heard Office so beautifully sung, being used to the horrible screechings of the old Maubuisson nuns.

In the meantime the wounded porter had reached Henri Arnauld, who speedily obtained an order for arresting Dame d'Estrées and a decree to re-establish Mère Angélique at Maubuisson.

Men fully armed, as if prepared for the worst, appeared at Maubuisson on September the 11th. The constable of the watch brought Angélique a hundred crowns from Catherine, for she knew she would be in dire need.

At 5 p.m. men and nuns watching from a tower at Maubuisson saw with terror an army of two hundred and fifty armed men marching along the road from Pontoise. They rushed down from the tower at top speed to warn Dame d'Estrées.

"Quick, quick," she said to Dame de la Serre, flinging off her Abbess's robes for the last time, "my lay clothes, my clothes." She tore down the stairs of her suite, and ran to a door in the enclosure which she had prudently unbricked the night before.

Dame de la Serre would have liked to escape with her Abbess, but it was too late. Quickly she seized a few provisions in a haversack, and a chamber pot. She climbed up a ladder to the top of a high wardrobe, and there hid behind a tapestry. She hoped to last out undiscovered for some time, up there.

Dom Sabbatier fled to the Jesuits at Pontoise. He was never to return to Maubuisson. The nuns who had been partisans of Dame d'Estrées trembled for their fate. They felt they would probably be dismissed to some penitential place for the rest of their days.

Dame d'Estrées and the Comte de Sanzai had fled in such a hurry that she left legal documents behind in a casket. When Angélique found them that evening, she saw that they contained many important papers. She wrote:

"The guard came to fetch me at Pontoise, and I left on foot just as I had come, with my nuns. All the priests of the town accompanied us, and a great crowd of people who loved us because of the alms we had given them. The guard were riding on either side."

This thrilling story is supplemented by Angélique's niece. It seems that this strange procession took place at ten o'clock at night.[1]

Directly the guard arrived, Mère Angélique judged that they must lose no time in taking possession again. The night would not prevent this, for it was changed into full daylight by the quantities of torches held by the guard.

"Each guard in the march, and they numbered a hundred and fifty, carried a torch in his hand and a musket on his shoulder. . . .

". . . One can picture the joy of all the good young nuns whom Angélique had received the year before, the quiet peacefulness of Anne-Eugénie and the weakness of poor Marie-Claire, already sick of dysentery, who had to be helped all the way and was nearly collapsing with fatigue. When she reached Maubuisson she was put into the infirmary, but Angélique was obliged to neglect her and poor Marie-Claire was often alone."

There was a great deal to occupy Angélique when she returned to Maubuisson very late that night. To start with, the guard had to be lodged and fed in the outside buildings. So many of the local gentry were furious that Dame d'Estrées was no longer Abbess, that they prowled around the enclosure at night and fired at the windows. Fifty armed men had to be garrisoned in the Abbey grounds for six months, that is until the March of the following year. And even a year after the assault, Angélique was still uneasy and never dared leave the place.

On that evening of September 11th, she tried to find Dame de la Serre. At length the men heard her behind the tapestry, blowing her nose; she had been crying her eyes out. An arrogant woman with a large bold face, she was very strong, quite capable of knocking a man down. It was very difficult for the men to get at her, and after vainly ordering her to come down, they threatened to shoot. At that she capitulated.

[1] I quote from the account by Sainte-Beuve.

Angélique searched her. Many papers which she had meant to steal were found hidden on her, even a letter from Dom Sabbatier to the Master General, Dom Boucherat. She was locked up in the dungeon. Then Angélique ordered that the guard should be given hot wine before they started their night vigil.

The other three nuns who had been partisans of Dame d'Estrées were caught inside the enclosure, chastised, and, by order of the Master General, sent off to the penitential places they had dreaded.

It took some time to restore the calm which had reigned at Maubuisson in the days of St. François de Sales. After a while, Angélique realized that she was not the Abbess for the job. She knew that she was only a barrister's daughter. If she had been a great princess, even a bastard of noble birth, protected by the King, the Comte de Sanzai would not have dared to come as he did. So that September, she planned to find such a blue-blooded successor, whose very presence would be a protection to the place.

But what would she do with her dowerless new nuns? A rich and aristocratic Abbess would never accept them. Angélique decided to take them away with her when she left.

(Amongst them was a very promising young nun, Soeur Geneviève le Tardif. She was among the very few who rose to mystical heights. Towards the end of her life, as she did not see eye-to-eye with Angélique, she was condemned by Jansenist historians, who looked on her as a rival. But in those early days of her novitiate, when no one guessed that she would eventually come to power and inflict a great deal of suffering on Angélique, this little nun looked calm, sweet and gentle. She was so perfect that even Angélique could see no fault in her. So one day when she was very ill, almost at death's door, Angélique and Agnès and two other nuns planned how they could humiliate her and try to catch her out in some imperfection. Only Jansenist nuns could have done such a thing!)

All this time Angélique was tormented about her father, who had fallen very ill with pneumonia that September—indeed he died at the end of the month. She used to wake up in the middle of the night and pray aloud, and Soeur Isabelle Agnès de Châteauneuf would hear her and finish the response. Recalling how her father had cheated the Pope and told many lies for avarice, she despaired of his salvation. However, on his deathbed he vowed himself to poverty and seemed to be completely converted.

Antoine Arnauld died at the age of fifty-nine. His body lay in state before a vast concourse of people, and he was buried in the Arnauld chapel at St. Merri. Madame Arnauld was left with very little money. In fact, she sold the family mansion to her son Robert.

One can just picture the Jesuits gleefully rubbing their hands after their arch-enemy's death. They had not forgotten his withering epithets—scorpions and suchlike—and they were not averse to taking their lawful revenge on his now defenceless daughter at Maubuisson. They had not long to wait.

The first thread of that immense arras was woven in the September of 1620, when Angélique's elder brother, Robert d'Andilly, made friends with the Abbot of Saint-Cyran[1] at Poitiers. Had it not been for Saint-Cyran, friend of Jansen,[2] this heresy would never have sullied the name of Port-Royal, nor would Angélique's name have fallen into disrepute. And if only Monseigneur de Genève had not died on December 28th, 1620, she would never have fallen a victim to such a man as Saint-Cyran.

She started trying to find her successor as Abbess of Maubuisson. At last it was suggested that she appoint Dame Charlotte de Bourbon-Soissons, bastard of the Comte de Soissons, from the Abbey of Fontevrault (where some of our English kings are buried). She had a great reputation for devoutness.

Dame de Bourbon-Soissons was expected in early February, 1622. The older nuns, twittering at the advent of a very great lady, reproached Angélique about her habit, which was, as usual, very dirty and patched in different colours. At last, they induced her to wear an entirely new one. Several times she interrupted herself at a conference she was giving to her nuns, to exclaim: "What a dress! Is it possible that I am obliged to wear this dress?" However, she endured it, for with the arrival of Dame de Soissons, she saw a prospect of future deliverance.

Another anxious old nun said to her: "*Madame l'Abbesse,* do

---

[1] Jean Duvergier de Hauranne, Abbot of Saint-Cyran (1581–1643).
[2] Cornelius Jansen, Bishop of Ypres (1585–1638).

not let Dame de Soissons see your cell under that ill-smelling drain. Besides," she added slyly, "it would surely be more perfect to keep one's austerities hidden."

"Do you know what has happened to Dame d'Estrées?" asked Marie-Claire one day.

"You shouldn't be so curious," snapped Angélique. "However, I might as well tell you that she has escaped again and been recaptured several times. Stupid nuns who look after her! Now, if *I* had her under lock and key, she wouldn't escape, I can tell you. The small pension allowed her for necessary food has been squandered on litigation for recovery of what she calls her rights."

Dame d'Estrées was seen in final impenitence by a monk who visited her in the grim, sombre mediaeval Châtelet prison in Paris. She was in bed, regaling herself on saveloys and red wine. The prophecy of the old courtier had come true. Eventually she died in misery and squalor in a tiny attic room in a Paris suburb. She was attended by one of her bastards, who used to bring her food. She was buried in the Paris Convent of the Poor Clares. When her effects were gone through, books of piety were found, together with title deeds stolen from Maubuisson.

Angélique had the Abbess's lodging prepared for Dame de Soissons.

The great day arrived. A magnificent coach rumbled into the courtyard. The coachman jumped down from his box, opened the door, with its armorial bearings, and let down the footboard: there emerged a most seductive-looking nun in a spotless white habit with a transparent veil on her head. A well-cut, heavily pleated cloak fell gracefully from her shoulders. She had arched eyebrows, a lovely complexion, a cooing, aristocratic voice, and . . . she wore gloves. Angélique, who had come to the door to meet her, felt her heart sinking.

Soeur Madeleine de Sainte Candide le Cerf, after speaking of Dame de Soissons' extraordinary attractiveness, her many natural gifts, her sweetness and affability, adds that she was a stickler for etiquette and wished the other nuns to recognize her high rank. That chill February day, when she received them in the Abbess's lodging with Angélique by her side, the nuns walked in as usual.

She threw up her hands in horror and cried, in her fluted voice, "On your knees at once, *mes soeurs!* Don't you know how to approach your Abbess?" Then she turned to Angélique. "Don't you make them speak to you on their knees?" Angélique imperceptibly shrugged her shoulders. (For ever afterwards, the nuns would drag themselves on their knees about the Abbess's room to speak to her, and always addressed her with ceremonious respect.)

In the refectory, Angélique quite expected Dame de Soissons to be fussy about her food. To her dismay, she found that she only ate vegetables. She was austere beyond her strength, thus allowing her penances to undermine her health.

Angélique told her it was her duty to eat, so that she would be able to rule the house. "There is much to do, apart from guiding your nuns, paying the bills every week, supervising your steward, keeping an eye on the monks. The financial side alone is quite hard work. I suppose you have been trained in keeping accounts?"

"Oh," replied Dame de Soissons, "the Lord will look after me. My heart is all His."

Her type of devotion did not appeal to Angélique, for it was demonstrative and romantic. At first Dame de Soissons showed great affection for Angélique, and then, alas, a trouble-maker entered the nest: a crony called Dame Bigot, brought from Fontevrault, who was completely against the reform.

"You should just see Madame Angélique's cell: it's a rat hole. The stench is unendurable. When she leaves, you will have to fumigate it. She doesn't seem able to keep clean at all. Have you noticed how all her younger nuns are frightened of her? Her sisters are completely in her power. She is really very hard. She does nothing for her poor sister Claire, who I am sure is consumptive. Her cheeks are on fire. As to that Anne-Eugénie, she'll die of green sickness, I'm convinced."

"Odd," pondered Dame de Soissons, "Madame Angélique always talks to me about being kind to the sick."

"She's a hypocrite."

"But," replied Dame de Soissons, "I think she likes me."

"Don't you believe it," said Dame Bigot in a whisper. "I've heard her putting the nuns against you. It's high time she left or you'll be having trouble here. I think she's annoyed because the monks have reminded her that you are of noble birth and have renounced more than she has. That riles her: she thinks she has renounced more than any other nun in France."

Dame de Soissons started treating Angélique rather coolly. Angélique tried unavailingly to melt this chill. She began telling her own novices that she feared for all the work of reform she had put in at Maubuisson. And then Dame Bigot would draw Dame de Soissons' attention to these dowerless nuns.

"Why, they will bring the house to ruin. We can't afford to feed these beggar girls. She seems to think we're a charitable institution!"

And then Dame de Soissons made a terrible mistake. She referred to the girls as "*des gueuses*"—paupers. Furthermore, she began to complain about Angélique outside the enclosure. The guest parlours were full of tittle-tattling Cistercians and highborn ladies.

However, Angélique was consoled in the February of 1622 by receiving a second visit from Mère de Chantal, and together they were able to speak about their beloved spiritual Father, recently dead. The effect which the new Abbess made on the Mère de Chantal is not known, but we may surmise that Dame de Soissons was effusive. Mère de Chantal, in spite of her loving heart, could not bear gush from fellow nuns, and withdrew into her shell.

"In the spring," declared Dame de Soissons, "I think it would be so *charming* if the novices could have processions in the garden. They could let their hair fall on their shoulders."

"What!" exclaimed Mère de Chantal, "they haven't yet cut off their hair?"

"Oh, tut, tut, *mon coeur*," said Dame de Soissons, "you are being very hard. I suggest they make a procession and crown themselves, say, with a crown of thorns, and sing hymns."

Freezing with distaste at the idea, Angélique said: "Madame, when I have left, you may do what you wish, but during the rest of my stay here, to instal you, I beg you to keep strictly to the reformed Cistercian Rule."

Mère de Chantal could see one thing in the new Abbess which she disapproved of immensely. She encouraged her own novices

to adore her. These girls whom she had recruited bore all the hardships of religious life, just because they adored the fascinating
Dame de Soissons. During her February visit, Mère de Chantal
got pneumonia. Angélique bled her herself, and then mopped up
the blood in several little napkins which she kept as holy relics.

"What exaggeration!" exclaimed Dame de Soissons, hearing of
this from Dame Bigot.

10. *MÈRE DE CHANTAL*

THE BARONNE de Chantal, nicknamed *"La Dame Parfaite,"* was so greatly beyond compare that the Abbé Bremond renounced speaking about her. Mère de Chantal and St. Margaret Mary are the only two people about whom he uses the adjectives—"exquisite and dolorous." No biography can surpass that of her beloved secretary, Mère de Chaugy, whose style is like nectar, and whose book must be read savouringly for long years. It is a pity that Sainte-Beuve has so much neglected the saint in his *Port-Royal.*

Briefly, her life. After a short but ideally happy married life in which she had four children, her husband was killed in a hunting accident. She must have been very lovable, for her husband, who had been very gay before his marriage, fell completely under her spell. She loved him so much that, though she was a lover of simplicity, she wore beautiful clothes to charm him. In her prayers, she renounced everything to God . . . except her husband.

During her widowhood she was obliged to spend seven years in her father-in-law's château at the mercy of his housekeeper, who was closefisted, mischief-making, rapacious, coarse, envious and evil-tongued. Thus was she trained to charity, detachment and self-control, for she herself was aristocratic, impetuous and high-spirited. She found an outlet for her loving heart by making an apothecary's room for the sick, a place whose neatness became proverbial in the countryside. She herself took home and nursed most tenderly, day and night, a leper boy, forsaken under a bush by the roadside. If she was unable, occasionally, to come to him, he used to weep when a servant brought his food. He said: "When Madame comes, she never holds her nose."

It is difficult for us to realize the full horrors of seventeenth-century poverty. Some poor creatures, thrown into barns to die alone, had become so weak that they lay unattended in their filth, day in, day out, and sometimes the filth froze to the ground. The Baronne nursed all she could find.

One day in Lent, 1604, hearing Monseigneur de Genève preach at Annecy, she recognized him as the director she had seen in a vision, and he likewise recognized her. Finally she left the world and founded, at Annecy, the first Visitation convent for widows and girls of indifferent health.

By the time of her first meeting with Angélique, Mère de Chantal's deep friendship with St. François had become muted, for it had been wholly offered to God. He had called her "the courage of my heart and the heart of my courage," but by then, all he wanted was her "advancement in most holy celestial love." Mère de Chantal was greatly reserved with Angélique when speaking of him, and that is why Angélique was so bold as to affirm, later, that he had given her the same friendship as to Mère de Chantal.

When in July 1620 Mère de Chantal had come to stay at the Abbey of Maubuisson as Angélique's guest, she was forty-eight years old, and living in the midst of continued and great trials. She had very little health: her illnesses always looked as if they had been sent to her, as if God meant her to understand that this Order she founded was for women in poor health. Otherwise, impetuous and austere as she was, she might have been tempted to expect them to live at her own high level of mortification.

She had borne many bereavements. Twelve years later came the most terrible trial of her life—a distaste for holy things which made every moment a crucifixion. She was to turn to Angélique, by then an old friend, for comfort.

On that July day, for greater privacy, Angélique led her friend into the garden. Angélique loved the exquisite kindliness of that clear glance, and her light-footedness. (But at the end of her life this agile walk hid an infinite lassitude.) Mère de Chantal took a few crumbs of sugar from her pocket and started calling the birds.

She said to Angélique: "I knew this as a girl—a madcap girl too—when I gave the starlings a little sugar, I could make them follow me high and low, wherever I wanted."

In the distance one of the older nuns was laughing uproariously. Angélique frowned.

"Oh, don't frown like that, my dear friend," said Mère de Chantal, "it does me good to hear them laugh. I hope you encourage them to be gay at recreation."

"*Ma Mère,*" answered Angélique, "the old ones still have their recreation, but we, the reformed ones, live apart from them, and we have no recreation."

Far from commenting, Mère de Chantal enquired particularly about the infirmary. She said, "We have a rule at the Visitation, that, when a nun feels she needs anything, she is simply to say so to her Superior. Really the nuns can't expect us Superiors, especially when we are harassed with many duties, to notice if they are ill, though there are plenty of them who attract attention by little coughs and sighs and groans."

"Yes, I suppose it would be a good thing," replied Angélique, "if we had that in our Constitutions. Very often a nun falls ill with us and we discover it too late."

Mère de Chantal said: "I call that a kind of false heroism on their part. In fact, it can amount to suicide and gives you all a great deal more trouble and expense in the end. We are very particular about the infirmary in our Institute, to keep it agreeable and fresh with green branches and flowers, and to see that the sick are visited by the others in their free time. We think it more important to attend properly to a sick nun than to go and hear Office even on great feasts."

Angélique said: "Please tell me about the early days of your foundation at Annecy."

"We began in great poverty in a tiny little house. The first day, our lay sister Jacqueline Coste was most perturbed about the first meal, so she went to borrow some milk from a neighbour and picked a few herbs in the garden for soup. We were just sitting down to eat it, when a bell rang at the turn, and somebody brought us meat, bread, and wine. Thereafter, we lived on Divine Providence."

"And did Monseigneur de Genève come and see you often?" asked Angélique.

"Oh yes, he came nearly every day, accompanied by his chaplain. He would see us all in the garden. It was in a tiny alley that he made us speak about our progress in prayer. We had a small orchard and a fountain and a trellis just in front of the refectory window. He used to sit down on a stool and we sat at his feet on the grass, while he discussed the Rule and the spirit of the Institute with us. He thought our headdresses most unbecoming, and said, 'Those poor ladies do not appear to their advantage.' So, one fine day, he cut our first veils from an old dress of mine. He wouldn't have crepe but coarse muslin, for he wanted us to profess great simplicity and poverty. The day we made our first vows we had nothing to decorate the chapel, so we hung up shrouds and white tablecloths, snowy white, and pinned little bouquets of field flowers on to them. I assure you that the effect was charming. Oh, I felt happy on that day. He saw that we were all rapt, and he said to the rest of the company, 'Let us retire and leave these brides to taste the gift of God in silence.'

"Many of our early nuns were like the bride in the Song of Songs, raised by God to a high state of prayer. In a short space of time I noticed that those who kept the Rule were called to the Prayer of Quiet, to a loving repose in God, to a very high union. Others had extraordinary illuminations on the divine mysteries, in which they were completely absorbed. Others were in ecstasy. In fact, Monseigneur de Genève and I became quite alarmed after a while, so we prayed that the Order should not receive extraordinary graces, for they are apt to nurture the little grubs of vainglory."

"Yes, I agree with you," said Angélique. "I too am much frightened of the danger of illusion."

During her visit, Mère de Chantal used to rise, as was her wont, at five o'clock, for her hour's mental prayer. Angélique would come and fetch her a few minutes before five. As she opened the door of her cell, she saw a text over her bed, "I sat down in the shadow of my Beloved, and His fruit is sweet to my taste." Angélique noticed too that the bunch of flowers she had given her the day before had been allowed to dry up and shrivel at the feet of her crucifix. Mère de Chantal used to say: "Colour and scent are the life of these flowers. I place them before the Blessed Sacrament, where little by little they fade and die. I want to be thus. . . ."

Mère de Chantal did not utter a word. She gave Angélique a nod and a friendly smile before walking downstairs to the chapel.

For a time Angélique came under the spell of the universal and kindly charity of this wonderful foundress. After she had left, the correspondence between them began. It is extraordinary to think that Angélique adopted a seal exactly like her friend's. It represented a heart pierced with two arrows on which could be read the monograms of Jesus and Mary.

Angélique to Mère de Chantal: "My dear Mother, for the love of God, love me always and achieve by your prayers and your maternal care, that I belong to Him always, for I am your true child who gives herself all, all, all entirely into your hands. May God keep you and be blessed."

Angélique continued to write most affectionately. She said that she was Mère de Chantal's little novice: "I am your true child." She had to bear with the monks who were jealous of Mère de Chantal's visit to Maubuisson, but Angélique told her that she treated them with great coldness. Her letters are almost too self-revealing, almost unashamed, for she tells her all her faults.

"My *chère Mère*, as I was writing this I'd just lost my temper and spoke with much contempt about somebody and said something else so that they should do my will."

Then she confesses to an attack of jealousy because some other nun had shown great affection for the Mère de Chantal, and said she would have been very happy under her care. "I was greatly vexed about this, as it seemed to me that she despised me. I said to her, 'Oh, it's only because it's a novelty.'"

Angélique confessed that she was often irritable with her nuns and wore "a vexed air." She had two or three times been a hypocrite and refused under pretext of abstinence to eat things which she really disliked, "and, had it been something I liked I should have taken it. I talk nearly all the meal time, and very often about news and follies, and I reprove the reader, either with mockery or impatience. I do not speak at all to my sisters: I find no time, because I waste it. My thoughts are against Charity, and yet I cannot conquer my ill-humour.

"Particularly I am not faithful to surmount the inclination that I have to raise myself above all the world by my own judgment, nor my brusque humour, which always makes me most unedifying and troublesome to my neighbour.

"I see my life always full of great infidelities of which many come from this great natural activity which our blessed Father and you had always advised me to mortify, to which I have been most unfaithful."

But it was not until 1637, several years later, that the letters from Mère de Chantal became at all intimate. Her biographer, Monseigneur Bougaud, has questioned the authenticity of these letters. He thinks that they have been falsified by the Jansenists, so that they should bask in the glory of the saint's friendship. This is most unlikely. True, the originals could not be found, but the editing was in the hands of Robert d'Andilly, an honest man, and one can hardly credit him with such a dishonourable action.

It appears that Mère de Chantal's connection with the Jansenists caused the Devil's Advocate at her process to postpone her beatification for fifty years. Monseigneur Bougaud was puzzled that she wrote so openly about her soul's dark troubles to one like Angélique. On the other hand, it must be remembered that at the time Angélique was not under suspicion, and Mère de Chantal took her for the most orthodox of abbesses.

11. *THE TERRIFYING ABBÉ DE SAINT-CYRAN*

BEFORE ANGÉLIQUE left Maubuisson for good, she nursed Dame de Soissons through an attack of smallpox, a disease which she had always dreaded. She caught it herself and nearly lost an eye. The physicians wanted to remove it, to put an end to terrible pain. Fortunately, she got better just in time.

Dame de Soissons did not seem at all grateful for Angélique's care. The relationship had completely broken up through the mischief-making of Dame Bigot, and Angélique longed for the day of her release.

In the meantime, in 1622, her married brother, Robert d'Andilly, successful as courtier and barrister, called on her at the guest parlour. Angélique was accompanied by Claire and Dame de Soissons. After the usual elaborate courtesies, he brought his important news.

"*Ma Mère,*" he said, "I met a most remarkable priest at Poitiers last year. I am anxious for you to meet him. If you are looking for a director when you return to Port-Royal, I can recommend him highly. He is the Abbé de Saint-Cyran, from the Basque country."

Dame de Soissons interrupted:

"Perhaps he would suit us here at Maubuisson?"

"Indeed, *Madame l'Abbesse,* who knows? He is a very learned and spiritual man, but also very humble. You would have to implore him before he came to see you. He is an authority on the early Fathers of the Church. While preparing a thesis at Louvain, he became friends with Jansen, a great scholar. Monsieur de Saint-

Cyran invited him to his house near Bayonne, and they did an immense amount of research together. They used to work through the night in armchairs specially designed to give them intervals of repose."

"How dreadful!" exclaimed Dame de Soissons. "I'm sure that under such conditions they can't have digested all their reading."

Angélique raised her eyebrows and Robert continued: "When I met the Abbé at Poitiers, we immediately became friends. Now he lives a very retired life in Paris, in a small house near the Carthusians. I really must read you the letter he wrote to me." He took out a paper from his coat, and without a smile, read a typical Saint-Cyran letter, misty, and complicated to the point of being ridiculous.

Angélique said: "My brother, this letter seems to me to be very . . . abstract."

"Oh!" Robert continued enthusiastically, "He is like that—ethereal, a pure spirit. There is hardly anything material about him. He will not have it that the Church is a concrete assembly of people, but says that it is a divine breath, an inspiration by the Spirit, and he affirms that without this Spirit, the Church would not exist at all. He said to me the other day: 'God has made it known to me that there is no more Church.'"

Dame de Soissons threw up her hands. "But this is heresy! He'll be put into prison, if the King and the Bishops hear of this."

Angélique said, "Wouldn't it be more prudent if you got some information about him from other priests in Paris? You don't know much about him, do you?"

"He is misunderstood, like all men of genius," said d'Andilly. "He wants to associate me in reforming the Church and bringing her back to her primitive simplicity. He aims very high."

Marie-Claire said bravely, "I think ambitious hermits are rather dangerous. Anyway, Robert, tell us what he looks like."

"His brow is vast and furrowed, his nose strongly pronounced, his mouth peremptory—even haughty and domineering—his bearing very masculine and his whole gait restrained. He is so detached from the world and from man, that he appears distant and rather set. I shall never forget the first time I saw him in the cloister of

Poitiers. He closed his eyes and raising his hand he exclaimed in a voice of thunder, 'Ignorance, ignorance, darkness, strange error, blindness everywhere.' I think he is going to become one of the great reformers of the Church."

Then turning to Angélique, he said: "I have spoken to him of the reform you have achieved at Port-Royal and here, and I have begged him to come and see you, but he refuses to do so."

This piqued Angélique, used as she was to receiving the compliments showered on her as a young reforming abbess of great renown. Had not the Pope himself praised her handiwork? She thought: "Who is this obscure Basque priest who refuses to call on me?"

Robert continued: "He often goes to see Mamma; he has become quite an habitué of our house. We all thought that Monseigneur de Genève was irreplaceable, but now. . . ."

At this point, the convent bell rang for Office. Angélique rose instantly.

"I must leave you now, brother. Give my greetings to our sister Madelon. I hope she is not so frivolous, and that she will eventually join us."

Jean Duvergier de Hauranne, very recently made abbot—*in commendam* and seldom resident—of Saint-Cyran, was to be the effective founder of the Jansenist heresy, for Jansen himself was dead before his *Augustinus* was published and there is no way of knowing how he would have reacted to its condemnation by Rome. Jansen, as a very young man at Louvain, meditated much on the condemned teaching of Baius, according to which man's nature was totally corrupted by the Fall, itself wrongly understood because of an insufficient distinction between nature and grace. He met Saint-Cyran, and the two worked together with incredible patience and industry on a study of St. Augustine, designed to restore what they conceived to be his teaching on grace and predestination to a Church which had forgotten it. They knew that the teaching would seem revolutionary, and that its launching must be most carefully planned.

It is tragic that a soul of Angélique's calibre, whose aims were so lofty, should fall into Saint-Cyran's snare. He spun his webs very skillfully indeed. His apparent reluctance to meet her was only part of his strategy. Had he not secretly planned with Jansen himself, that the best way of spreading a doctrine in France was to see first that it was enthusiastically adopted by an abbey of nuns? He knew that Angélique was ignorant, that she had received no education. He found out all about her before he eventually met her three years later. And when the time was ripe he pounced. "Beware of wolves in sheep's clothing," says the Gospel. In May, 1625, Saint-Cyran cleverly contrived an excuse for introducing himself.

He had heard from Madame Arnauld that Angélique had taken all these young nuns without a dowry, and he wrote to congratulate her on this. And then he faded into the background until his hour was ripe.

A note of impending doom is heard in the distance. The springtide of the early nuns is soon to end. Souls so fresh and pure would wither with a breath from Hell. They would be tormented by a religion of despair, a growing disbelief in man's goodness, a distrust of the world: most of the souls in and around Port-Royal were to be blasted by this terrible personality. They came to imitate his trembling before the Eternal: ceasing to see God as a loving Father, they quaked before Him as a judge.

Saint-Cyran was born at Bayonne in 1581. Therefore he was ten years older than Angélique. Quite apart from his association with the anxious, grim Jansen, with his long thin profile and his enormous nose, he caused other men in Paris—and great men at that—to be worried about him. And not only saintly men: Richelieu, who, along with his ruthlessness, had a lot of common sense and an astonishing perspicacity in reading characters, thought him very dangerous.

He was more fascinating in the flesh than in his writings. We are at a disadvantage in judging him, for we do not see the man or hear him, we do not feel the magnetic appeal which he certainly exercised on many men and women of his day. He had his adoring disciples who wrote most naively about his holiness. There must have been something impressive about him, for him totally to subjugate a woman like Angélique.

A story told in Mgr. Knox's book *Enthusiasm* illustrates Saint-Cyran's terrible self-consciousness, the absorption in self which he bequeathed to Angélique. And this of course she passed on to the members of her own convent and family, in which there was a kind of intellectual inbreeding: no window was opened to let in a little fresh air from outside influences. Anyway, this is the anecdote.

One day a peasant came up to him and told him that his wife had just given birth to a stillborn child. What does Saint-Cyran do? Console the father, send a message to the mother? Not at all. He entered at once into some fine considerations of the fact that the child is in Hell since it was unbaptized, and then he went on to explain what an interest he, Saint-Cyran, had always taken in the education of the young.

"I love extremely all kinds of children."

As Mgr. Knox has said, he always brings the conversation back to the enthralling topic of himself. He never allowed any of his austerities to be hidden from the world. He told his biographer that in the winter he always prayed without wearing a pair of socks, even if it was very cold.

Bremond has said of Saint-Cyran that he was not the man to allow one inch of his holiness to be missed.

He was indeed a paradoxical character. On the one hand he was generous to the poor and forgave his enemies, and yet he was capable of small meannesses which are hard to forgive. Here are some instances.

Every afternoon, he went for a walk near the Chartreuse with one of his disciples and was immediately assailed by a crowd of beggars. He would say to the disciple. "I have no change on me. Would you be so kind as to lend me a few pence for these poor people?" The disciple eagerly obliged. When they returned home and Saint-Cyran offered to repay him, the disciple would say "Oh, no, allow me to give the alms." Saint-Cyran would accept, although he had promised to repay.

And then there was the notorious incident which made Riche-

lieu roar with laughter and exclaim: "But he's a visionary!" When
they were friends, Monseigneur Zamet, Bishop of Langres, sent a
magnificent Bible to Saint-Cyran. He, very much touched, asked
the porter who had brought the Bible to carry to Monseigneur
Zamet a superb cabinet encrusted with mother of pearl. The porter
was just going to leave, and in fact had reached the door, when
Saint-Cyran stopped him quickly, assuring him that God was satis-
fied with his good will and did not ask for anything more.

Saint-Cyran upbraided Angélique for wishing to leave Port-
Royal des Champs because it was so unhealthy and she had lost
twenty-five nuns in three years through epidemics. She replied
that they spent more time in the infirmary than in choir. He said:
"You could always serve God in the infirmary just as well as in
choir." But when he himself stayed at Port-Royal, he left in a very
great hurry, saying that the climate did not suit him.

The nuns finally settled in Paris, and were so poor that they were
assailed by creditors and living from hand to mouth. One day,
Saint-Cyran was talking to the harassed Angélique in the guest
room: some court friends were bewailing her poverty, for indeed
her nuns were on the point of starving. Saint-Cyran, who was himself living quite comfortably in his snug little house, all of a sudden interrupted the talk by exclaiming: "But nobody pities poor
Monsieur de Saint-Cyran!"

He condemned all artistic pleasures, saying that the most ugly
and deformed images are the most suitable for representing God.
This most appalling heresy could do such an immense amount of
harm.

When, towards the end of his life, he was released from prison,
he went straight to the convent parlour of Port-Royal. Alas, something very unfortunate happened there. A young nun on the
other side of the grille suddenly got a terrible attack of the giggles,
indeed, a *fou rire*. Apparently she had been tickled by the look of
a myopic ecclesiastic who was trying to peer through the grille.
She was probably overtired, and this was just too much. All the
other nuns started laughing at once. Saint-Cyran was wounded and
left immediately.

When he returned in eight days, he asked to be alone, but of course, as Mgr. Knox points out, you were never alone at Port-Royal. Two adoring men disciples watched him from a place of hiding, saw his tears and prostrations as he sang a psalm, a most suitable one about God avenging him from his enemies.

And as Mgr. Knox again so aptly points out, his self-importance was inherited eventually by Angélique, and this communicated itself to her nuns "in a kind of corporate self-satisfaction over the glories of Port-Royal." This is the temptation of all foundresses, but "at Port-Royal worship of the Institute seems to grow into a kind of mania; the more its inmates find themselves cut off, by the peculiarity of their views, from the rest of Christendom, the more freely their tears flow that the rest of Christendom should be so wrong."[1]

Saint-Cyran was very clever in the way he flattered: he told Angélique, when he met her for the first time, that he had known many reforming abbesses, but few who had reformed themselves —thus sweeping aside, at one word, all the remarkable reforming Benedictine abbesses, to say nothing of the others.

It would be a good thing in order to make it quite clear, here and now, why the Church has condemned him and all his disciples, to give a few instances of his heretical leanings and explain how he cast himself of his own accord from the sheepfold of St. Peter.

He behaved very often like a revivalist preacher. For instance, he carried too far his belief that he was directly enlightened by the Holy Ghost and that he ruled his behaviour by this interior voice. For example, sometimes in the middle of saying his Mass he would abruptly leave the altar and go back to the sacristy.

His ideas about confession of sins and the absolution given by the priest are extraordinary. In the Gospel Our Lord, who was after all talking to simple folk, said to St. Peter and the other Apostles: "Whosoever sins ye forgive, they are forgiven." But this was too plain, too easy for the ungenerous and tortuous Saint-Cyran, who could not accept such an outpouring of mercy. He decried the whole principle of sacramental confession before a priest, which is one of the great institutions of the Catholic Church. One of his favourite practices was to hear confessions without ab-

[1] *Op. cit.*, p. 195.

solving. According to him, absolution did not efface sin. It was only a kind of declaration that repentance had been sufficient to obtain the forgiveness of God.

And as for Holy Communion, it was much worse. He would leave harassed, sick souls for months on end without allowing them to approach the holy table. He even advised people on their death-beds to mortify themselves to the last degree by dispensing with the ministrations of a priest. He said that devout utterance of the name of Jesus could give to a soul occasionally almost as much, and sometimes even more grace, than could be received from the Blessed Sacrament. Had that been so, Our Lord would have said so, clearly. He was quite plain in His invitation to Christians to come and feed on Him.

According to Saint-Cyran only the spirit counted. To Marie-Claire, dying of consumption and despair at the end of her life and deprived of Holy Communion, he said, "You have no ill reason to esteem that you have communicated, because there is a communion in spirit."

The pose of mystery adopted by Saint-Cyran got on Richelieu's nerves. Mgr. Knox has said: "Saint-Cyran went round saying rather ordinary things about the decadence of the Church and then imploring you not to repeat them; if you did, he would deny having said them. He would give his correspondents strict injunctions to burn his letters."[1] Richelieu thought the man "more dangerous than six armies." As for Louis XIV, the incessant buzz of Port-Royal managed to get on his nerves. "They were perpetually explaining things, justifying things, issuing (at great length) answers to Monsieur So-and-So's Answer to Monsieur Somebody-else; their friends at Court were never out of his antechamber."[2] Louis XIV found nothing but Jansenists wherever he went. "*Ces Messieurs de Port-Royal, toujours ces messieurs,*" as Sainte-Beuve says.

A crude temptation would not have appealed to one like Angé-lique. It was her fate to be deceived by her extraordinary desire for perfection. There were two things in her nature which were

[1] *Op. cit.*, p. 184.
[2] *Op. cit.*, p. 186.

akin to Saint-Cyran's, and on which he probably built. One remembers how, in her early days as a nun, she had been given a book which filled her with a great fear of being deceived by extraordinary graces, and thereafter she looked upon them as illusions sent by the Evil One. Similarly, when Saint-Cyran was told by a friend about the life of a very poor holy woman, and how angels used to light her way at night and hold a torch for her while she prayed in her oratory, he interrupted, saying he did not even want to listen: "All this is extraordinary—all this is extraordinary"; and thus he shut his mouth.

How much Angélique missed of the wonderful devoutness of seventeenth-century Paris! All those delightful anecdotes collected by historians like Bremond, about the coalheaver praying in church with tears streaming down his cheeks, or the poor man who, like St. Benedict Labre, used to go on foot to all the churches without shoes or hose, even during terrible cold winters, and how he used to sing hymns. The Paris of the day was crowded with remarkable souls like these. And there were plenty of them in the domestic class too.

Saint-Cyran used to say that even to look at one single person of the world was enough to enfeeble our soul, or at least to instil an infection which would tarnish its clarity. He was quite unmindful of all the remarkable men and women living at court who had been inspired by St. François de Sales' great book *Introduction to the Devout Life*. St. François had a beloved spiritual daughter, a poor laundry woman, who carried his *Treatise on the Love of God* in her arms. But because she was a woman Saint-Cyran would not even look up at her. Saint-Cyran had been warned by Jansen to beware of "*cette race là*," the race of the fair sex, and not to get mixed up with them.

However, it was a long time yet before Angélique was to be subdued by his influence, and in the meantime God gave her many chances to listen to more prudent advice.

12. *MÈRE ANGÉLIQUE RETURNS TO PORT-ROYAL*

In 1623, there was a little incident about a lay sister which is usually described by other authors as instancing Angélique's greatheartedness. A lay sister, Soeur Marguerite Agathe du Chesne, had been afflicted for years with very bad toothache. One can imagine her tortures—unable to sleep, unable to eat, her cheeks swollen and throbbing, her nerves on edge. It would have been so easy for somebody to arrange to have her bad teeth extracted. But no. That had occurred to no one, least of all to Angélique. This sister Agathe had been seven or eight years a lay sister in the kitchen. One day, she was very irritable when Angélique was about, and Angélique, to teach her a lesson, forbade her to receive Holy Communion and then moved her to some other employment, perhaps to give her a rest, who knows? Perhaps to mortify her.

After a while, Soeur Agathe could endure it no more. She planned to escape, just as Angélique herself had planned to escape as a young girl. She stole some secular clothes belonging to one of the novices, and she took with her the relics from a cross on the church altar. Then, when everybody was in bed and fast asleep, she climbed over the walls. It was a pitch dark night, and the dear soul was frightened of wolves. She found shelter in the cottage of a poor woman who gave her hospitality very unwillingly, alas. Perhaps she was afraid of being blamed by Angélique when the whole thing leaked out.

In the morning before dawn, she walked to Paris. She walked all

that long distance and could not have reached Paris before night-
fall. She went to a sister of hers who was employed at a great house.
And alas, this sister—instead of trying to hide her and do something
about her toothache, and generally set her on her feet—was afraid
because she had committed a theft. She took her to the Bernardines
in Paris and then sent word to Maubuisson.

In the meantime Angélique and the whole community were
praying for this nun with incredible fervour. When the culprit returned, Angélique embraced her and said: "Oh, my dear child."
She reclothed her herself in her nun's dress.

Soeur Agathe tried to escape again and was eventually trans-
ferred to another house, where she died.

At the end of February 1623, having recovered from smallpox,
Angélique climbed the turret of the Abbess's suite and had one last
look round at this domain which she hoped never to see again.
Memories which had sickened her in childhood ever remained. As
clearly as if it were that first morning she recalled looking out of
the window and seeing a man on horseback leaving at dawn. No,
she could never have occupied those hideous rooms. She preferred
the rat hole. How sad that she had never instilled her love of
poverty into those old nuns.

To the right was the patch of ground which had been Henri IV's
melon bed. She had soon destroyed this memento of his baleful
visits. She turned and looked at the door in the enclosure through
which she would leave in early March. Through it she had gone
that horrible September afternoon when Dame d'Estrées had
turned her out. It was at that door that many a young postulant said
good-bye to her parents, in tears before she left the world forever.
Angélique turned a little and looked at the church, so beautiful, so
crowded with lovely tombs. And yet, in there she had continued to
endure her usual aridity! Never since Père Basile's sermon had she
found any spiritual consolation. How she envied her sister, Anne-
Eugénie, who always seemed to live in ecstasy.

From having abstained so unwillingly, Angélique had begun to
hate and despise the flesh. Every time she heard of the birth of a

new nephew or niece, she shuddered. She would shake herself. "I mustn't think like that. I'm envious. I'm vowed to chastity."

She gave a last look round. Very soon it would be spring here, with all its beauty. Flowers would bloom unbidden. Flowers were not necessary for souls doing penance; a penitent's only need was a cave in which to bewail her sins.

The park trees were beautiful here, but not so beautiful in her eyes as those of Port-Royal, that abbey to which she was so eagerly returning. Ah, that little desert had no worldly riches. Port-Royal was her own country from which she had been exiled, and for which she longed continually. She glanced at the hour glass which she had brought with her (it was against poverty to carry a watch), and recalling that she had ordered her young novices to come to the Chapter House when the older nuns and Dame de Soissons were having their midday siesta, she hurried down the turret steps.

In a short while she was speaking in a whisper to all her young nuns crowding around her.

"When my mother comes this afternoon, I want you to go down on your knees and beg her to hire six coaches to take us to Port-Royal on March 3rd. I will join you there a few days later, as I will stop in Paris on the way."

"*Ma Mère!*" exclaimed Soeur Geneviève le Tardif. "Without you we will feel so lost. We won't know how to explain."

"Aha," smiled Angélique, "you won't need to explain anything. I don't want you to talk until I return. I'm going to put you under obedience not to say a word."

"But," asked Soeur Geneviève, "how will our new sisters know our names?"

"I have provided for that." She opened a box. "I have written all your names here on bits of parchment. You will stitch them onto your sleeves the night before. Directly you see the church spire, over the brow of the hill, you are to say the verse of the Psalm 'O Lord, place a seal on my lips,' and from that moment onwards . . . not a word."

"Yes, yes, *ma Mère*," they all cried obediently, though they regretted a little that they must keep silence with those kind Port-Royal sisters, who had all signed a petition to welcome them. The

novices feared their presence would bring starvation. Mère Angélique had warned them that she could only provide them with
herbs, soup and bread.

On March 3rd, trying to hide her delight, Dame de Soissons bade
Angélique good-bye. "Thank you for your help during this rather
trying time," she said, in her charming voice. And what was her
amazement and fury when all Angélique's young nuns came to say
good-bye as well.

"But this is a trick. You never warned me."

"Ah," said Angélique, "but you told me they were paupers. I
didn't want to inflict them on you any longer."

"But what will the Master General say!" exclaimed Dame de
Soissons. "I'm sure he'll say that we were rich enough to keep
them."

"I daresay you could, had you wanted to. But we prefer to eat the
bread of hardship, amongst those who love us, rather than to live in
luxury amongst nuns who don't want us," said Angélique haughtily.

Dame de Soissons exclaimed, "But Port-Royal has only six
thousand livres income per year. You're going to bring your community to starvation. I'm not going to lend you any horses or
coaches. You'll have to go on foot."

"That is all right," said Angélique, almost smugly. "My mother
is in the great alley with six hired coaches. Good-bye, my friend,
may God look after you."

Angélique would not have been human had she not felt a little
pleased with her act of diplomacy. Alas, this was not the last of her
little acts of diplomacy.

13. *MÈRE ANGÉLIQUE MOVES TO PARIS*

As THE coaches trundled away with the young nuns to Port-Royal des Champs, Angélique went on in another coach with her mother to spend a few days in Paris.

Whilst Angélique was enjoying the luxury of homecoming, denied to her own nuns, the poor young things in question were having a rather difficult time in settling down, through having to keep silence. Angélique had not ordered them to be quiet through love of monastic silence, but because she wanted to be the first to bring all the Maubuisson news to Port-Royal. Of course, strictly speaking, she should not have gone on this visit to Paris. The nuns were in her charge, they were very young; she ought to have accompanied them to instal them properly into overcrowded, unhealthy Port-Royal, and make provision for their bedding.

When at length she returned, the inevitable happened. They fell ill with spring epidemics, and in three years' time, twenty-five of them had died. It must have been awful to live in those days at such close quarters with nuns who coughed and coughed and shivered all night, dowerless young creatures in a state of collapse, afraid to go to the infirmarian because of the trouble they might cause. The dormitory was divided into partitions in each of which six nuns were crammed.

When she eventually came, Angélique ordered a carpenter to make more partitions and got more straw for the beds. All this should have been seen to before they came. One lays the deaths of those nuns at her door, though she says that she bore it all with great indifference.

When Angélique saw her sixteen-year-old sister Madelon whom she had so longed to entice into the Order, she was not pleased with her at all. She argued and answered back, and Angélique struck her face. (How unlike Mère de Chantal's little love pat, "*petit soufflet d'amour*," gift of a motherly heart.)

The poor child became rather weak in the head—at least that is how one interprets the nun's phrase: "she was plunged in vapours which mounted to her head and which made her forget almost all things." Indeed, she was always ill and, being unable to work, spent her time in prayer. She sacrificed seeing her sisters, because she loved them too much.

Of all the exquisite Arnauld sisters she is the most forgotten, the least known.

How merciful Nature is! When she sees one struggling untended with a hopeless illness, she brings release by death. Almost all those who died so young had consumption or marsh fever. It is sickening to think of all they endured, without physician, without proper medicines and with that terrible infirmary, fireless except when it was impossible to do without a little flicker of warmth, no proper food, no good bed or bedclothes, nothing to warm or to comfort them.

On June 9th the rest of Angélique's professed nuns left the Abbey of Maubuisson to come to Port-Royal, much to the fury of Dame de Soissons, to whom this also was unexpected. And on July 4th Angélique received her first letter from Saint-Cyran, congratulating her on taking all those nuns without dowries.

It is extraordinary that Angélique, who was so anti-intellectual, so anti-mystical, should still have been so thoroughly impractical. If she had had a grain of sense, she would have moved heaven and earth to drain the marshes, as they were eventually drained by the solitaries who settled at Port-Royal.

She would have known that prevention is far better than cure. It is hard to imagine that no one gave her any advice. French women are notoriously sensible. They can't all have been simpletons in that place, but one cannot see Angélique ever taking advice.

She said she became ill when she was crossed in anything. And from the age of thirty to forty, that is during the fullest and most decisive years of her life, she was without a director. She was the mistress of life or death, with no one to control her.

So idiotically enthusiastic was she about the law of silence (for others, of course), that she allowed exaggerations from its too strict keeping. For example, at Maubuisson, after a barefoot procession, one nun, not finding her shoes, thought it was better to do without them than to break the Great Silence. For several days, in the heart of winter, she walked barefoot in the gardens and on the cold stone tiles. No real mother could have allowed a thing like that.

Lice soon began to settle in and were almost ineradicable. The stench *en masse* of all those sick young girls kept away from proper ablutions must have been overwhelming. And that heavy greasy habit in summer, for girls sweating with fever and not allowed to change a habit which spread infection simply by contact. . . .

Angélique was always ready to pounce. Once, a nun showed an invincible repugnance to exchanging her bed for that of a filthy sister. Angélique exclaimed, "Oh, this damned cleanliness, how it makes you commit faults. Don't you feel that this is enough to make God deprive you of His grace?"

When she reproached a sister for having a bedcover which was less coarse than the others, the nun replied: "I assure you I did not ask for it."

Angélique said haughtily, "I believe you. But you're not ill pleased at being presented with it. Know that, for our condemnation, God allows us to be given things which we would not dare to ask for."

Some poor souls took refuge in compiling little anthologies of their Sunday spiritual reading when they had more free time. They used to feed on the historiettes found in the lives of the saints. Angélique heard of this and forbade it. She used to go round the cells to look for these anthologies and destroy them. She spoke of them as *"des niaiseries"*—sillinesses—and deplored the waste of time, when the nuns should be adoring the eternal repose of God.

Unlike Mère de Chantal, who encouraged her nuns to laugh heartily at recreation because it would do them good, Angélique was against laughter. She said: "If a nun is gay and imperfect it is a bad sign . . . the malediction of Jesus Christ was fulminated against those who laugh."

When Angélique heard young pupils at Port-Royal singing, she exclaimed in horror against it . . . "this joyful singing of children seems to me terrible."

In contrast with Mère de Chantal who loved Madonna lilies, for they reminded her of God's Providence, and who used to watch a bee probing a flower with "*sa petite bouchette*," Angélique disregarded nature; her thoughts turned even more and more to sombre things. She wrote to a nun: "Is it not true that the everlasting fire which has been lit since the beginning of the world, will consume us eternally if we do not extinguish it by our tears and our sufferings?"

There was not much resistance against her rule, for Angélique had taken care to admit only the "docile, simple, humble and penitent" postulants. She railed against the stupidity and "imbecility" of nuns, forgetting that she herself always chose that sort, because they were easier to deal with.

On Februrary 4, 1629, Angélique's old mother, Madame Arnauld was professed at the age of fifty-six, taking the name of Soeur Catherine de la Félicité. Almost immediately she began to lose her health and, what is still more serious, her eyesight. If Angélique's lamp smoked and gave out very little light, it can be imagined that her mother's was no better. At length the poor woman told her daughter that she really could not see properly to say the Office, the print was too small, sometimes practically invisible, and the light flickered: could she please be allowed to say the shorter Office of Our Lady, which she knew by heart?

Angélique replied icily, "Do as the others do." And in the end Madame Arnauld went blind.

Catherine Le Maître, in Paris, was unable to enter religion because her husband was still alive. When she heard that her mother was professed, she was so delighted that she rose from her sick bed and begged Angélique to find a house in Paris. "Then we would all be together and I could keep an eye on the boys' education and visit the convent. Also, did not all the recent deaths prove that it was dangerous to live at Port-Royal?" Monseigneur de Gondi, Archbishop of Paris, was approached. He hesitated because he said it would create an unwelcome precedent for nuns from outside to come pouring into Paris. Also he did not relish having nuns in his diocese who were under the jurisdiction of Cîteaux monks, instead of under his own. After a while he gave in, stipulating that Port-Royal des Champs must be given up altogether, and that the whole transfer from one house to another be completed within a year.

After helping in the reform of Lys and Poissy, where she won admiration for her intelligence and strength of persuasion, Angélique, who had on that visit reduced her sleep to three hours, fell into a state of despairing exhaustion. She would have collapsed had it not been for her sister Catherine.

In May of that 1625, she met Saint-Cyran for the first time. There is no record of what happened at this momentous first meeting, except that Angélique says that she was afraid of him.

In May the Arnaulds found just the right house in Paris, in the Faubourg St. Jacques, the oldest and most romantic quarter of Paris, surrounded by all the other convents and their gardens— Oratorians, Carmelites, Visitandines, Carthusians. Angélique noted with approval that the Faubourg St. Jacques could be reached from Port-Royal des Champs without having to go through Paris itself.

However, the site did not prove to be as healthy as they had imagined. The monastic cloister, the buildings and the church exist to this very day. The house is now a lying-in hospital, and the choir is heaped with stores of linen; under them, beneath the flagstones, Angélique is buried.

It is most impressive to see the grand seventeenth-century architecture of this convent with its little dormer windows, to walk in the quiet dark cloister, still quite intact, to see the red tiled floor leading into the chapel, all just as it was in her day when they made barefoot processions.

This Hôtel de Clagny, as it was formerly called, was surrounded by large gardens. The narrow rue de la Bourbe separated it from the Carmelites. It was much too small for the nuns, and they had to be overcrowded as usual into the attics. Afterwards the liberality of a pious lady, Madame de Pontcarré, enabled Angélique to build the cloister and the dormitories. These constructions were heavy, bare and of severe architecture, in accordance with the spirit of St. Bernard.

And here are Angélique's ideas on architecture. One day at Port-Royal des Champs, M. Hamon, a hermit there, had brought to her notice the irregular aspect of one of the buildings. She replied, *"Mon Dieu,* how I love that! If one is not actually living in poverty, at least one should keep its likeness."

The buildings rose on the rue de la Bourbe, which, considerably enlarged, is now the Boulevard de Port-Royal. At the back was the kitchen garden, in the space comprised between the Faubourg St. Jacques, the rue Maillet (now the rue Cassini) and rue D'Enfer (now the Avenue de l'Observatoire).

We read in the constitutions of Port-Royal: "The nuns will have nothing, either in their houses or in their gardens, which serves purely for beauty and not for necessity. There will be no unnecessary flowerbeds. No fountains, no other things which serve only to distract and content the senses." These constitutions were obeyed; the garden became one of the resources of the monastery, which, like so many other communities, sold its vegetables to the Paris markets.

In the church itself, the great grille which separated the church in two has recently been set free from its plaster partition. Above the altar were two little grilled openings. These gave onto two small staircases leading to the parlours. The openings enabled the passing nuns to adore the Blessed Sacrament exposed in the church.

Port-Royal possessed a very precious and celebrated treasure, now in the Louvre—the alabaster vase of the wedding feast of Cana.

The wide staircases with their wooden bannisters still exist. The parlours, in the east, were very large, for often the whole community assembled there. The kitchens and refectory were on the south side. The Chapter room was at the north east angle, and a vestibule separated it from the nuns' choir.

The cloister-garth, which was the nuns' cemetery, has been transformed into a tiny little Parisian garden, ivy-clad and full of melancholy charm. There still breathes, in Port-Royal of Paris, that ineffable something which lingers in old buildings.

Angélique moved into the house on May 29th, the feast of Corpus Christi. Catherine was her right hand, carrying out her orders with joyful, loving alacrity. She provided all the linen and crockery, and generally saw to it that things were as convenient as possible.

The enclosure was not yet established, though no men other than priests were allowed in. The exhausted Angélique was grieved when another guest was announced in the parlour. At the end of the day she would exclaim: "My God, how tired I am of the world. When will we have our enclosure?"

Solemn enclosure was imposed on June the 16th, and on June the 18th the first fifteen nuns arrived from Port-Royal des Champs. The attics were wainscotted, so that some of the nuns could sleep in them, and they turned a downstairs room into a temporary chapel. The church which we see now was not finally consecrated until June the 11th, 1648.

It is amusing to recall how Angélique, who had always blamed the Carmelites for filling their convent with such beautiful pictures, herself accepted paintings by Philippe de Champaigne.

In order to hear the muted music of a holy place, one must know how to listen. Bereft of all outward charm, the grandeur of Port-Royal is appreciated only by the listening ear. Once upon a time, the spirit burned here, and nuns suffered and exulted. Philippe de Champaigne has that listening ear.

Sainte-Beuve has said: "De Champaigne's pictures are the only artistic luxuries which the Port-Royal nuns allowed themselves. Music, although the most angelic of the arts, was neglected by them. They had no organs in their church and did not want anything else in honour of God, but a grave and simple chant. No bouquets, no flowers on the altar. No curious handiwork. . . . But the painting of Champaigne was an exception and seemed to the monastery just as if it were a domestic and natural decoration. It was in accord with the tone and spirit of the place. Everything in it is sincere. The painter and the models, they are all friends of truth."

On Ascension Day of that year died Dom Boucherat, the Master General of the Order, who had supported Angélique in all her reforms. The nuns were anxious; who would be his successor? Day and night they prayed before the Blessed Sacrament that this successor would be friendly to the reform.

Their prayers were answered in an unexpected way. Dom Nivelle, who was elected, immediately made it known that he would allow no "innovations." Angélique went to discuss it with Mère Madeleine de St. Joseph, the first Prioress of the Carmelites in Paris, quite near her, and decided to imitate her by removing the Order from the jurisdiction of monks and placing it under the Archbishop of Paris, never dreaming that a future Archbishop of Paris would destroy Port-Royal entirely. Eventually she received permission from Pope Urban VIII.

By May 1626 all the other eighty-four nuns had come from Port-Royal des Champs. And it was in that year that Madame de Pontcarré, at first so humble, so self-effacing, asked for just one room near the nuns and offered in return to build the cloisters and a new dormitory.

The Jansenists have written against Madame de Pontcarré, and at first, one is prejudiced against her. However, it might be a good thing to look into the whole case. Little by little, she assumed the dignity of benefactress, and out of the large gallery allotted to her above the parlours, she constructed a drawing-room and an oratory, all painted in cameo, as well as a study. She had a terrace constructed in front of her windows for her orange-trees in tubs. The nuns were obliged to water them with eighteen to twenty pails a day. She laid the cornerstone of the new constructions, and only paid for little more than the foundation. Afterwards she urged ruinous expenditure for the rest of the building.

She performed beautifully on her lute. When eventually she played to Monseigneur Sébastien Zamet, Angélique's director, he spent hours listening to her. So charmed did he seem, that even the servants tittle-tattled, and Angélique began wondering whether she should ever have allowed this holy Madam to gain a foothold in the place. But the prelate put a stop to the lute-playing of his penitent by saying: "You must sacrifice this satisfaction to God."

The Jansenists have always attributed the ruin of Port-Royal to Madame de Pontcarré. Her expensive building projects caused Angélique many a sleepless night. She had never known before how torturing it is to be in debt. Very soon, creditors were at the door, and the workmen refused to work till they had been paid. Angélique felt she was living on the brink of a precipice.

Sébastien Zamet finally tipped the scales of Angélique's sanity. Strangely enough, he had called on her on the advice of Mère de Chantal who, seeing that he wanted to reform the Cistercian nuns of Tard, in his diocese, had told him about the great reforming Abbess of Port-Royal.

Hearing of unreformed abbeys, Sébastien Zamet made up his mind that his Abbey of Tard would not be in the same case. Among his nuns he chose a Dame de Pourlan to lead the reform. (Eventually she went to Paris, where she became a thorn in Angélique's flesh.) Now this aristocrat had been sacrificed to her brothers by her father, and forced by violence to become a nun. Half the year she was absent from her convent, and on her profession day she publicly snatched off her veil and trampled it underfoot.

But after she had reformed, she became very austere. She took a habit of thick wool serge. Trembling with misery, she cut off her beautiful hair and threw it into the fire. And last of all, she gave up her lacquer cabinet replenished with perfumed sachets, flasks of essences and all kinds of exquisite scents.

Monseigneur Zamet arranged that Mère Agnès Arnauld and Soeur Geneviève le Tardif, nicknamed the Saint, should be sent to Tard to help Dame de Pourlan with the reform.

Monseigneur Zamet's great ambition was to found an Order devoted to perpetual adoration of the Blessed Sacrament, just as Monseigneur de Genève had founded the Daughters of Sainte Marie for his Order of the Visitation. (The Jansenists mock Zamet, because they try to make out that he was simply ambitious.) To achieve this Order he wanted to unite the two houses, Tard and Port-Royal of Paris, and place them under the rule of St. Augustine. He appealed to Angélique, for her fame as a reforming abbess had spread throughout the kingdom.

14. *MÈRE ANGÉLIQUE MEETS MONSEIGNEUR SÉBASTIEN ZAMET*

WHEN MONSEIGNEUR Zamet met Angélique in 1627, he caught her at a moment when she was open to suggestions of change. She was homesick for Port-Royal des Champs, and terribly anxious about finances. This unquiet spirit was still troubled about her own vocation, still haunted by scruples as to whether she should be an abbess at all, still wanting to leave and enter another Order as a lay sister, still suffering from fear and a spiritual inferiority complex which forbade her to aspire to any heights in the life of prayer. He only had to show a little sympathy, only had to mention that he had been a friend of dear Monseigneur de Genève, that he had gone on a pilgrimage to St. Bernard's Clairvaux with a great friend of Monseigneur de Genève, and she listened to him sympathetically.

Monseigneur Zamet was a man of psychological finesse, and he very soon saw through her completely. How is it that so shrewd a person as Angélique should have put herself under obedience to a prelate who was completely unlike her in temperament and ideals? Probably she realized that she was too independent, that for many years now, since the death of Monseigneur de Genève, she had directed herself, that she had been difficult in her choice of directors, only asking advice when she knew that she would like following it. In a word, she thought she had better give up her judgment entirely to Monseigneur Zamet.

At first, she may have been influenced by the enthusiasm of her sister Claire, who from the very beginning thought that he was

the holiest priest she had ever met. So did Madame de Pontcarré.
One can imagine all three talking together in the guest room,
Monseigneur Zamet in his beautiful bishop's robes, his amethyst
ring gleaming on his delicate hand.

Monseigneur Zamet had an agreeable manner, his features were
delicate and refined. Though his nose jutted out, it was not pointed.
He had a fine presence and a good figure, and his clothes were
well-cared-for. He ruled his household excellently. Sometimes he
could laugh in a joking, pleasant way. He was usually in a gay
and accommodating humour—the very antithesis of the Abbé de
Saint-Cyran. Directly he became Bishop of Langres, he issued or-
dinances exhorting priests to remove from their churches all statues
of the saints, or images, which were deformed, broken, mangled or
worm-eaten, since they only caused contempt and laughter, and
to replace them by others more suitable. It is not surprising that
this Italian loved beauty. Perhaps he did not show this aesthetic
side of his character in those first interviews with Angélique. Indeed, she hints that she was rather misled at the beginning.

One recalls that his father had been Henri Quatre's great friend.
The King called him "*Mon cousin d'argent*," and it was in his house
that the King's mistress, Gabrielle d'Estrées, had died such a painful death. This Italian had an innate taste for harmony and perfection of form. His father's house had been magnificent, with its pictures, priceless tapestries, and its gardens full of statues. He had
pavilions with marble vestibules and bathrooms, which enchanted
the guests of the day. This would, of course, have shocked Angélique, who would quite fail to take into account that this great
financier greatly helped the poor, as one can see by the accounts of
the Hôtel-Dieu.

Monseigneur Zamet wished to pour all this inherited love for
beauty into his new Order devoted to Our Lord in the Blessed
Sacrament. For Him, no splendour could be splendid enough. And
if Judas, in the form of Saint-Cyran, seeing Mary Magdalen pouring precious ointment on Christ's feet, were to say, "Give all the
money to the poor," one must remember Christ's answer: "Leave
her alone, for she hath done a good work."

After a while, what must this *parvenu*, fastidious prelate of humble origin have thought of this middle-class abbess who stank, and who looked so dishevelled? Secretly, he made up his mind to use her as far as he could, have her deposed when she was properly established in the new Order, and then get somebody else to take her place as Superior.

Did she think that here at last was the twin soul who would turn the thin, pale water of her life to wine? For twenty years now, she had had no spiritual consolations, while others all around her had lived in joy. And of these joys he spoke.

His counsels to Angélique were very like those given her long ago by Monseigneur de Genève. "I advise you to be extremely gentle; let there be nothing bitter in your expression or words. That will be very useful to you, and will also serve others. People given to sudden outbursts of ill-temper and to varying moods are a bad example, and always cause trouble in a community. Besides, it's a proof of being unmortified: the spirit of Jesus does not live fully in that soul. His spirit is so gentle, so patient, so humble and full of regard. O my sister, what a model! Gaze at it often: in this pure looking glass, you will know your thoughts."

M. Prunel, Monseigneur Zamet's biographer, counteracts the Jansenist sneers. He shows him to have been an exemplary Bishop. Very often he would make his pastoral visits on foot, hearing confessions and consoling the sick. All his letters prove that he was greatly attracted to the interior life.

True, in his early days, he had been rather worldly, but in 1624, a great change came over him. He renounced his post as chaplain to the Queen Mother and lived a very austere life, giving up his personal luxuries. To the criticisms of the Jansenists we must oppose the good opinion of many of the great men of his day—Père de Condren, St. Vincent de Paul, Cardinal de Bérulle, M. Olier, St. François de Sales.

Through a manuscript in which he made a rule of life for the Ursulines in his diocese, we get a hint of the kind of reforms he suggested to Angélique. She, for example, would not have approved of this clause: "Suitable syrups are violet, rose, maidenhair fern, cherry and bitter limes. . . . The honeys are violet and rose.

. . . The nuns will also prepare oils, and those are of roses, camo-
mile, and rue."

Ablutions are described without any prudery. Neatness and exterior cleanliness are the object of a long article. He must have
agreed with St. François de Sales, who said that outward cleanliness was a sign of inward composure and mental health. Here are
a few lines which make one dream about the seventeenth century's
horror of cold water:

"In summer, those nuns who need it will wash their feet once
every two months, and more often if it is necessary, which they
will do in silence in a place set apart for that. The Superior will
tell a lay sister to heat the water, throw in some good herbs, prepare the cloths, and warn the sisters of the day they will have to go
there. They will also have to cut their nails," etc.

". . . The nuns will wash their hands and mouths in the morning
in the wash house, and do the same, if they wish, after dinner and
supper as they come out after saying grace."

However, at first, Monseigneur Zamet was probably clever
enough not to stress these rules of cleanliness to Angélique, or she
would have dismissed him instantly. At the beginning, their relationship was entirely one of spiritual direction. He advised her to
go and see the Carmelites and become more friendly with Mère
Madeleine de St. Joseph. Perhaps he hoped that this association
with the Carmelites was to prepare her (though he said nothing
about it at the time) to model the new Order on Carmel. But Angélique, apart from her disapproval of the Carmelites' rich house, did
not feel at home in their way of prayer which, according to the
Spanish nuns, was very French, very nebulous. She was like the
great St. Teresa herself, much more practical, much more devoted
to the Humanity of Our Lord (or so she thought), and instantly
would see the connection between interior prayer and resulting
action and austerity.

The nuns on the day of her visit flattered her a great deal; they
called her the second Teresa, saying that she resembled their holy
Mother because she had moles on her face in exactly the same
places. But Mère Madeleine, who had watched her intently and
who had an especial gift for discernment of spirits, said after-

wards that she thought Angélique was in a profound state of illusion, and that she would never be rescued from it. In *La
Vénérable Madeleine de Saint-Joseph*, by the Carmel de l'Incarnation, we see that Mère Madeleine even went so far as to say that
she was singularly self-opinionated, and rooted in a determination
not to renounce her illusions.

(Incidentally, the life of Mère Madeleine, born in Touraine, is a
great contrast to Angélique's. What a wonderful girlhood, devoted
to prayer and to care of the poor and sick!)

When, afterwards, she told Monseigneur Zamet about her time
with the Carmelites, Angélique let him see that she had always
pined for the Visitation. Hearing this, he forbade her to write any
more to Mère de Chantal, and the correspondence ceased for some
years. There is good reason to think that letters were intercepted.
Moreover, he forbade her to write to her sister Agnès at the Abbey
of Tard.

When she confessed to him that she had pronounced her vows
with a mental reservation as to the Order in which they were to
be kept, he commanded her, under obedience, to pronounce her
vows again, aloud, in front of the whole community.

This restored her to some kind of peace and calmed her scruples.
Now, she was committed, and there was no turning back. She
imagined that she liked obeying against her will.

From then on, his direction began in earnest. From the first, she
really did not take to his style of spirituality, which reflected, to
so great an extent, the group which had surrounded the first French
Carmelites—this nebulous mysticism "in which everything took
place in God." Monseigneur Zamet spoke of the way of ignorance
and unknowing, the way of obscurity. This would have suited the
abstract Agnès at Tard much more than Angélique.

He had noticed her fear of illusion. He said that it filled him with
pity to see souls miss a fine destiny: because souls don't realize
that they are called to it, they prefer wretchedness to opulence. He
exhorted her to keep up her dignity of Abbess and to show more
proof of ambition in the spiritual life.

Now a simple soul would have taken him at his word and been
glad at the voice which said, "Friend, come up higher." But no,

Angélique could never do anything but look at herself, and then regret the fact that she looked at herself, and twist and turn herself into all manner of complicated involutions. She went back to her cell to lament and to indulge in introspection. When she saw him again, she accused herself of feeling vain at the idea of the spiritual grandeurs prepared for her. He replied by saying it was madness to be so much obsessed with one's own unworthiness that one refused the graces and the favours of a prince.

"Precious stones are usually enclosed in poor cases," he wrote. "The oyster who carries pearls in his breast does not, for that reason, change his nature or form. It remains always dirty inside and rugged outside."

The rest of this letter shows the same finesse: "I beseech you to believe me and to *occupy yourself less with virtue than you do*, for you are too much attached to it, and you are more concerned with it than God asks you to be. It will never be by your cares or your attention to yourself that you will be virtuous. It is a gift from on high, for which more than your industry is needed."

He often repeats this. He has well understood the character of Angélique, this ardent soul, impassioned for action, who could not bear what she called "uselessness," and at the same time, given to analysing herself too much, being almost irritated by her imperfections, and wishing to conquer virtue by combat, and quickly too, by her own efforts.

". . . Let her be led to God, and if her angers and her hasty ways displease her, let her endure them in that they are very excellent for ruining her self-love."

Feeling herself so well understood, Angélique began to expand a little. She was therefore more prepared to listen when he started speaking about the Order he wanted to found.

"You see, my dear daughter," he said, "as a result of their quarrel with Cardinal de Bérulle, the Carmelites have not wished to undertake perpetual adoration of the Blessed Sacrament. There is no Order devoted to this end."

At first Monseigneur Zamet deceived her, though perhaps only unconsciously, when he said that the nuns of his new Institute must be extremely retired, hidden, austere and poor. And in imagina-

tion, he made her tread a way of sacrifice and renouncement designed to suit her ardent nature, so passionate for perfection.

When he spoke of the mortification of the nuns, this appealed to
her, too. Monseigneur de Genève had always wished his penitents
"to ally mortification to a gay and sprightly exterior." But Monseigneur Zamet's interpretation would have been: "to mingle the
blood of flagellations to the intoxication of incense."

The rule of the Cistercians would be abandoned and that of St.
Augustine adopted. It is hard to see how, after belonging all her
life to the great Order of St. Benedict, reformed by St. Bernard,
Angélique could have dreamt of renouncing it. She must have
been one of those wandering spirits whom the mediaeval moralists
describe, gyrating from town to town like lost souls. Fundamentally
she lacked the stability which St. Benedict wished to inculcate in
his monks and nuns.

But in those early days she was all enthusiasm. She wrote that
it was the eternal will of God that Monseigneur Zamet should be
Superior of the new Institute. (She was no less sure, when she discovered that he did not suit her purpose, in affirming that his departure was "ordered by God.")

When her nuns commented on the severity of the Tard reform,
Angélique would say with unspeakable fervour: "Oh, my children,
we must not say that. Are we not happy to have found the real way
of perfection? For myself I am enchanted. M. de Langres [Mon-
seigneur Zamet] is a man of God. Whatever he does, he will always
do well, and I find it impossible to criticize. Are we not too happy
to have found a man who will lead us in the way of truth?"

This enormous esteem, however, was not reciprocated by Monseigneur Zamet, Bishop of Langres. He had mistrusted her secretly,
almost from the first. Having become the director of her nuns, he
must have noticed many things. For example, one poor little nun's
complaints had been stifled by Angélique brusquely threatening
that she would tell the rest of the community what she was like.
Another nun, who had asked to fast on bread and water, had been
put on a liquid diet because it was more humiliating. Yet another
nun was threatened with a spell of the convent prison. A fourth
complained that she had always been treated by Angélique like

a poor slave. He had seen nuns whose cheeks were swollen with the blows of Angélique's hard hands. He must have noticed her own mother going blind, her sisters ailing and heavily laden with affliction. Particularly did he pity her fragile little sister Claire, coughing painfully. "Ah yes," he thought to himself, "when the time comes, some other Superior will have to be found." Angélique would not do.

He was dismayed at the way she kept her nuns in ignorance, even of spiritual things, burning their spiritual notebooks, depriving them of books. That excellent Mère Madeleine de St. Joseph at Carmel had reminded him of the words of Mother Teresa of Avila to her daughters: "Alas, we are so silly by nature that we must not become more so by grace."

When he himself had spoken to some of the nuns in the guest room, he could not help being struck by the simplicity bordering on stupidity of some of these poor girls, who had kept the law of silence for so many years, and who had lived under the shadow of that domineering woman, their Abbess. They never seemed to have a thought in their heads. They certainly could not express themselves, their diction was bad; sometimes, he could hardly hear what they said. So different from the Carmelites, so many of whom had been aristocratic women of the world, and could, therefore, influence others to good in the guest rooms. That was one of their great missions in the Paris of that day. They brought many souls to God by their eloquence and the odour of their virtue.

He secretly planned to recruit some of the members for this new Order from the aristocracy. Angélique seemed to hate them. She had clung far too much to her own class—a good deal, perhaps, because she knew she could hold her own with them.

He spoke to her about her nuns' way of speaking, "that they might observe decency and religious modesty."

"You must avoid coarse and trivial words. Use few proverbs, unless they be rare and significant. . . . You must pronounce your words carefully. Your speech must be neither slow nor precipitate. Open your mouth to a moderate extent, unclench your teeth so that the word is clear and that you speak neither down your throat nor through your nose."

Angélique listened with her eyes down, breathing disapproval. She stored all this in her mind, and, a long time afterwards, and after reporting it all to Saint-Cyran, she said, "Monsieur de Saint-Cyran took great exception to instructing the nuns to speak well."

Monseigneur Zamet tried to devise a plan whereby he could get Angélique out of the way before founding his Order, while using some of her best nuns. Ah, he had it! Cleverly, when she sighed at being an abbess and groaned that she was not a humble lay sister, he took her at her word.

"If only abbesses could be elected by vote," she said.

"That's quite easy," he said. "The first time the Queen Mother comes to see a new abbey, she always grants a request. When she comes here, ask her if you can't make your abbey elective. We will then have an election. You will probably be deposed and you can then retire into obscurity."

15. *MÈRE ANGÉLIQUE IS DEPOSED AND HUMILIATED BY HER FORMER NOVICE*

ANGÉLIQUE HAD to put a good face on it. In her own mind, she was pretty sure that her nuns would elect her: that, of course, would be a great victory.

The Queen was approached. She in turn asked King Louis XIII; he had already given glowing praise to "the zeal and care of Soeur Angélique Arnauld, who by her conduct brought about a complete reform of the Abbey." In this way, Queen Marie de Médicis (who declared herself the foundress of Port-Royal without, however, giving so much as a groat), gracefully saved her face by granting a request which cost her nothing financially.

And so, after Angélique had been Superior for close on twenty-eight years, in July 1630, Agnès and the Tard nuns now having returned to Paris, a solemn election was held in the Chapter House of Port-Royal. A few nuns were in floods of tears. The result was declared by the Prioress in a clear voice. Unbelievable! The nuns had chosen for Abbess the saintly Geneviève le Tardif, and for Prioress, Soeur Jeanne de St. Joseph de Pourlan (the one who had publicly trampled her veil underfoot on her clothing day).

Dismay overwhelmed Angélique. Many years afterwards she says that nuns are ungrateful by nature: on this day, she felt their ingratitude for the first time.

Unfortunately, a few of her past victims, the ones who had suffered most heavily at her hands, were very tactless at that time, and started praising the new Superior in front of Angélique, perhaps with meaning glances.

191

In the old days she had been envious when Mère de Chantal was praised. How much more, when they lauded Dame le Tardif, who had been nothing more than her novice, and who had in no way helped to launch the reform.

Acting no doubt from the best motives, these two nuns, Dame le Tardif and Dame de Pourlan, began to humiliate her so much, that the only way Angélique could react without losing face was to pretend she had not noticed some of their insults.

As we recall, Soeur Marie Geneviève de St. Augustin le Tardif had a reputation for saintliness. (Angélique had refused to let her appear when the King's brother asked to see "the saint.") Coming from an impecunious Paris family, she had been a novice at Maubuisson, and later professed at Port-Royal.[1]

Her father thanked God for his poverty, because he knew it meant salvation. Her mother did not love vanity and therefore brought up the girl very simply. She heard that Maubuisson was taking girls without a dowry. Directly Geneviève appeared at Maubuisson, she pleased Angélique so much that she admitted her. She said that "she had a way of succeeding very well."

Geneviève was in transports of joy. She had so great a respect and so much friendship and trust for her Superior, that she opened her heart to her. She was one of the twenty silent novices sent ahead to Port-Royal des Champs when Angélique returned from Maubuisson in 1623. She soon gained a great reputation for virtue, being recollected, grave, modest and humble. So great was her gentleness, that she was beloved at first sight.

We must also recall that she was the nun whom Angélique, Agnès and a novice mistress had sought to mortify when she was extremely ill, to see if they could surprise her in any way, for hitherto she had stood all tests. Eventually, she made an excellent novice-mistress.

When she became Abbess, she fell in with her old Superior's desire to submit to humiliation. The nun who wrote an account of Angélique's resignation said: "They gave her the means of satisfying her desire, under the pretext that she would derive great

---

[1] Her life was written by Mère Marie de l'Incarnation le Conte and Mère Angélique de St. Jean Arnauld.

spiritual benefit by being as much humiliated and debased as she had been exalted. The principle of charity was the source of the wish to deprive her of knowledge of the affairs of the house, as well as those of her family. Her advice was never asked for, except when it could not be dispensed with."

Many years later, Angélique herself wrote of this, an account which alternates between bristling anger and subdued sneering.

Several sisters, as we know, did not know how to write. Monseigneur Zamet judged it necessary for them to learn, so the cells were provided with inkstands. "It was said that all the sisters must be capable of everything. Many did not stir from the parlours, from talking to the Fathers of the Oratory, and then had to write to polish their minds. What distressed me most was that they gave charge of the turn and sacristy to the most imperfect. They were unwilling to receive any more pupils unless they were the daughters of marquesses or counts. We had to have a daily change of soup, and highly spiced sharp sauces, unknown to us, had to be made with all sorts of seasonings to which we were not accustomed.[1]

"In church, many scents, elaborate pleatings of linen, bouquets. There were extraordinary austerities of fasting on bread and water, terrible disciplines, most humiliating penances. Those who had been most fastidious with their food, afterwards ate caterpillars and other filth. . . . During recreation, they made fun of one another, mimicking one another. This was called 'sharpening their wits.' I was often in distress at this, but I said nothing.

"When I asked myself secretly, 'What is the good of it all?' I said, 'To destroy my own judgment.'"

Dame du Fargis says that, after Angélique was deposed: "I was wearing some very old shoes. She asked me why they did not give me new ones, and then added, 'My God, how very wretched, to be always meddling in what does not concern me.'" She had exercised initiative so long in her good works, that now it was almost impossible to abdicate. Angélique was horrified at first that the nuns

---

[1] How greatly this resembles St. Bernard's sarcastic tirade against Cluny's many different ways of preparing the monastic egg!

should be scourged by other nuns, but later she was advising it herself.

Then began terrible humiliations in front of all the other nuns. On the eve of All Saints, three months after she had been deposed, Angélique was made to attend Chapter, bareheaded and barefoot. She was ill as a result. "The sisters were forbidden to speak to her. She obeyed with exactitude. If some sisters came to look for her, she excused herself from speaking to them until they had asked the Abbess for permission. Some showed great esteem and affection for Dame de Pourlan, who was in control, even occasionally before Angélique, in a contemptuous kind of way. She showed no distress but was glad.

"Three or four months after the election she was made mistress of the pupils. She swept the room and did other disagreeable tasks. There was a girl there of troublesome temper who objected to all that was done. Mère Angélique always felt a kindness for her, whatever she might do. She always spoke to the Abbess on her knees, and knelt when she met her. She was made to undergo all sorts of humiliations.

"Accounts of her life were read aloud in the refectory. All manner of debasing things were put into them, that might have made a less humble person extremely angry. Among others, she told me they once read that she held herself badly in church, wallowing like a pig, and that if she were elected Superior of the monastery of the Holy Sacrament, she would make it a house of misrule, like Port-Royal.

"As she listened to this, she went on with her dinner. Mère Jeanne asked her why, and she replied that she had not thought about it at all."

(This was untrue, for she had remembered it sufficiently to tell the recording nun afterwards.)

Young girls in the refectory were made to hang a basket of filth about Angélique's neck and she was led from table to table while they said: "My sisters, look at this wretched creature, whose spirit is more full of perverted opinions than this basket is of filth."

And all the time, Angélique looked very devout, as if she recognized that it was all true. On some other occasion, she was made to come into the refectory wearing a paper mask, and told to say: "My sisters, pray to God that He may convert me truly."

The new Superior gave her to understand that it was no great deed to have resigned her abbey, she had done nothing more than she ought; and various other things which "she endured with joy."

But the thing which touched her to the quick and which she mentions in her relation of it all, is that her letters from Monseigneur de Genève, the letters which probably had been lent to the inquisitors in 1628 when she deposed on his holiness in preparation for the process of his beatification, these precious letters were treated with disrespect.

"I kept these letters carefully until my resignation of the title of Abbess. But subsequently the mothers from Dijon who thought their own spirituality far above that of M. de Genève, and all his letters a slight thing in comparison with their pre-eminent devotion, took them from me. They set so little store by what I looked upon as relics, that they made use of them to cover some pots of preserve, as I myself saw without venturing to complain. *Some, however, were saved from this shipwreck.*"[1]

And when she asked: "But what good does it serve?" God gave her the grace to reply: "It makes me die to myself." There had been two girls in a village whom the lord of the place had resolved to ruin. When told of it, and advised that it would be a charitable deed to save them from this peril by finding a place of refuge for them, Angélique had taken them into the house. Mère Geneviève went to her, asked where they came from, and said it was in order to send them back. Angélique named the place and said nothing else, but she felt it acutely and shed many tears, still saying nothing.

The day that Angélique for the first time took the rank of simple nun, she went through her cell to see if there was anything in it which she should not possess. She found the packet of Monseigneur de Genève's letters. She knew no nun was allowed to keep any correspondence in her cell, but . . . to have to give up these. . . . What would *they* do to them? Would they appreciate their value?

---

[1] The italics are mine.

Of course they would, for they had been used for the process of beatification. She had not sent them all, because so many of them contained flattering references to herself. She thought, perhaps, it would be a wise thing to say that they had been used in the process, and then the Superiors would treat them with care.

Angélique kissed the letters and said good-bye to them, and then bravely went to Mère Geneviève le Tardif. She was not in, but the Prioress, Dame de Pourlan, was there.

"Can I do anything for you, Soeur Angélique?" she asked, with, perhaps, a trifle too much emphasis on the *Soeur*.

Angélique hesitated: Dame de Pourlan noticed this.

"No thank you, *ma Mère*, I will return again."

"What's that packet you are carrying?" asked Dame de Pourlan sharply.

"I was just going to return Monseigneur de Genève's letters."

"You may leave them here. I will explain to our Mother Abbess when she returns. That will do. You may go."

And Angélique, who had never been dismissed in her life, was obliged to leave the room. She was humiliated and very anxious, and continued being so for several days.

The two Superiors knew quite well that this packet of letters would be a test to her, a kind of sacrifice of Abraham, and they decided to use them to put her through her paces. After unfolding them, they covered jam pots with them and pots of ointment in the apothecary's room. Wishing to see the effect on Angélique, they watched in the apothecary's room when she came to bring them something they had ordered. They then asked her to fetch a pot of ointment from a shelf, and looked carefully. Probably Angélique knew she was being spied on, for she did not flinch. She had seen the handwriting, she had seen the letters torn and all but ruined, but she handed over the pot, made a bow and left the room. She was far too proud to wince before "*ces mères de Dijon*," as she so scornfully calls them. Did they expect her, an Arnauld, to burst into tears, fall to her knees, sob and weep like any fool of a nun and beg for the return of those letters? Not she! She had put her hand to the plough and she was not turning back. They wished to destroy her. Let them. She also wished to destroy herself.

But she says, in her relation about the letters: "Some, however, were saved from this shipwreck." So she managed to rescue some of them. This only proves how imperfect her sacrifice and obedience had been. To imagine Angélique rescuing the letters of Monseigneur de Genève makes a strange picture. . . .

Somehow, at dead of night, she must have found her way down to the apothecary's room. She looked up at the shelves. Yes, the letters were there. Perhaps she would also have time to get to the kitchen and rescue a few of those on the jam pots. If she dared not rescue them, at least she would be able to read them for the last time and try to memorize them.

An owl hooted in the garden. Hush, what was that—a creak of a board upstairs? No, it could not be a footstep. Perhaps just a mouse, though mice and rats soon left any reformed Cistercian abbey, for there were no crumbs left about for rodents, let alone for nuns. Perhaps it was a nun taken sick with summer dysentery? Anyway, she would not want to come downstairs.

Turning up the wick of her tiresome little lamp, Angélique took a pot down very carefully. Confection of Senna had been covered over with this letter.

"Sprinkle all your conversation, exterior and interior, with sincerity, gentleness and joy. O God, my daughter, I see your entanglements . . . in those thoughts of vanity. Fertility joined to the subtlety of your mind lends a hand to these suggestions. . . .

"Try to get used to speaking a little softly, to do what you do gently and softly, and you will see that in three or four years you will have put order completely in this so unexpected suddenness. . . ."

Her eyes filled with tears. Three or four years indeed! She had received this advice twenty-one years ago and she had never made any use of it. She peered closely in the dim light and saw his phrase:

"This too active disposition will always spurt out."

She went red with shame, as if somebody had overheard her in the confessional. How terrible to think that her Superiors had read these letters, and that now anybody could read them, lay sisters, servants and all—anybody who came to the apothecary's room or the kitchen. They were far too intimate. She should never have let them out of her hands.

"For prayer, my very dear daughter, I find it a good thing that you should read a little in your copy of *The Treatise on the Love of God.*"

Yes, but she did not possess this book any more, and she was not going to humiliate herself by asking for a copy. Ah! she was being repaid in her own coin. She remembered the times she had snubbed her nuns when they had asked for books. And now how badly she needed *that* very book! She took up another pot, a decorated majolica pharmacy jar of the period with the Latin name in exquisite calligraphy. Confection d'Hyacinthe—the sovereign remedy of the day, given only in extremities, and so precious that it was usually kept under lock and key.

"You see, my daughter, these inclinations to pride, vanity and self-love, they are mixed up everywhere and they slip in imperceptibly, but for all that, they are not the motives for our actions."

And here, over the jar of Ground Ivy for stomach trouble, was the letter he had written to her about her severity to one of her nuns:

"But you see, my very dear daughter, that you are a little too severe with the poor nun. You mustn't reproach her so much, for she is the daughter of good desires. She looks up towards Our Lord, who, from the height of heaven, looks down at her as a father does at his child who, still weak, finds it difficult to walk steadily."

Angélique brushed away the slow, difficult tears of middle age. She climbed up on a chair and lifted her lamp to see a pot labelled "Black alder and clematis pods for purging." What a disgrace! This priceless letter was all stained and torn.

Of course it was the letter in which he said that it took seven years to break in a young horse.

"Tame little by little the vivacity of your spirit to patience, gentleness and affability amidst the trifling and childishness and the feminine imperfections of sisters who are difficult about themselves and given to pestering the ears of the Mothers. I could have wished that you had not railed at and mocked those persons, but that with modest simplicity you had edified them by the compassion they deserve."

Ah yes, that was about the time when Dame d'Estrées had escaped and she had called some bad nuns fools.

"But go to the Royal Port of the religious life by the royal road of the love of God and of one's neighbour, of humility and of genial courtesy."

No, during all those twenty-one years she had grown much less tolerant. There was no "genial courtesy" in her, alas. Here, over the pot of Horehound for feverish coughs was a letter dated May the 25th:

"For myself, I think that we should not call down griefs into our hearts in the manner of Our Lord, for we cannot master them as He did. It suffices that we suffer them in patience."

Though he had told her that she must have half an hour's prayer, she was still as unprayerful as ever. This she had realized when Mère de Chantal had come to stay at Maubuisson and had risen early for her hour's mental prayer. How this had put her and the other Cistercian nuns to shame! Even when Mère de Chantal was ill and exhausted and had nearly fallen asleep again when getting out of bed, she would rise with the alacrity of an angel, and say her prayers standing, to prevent herself from dropping off.

Here was the letter in which he began:

"Madam, no, I beg you never be afraid of importuning me by your letters. . . . God has given me a very singular affection for your heart, and I pray that His divine majesty will fill it with blessing."

Angélique stifled a sob. How heart-rending: she who had never experienced the joy of being a beloved child, to have known for so short a time this incomparable spiritual father, and then to have lost him. And what was worse, she had not heeded his counsel. Here was the letter in which he begged her to try and get at least six hours' sleep. Yes, she must attempt to do that, at least. In the distance the clocks struck the half hour. Here, on the pot of Shepherd Purse for enriching the blood of novices, was the letter in mid-June of that heavenly year when she had been his spiritual child:

"Therefore there will be no more *Monsieur* for you, nor *Madame*

for me. The ancient cordial and charitable names of Father and
Daughter are more Christian, more sweet and of greater power to
show the sacred love which Our Lord has established between us.

"And if possible, be even-tempered, and let all your actions re-
flect the resolutions which you have made, constantly to love the
love of God.

"I do not know why I write to you at such great length. It is my
heart which never tires of speaking to yours. . . ."

How well he had understood her need for peace and sweetness.
He kept telling her not to wonder whether she would be amongst
those highly placed or low, at God's banquet. He simply advised
her to rest in God, that she was not to look whither she was going,
but with Whom. He urged her to go to Holy Communion, quite
boldly. And here was advice which would help her in her present
trouble:

"If they grumble, endure it humbly and lovingly. The grum-
blings will then be turned into blessings. . . . Do not take care to
construct your letters well, for I am not looking out for fine struc-
tures or the language of angels, but for the nests of doves and the
language of love."

The language of love. And she remembered that this very letter
had arrived on a day when she had very sharply interrupted and
reproved the reader in the refectory in front of the whole community. The poor girl had gone as crimson as a coxcomb, and Angélique had continued to make a fool of her.

She held her lamp higher. Here, most suitably covering the pot
of soporifics such as Angelica and Poppy, was the letter advising
her to practise calm demeanour when going to bed, rising, sitting,
eating and talking to her sisters; do it all quietly:

". . . That she slows down all her exterior actions, her carriage,
her step, her countenance, her hands, her tongue."

He had poured a beneficial balm over her, calming her holy
impetuosities, trying to make her take the path to heaven step by
step.

"Cherry trees bear their fruits quickly because these are only
ephemeral cherries, but the palm tree, that prince among trees,
bears dates only a hundred years after planting."

Here on the pot of Ash Leaves for skin diseases, he had called her *"sa toujours plus chère fille de Port-Royal."* And this one, over the Wild Thyme for headaches, "Your letters, my daughter . . . they are refreshment and unburdening for my soul."

"Ha," she said angrily, "let's hope that those supereminent superiors, Mère de Pourlan and Mère le Tardif have seen *that* one. How much ashamed they will feel when he is beatified and they remember that they used his letters shamefully."

It did not prick her conscience to steal some of the letters and hide them. She would replace them with plain paper the following morning.

How could she hide them in her cell? Impossible: she would have to keep them on her person, always. And then, of course, there was the danger of being stripped and searched. *They* were not beyond that, just as she herself had not been beyond it, when she had been Abbess.

A creak upstairs, the sound of a door opening, someone pausing to listen. A firm footstep came down the stairs. Angélique blew out her lamp and hid behind the curtain, trembling with fear. The door opened. Somebody holding a candle peered in. A long shadow fell across the floor.

"Is there anybody in here?" asked a cold voice.

Angélique held her breath. After an eternity, the door closed again, and the footsteps retreated. A monastery clock struck one. Angélique decided to stay in hiding until two in the morning, when the bell would ring for Matins.

The petty persecution continued: a nun wrote of it: "One day at a Chapter meeting, when Soeur Marie-Claire was next to her [Angélique], and Soeur Marie-Claire not stirring when she was spoken to, she pulled her dress gently, to point out to her what she was to do. Whereupon she was reproved and asked why she was meddling. Everybody took sides in the matter, indignant against the persons who had treated the Mother in this way."

It is almost impossible to believe that Monseigneur Zamet was responsible for causing such turmoil in the dovecot. These ideas

could not have been conceived in a man's brain. They all smell of
unredeemed woman. One suspects Dame de Pourlan. Dame le
Tardif was too holy to think on those lines.

One day a nervous postulant, whom Angélique had wheedled
into coming to Port-Royal, opened a door by chance, and saw that
the discipline was being given to a sister. She recoiled in dismay.
Angélique saw her horror.

The girl declared: "I testify to my aversion for all these sorts of
penance."

Angélique assured her that when she was a nun, God would
require of her only the practice of St. Benedict's rule.

Port-Royal was just next door to the Oratorians, and Monseigneur Zamet asked them to direct his nuns. In her account of all
this, Angélique accuses them of forcing the nuns to open their
hearts completely:

"And thus one became inclined to be sorry for one's state, one
thought that God had great designs on us, and one amused oneself by constant talking and never doing anything to correct oneself.

"If they did anything, they were praised as if it were an heroic
action. If they did nothing . . . they were sorry for us because we
had so many troubles."

The nun who writes the account of these thorny happenings puts
them all down to the Evil One. It all upset a nun of Angélique's
who went with her everywhere. She became a very imperfect nun;
in fact, she went a little off her head. There were furies and attacks
of temper which were quite frightening, and "these were called
the ways and the leadings of God. . . . The young nuns became
dissipated and walked about without permission. They talked
when they wanted. The most imperfect were those who talked
most to the Fathers."

The relation was interrupted and brought to a close by Mère
Angélique de St. Jean, many years afterwards, in 1678. She said
it was a pity that all the nuns consulted Dame le Tardif as if her
thoughts were movements of the Holy Spirit. "These thoughts on
the Institute of the Holy Sacrament came to her during her prayer-

time, but the majority of them were not very reliable. But one admired all that." It is easy here to see that all the Arnauld's *esprit de corps* is bristling! The niece up in arms for her aunt, dying in the odour of sanctity. Beside her, Dame le Tardif was a nobody.

16. *MÈRE ANGÉLIQUE IS MADE SUPERIOR OF THE INSTITUTE OF THE BLESSED SACRAMENT*

AFTER THREE years of this kind of treatment, Angélique began to wonder if this Institute of the Blessed Sacrament would ever be founded and if there were any chance of her being the Prioress there, as Monseigneur Zamet had intimated at first. But by now this was very far from his thoughts.

The Order was to be ruled by three great prelates: Sébastien Zamet, Bishop of Langres; Monseigneur Gondi, Archbishop of Paris; and Octave de Bellegarde, Bishop of Sens. These three were at daggers drawn. Paris and Sens disliked Langres. The Archbishop of Paris was not at all pleased at having two associates. He would have preferred to be the only one in charge. So when Monseigneur Zamet announced that he had chosen Dame le Tardif to be Superior at the Saint-Sacrement Convent, he flatly refused to appoint anybody but Angélique. She must have heard this news with some relief. At last she was to get away from her torturers.

Monseigneur Zamet was upset: he sensed that she was not in sympathy with his ideas, and that the Institute would crash under her influence. Monseigneur de Bellegarde probably reported Mère Madeleine de St. Joseph's opinion of her, "that her spirit was full of pure illusions, and what was even more unfortunate, [she was] of an obstinacy and a determined will not to leave them."

"You really trust the judgment of the Prioress of Carmel, then?" asked Monseigneur Zamet.

"Yes, indeed I do. I believe she has a special gift for the discerning of spirits, so that she can see quite easily if someone is not in the true doctrine of the Church. I particularly asked her opinion of Mère Angélique, after the visit she paid her, during the transfer from Port-Royal des Champs."

Thereupon, Monseigneur Zamet asked a protégée of his, Mademoiselle de Chamesson, who was only a postulant and whose name in religion was Soeur Aimée de Jésus, to supervise Angélique and initiate her into the ways of the Order. Angélique at once realized that she was being watched.

It was indeed clumsy of the Bishop to provoke feminine rivalries, but he was worried, and he had had enough of Angélique's whole attitude at Port-Royal. True, she had suffered all her humiliations in silence—but oh, such an eloquent silence!

He said to her: *"Votre ombre nous nuit"* ("Your very shadow harms us"), and she replied:

"Send me away anywhere, and I will go."

Now the house which had been chosen for the new Institute was in the rue Coquillière, near the Louvre, in the fashionable quarter, therefore very noisy. Like the other convent at Tard chosen by Monseigneur Zamet, it had no garden. The exact site is not now certain, but it was probably at the corner of the rue du Bouloi. The street exists to this very day and leads straight to the Louvre. The Blessed Sacrament was installed with all solemnity by Monseigneur de Gondi on May 10th, 1633. Quite soon, because it was so near the court, it became *the* fashionable Paris chapel. Angélique heard coach wheels stopping outside the whole time and knew that footmen would be opening doors for rustling ladies and their friends.

One also heard street cries and the soldiers' jokes; Mademoiselle de Chamesson, who was after all very young, used to laugh at these, and this horrified Angélique. She had been used to the quiet, austere chapels of Port-Royal des Champs and Port-Royal of Paris, and was aghast at the kind of people who came to the rue Coquillière. There were the mothers with their children who chattered and made a noise, there were the great ladies in their silken gowns, and above all, there were the crowds who came, not so much to adore the Blessed Sacrament exposed, as to gape at the altar decked with fine linen, flowers and lights, and at the jewels which the court ladies had lent and which were streaming and glittering

on the altar. The house of God had become a show piece, drama-
tized by an Italian prelate, and Angélique was angry.

When she complained, he was adamant. He said that exterior
pomp in worship helped the soul to raise itself with dignity and
majesty. He himself officiated in the chapel with great devotion,
and somebody said that it was impressive to see him incensing the
altar, for he had a gift for performing ceremonies with due rever-
ence.

Angélique found many other things to disapprove of. Monseigneur Zamet insisted that piety was not incompatible with good
humour: he wanted to make the recreations sprightly, to polish the
behaviour of the nuns and educate them in the ways of the world.
Therefore, they were encouraged to be amusing at recreation, even
at one another's expense, and to imitate one another. "O silence, O
solitude!" groaned Angélique when she recalled the quiet of Port-
Royal des Champs, where all one heard was the cooing of doves. At
meals, Monseigneur Zamet wanted everything to be done properly.
He would not have coarse earthenware, but insisted on good china
goblets. And so they used the ones which had been given several
years back by Madame Arnauld.

Angélique, who wrote an account of this a long time afterwards,
substituting her own sensations of irritation, quite forgets to mention that of course they used the cups given by Madame Arnauld,
She said, "*Au grès on substitua la faïence.*" This incisive little
phrase has a far more effective ring in her indictment against Monseigneur Zamet. She was a worthy child of the clever barrister,
Antoine Arnauld.

And so this uneasy situation might have continued for ever and
the Port-Royal nuns would have avoided Jansenism. But a domestic
quarrel between the envious prelates who ruled the convent
opened the door to Saint-Cyran, and with him entered the full
spirit of Jansen. This is how it happened.

Agnès Arnauld was urged by her Oratorian director, Père de
Condren, to write all the thoughts inspired in her by the Divine
Mystery on the altar. What she produced was fervent and harmless
but pretty well unintelligible, and should indeed have been rele-

gated to the obscurity for which it was intended. It should never have left her cell.

It was not printed, that is why it was called "*Le Chapelet Secret.*" We will remember that she was a little conceited and had an innate tendency to preciosity: she would have been at home in the blue drawing-room of Madame de Rambouillet which her brother Robert frequented. She has been called "*une Julie d'Angennes mystique,*" for the subtle quintessence in her imaginings was very confusing. This Sacrament which God has instituted as a seal of His love for men is represented by Agnès as terrible, frightening and inaccessible. For example, among the sixteen attributes which her soul adores, there is not one which glorifies the ineffable goodness of God, refuge and friend, the food of man in exile. All the attributes which she speaks of inspire fear before the implacable holiness of the Lord—inaccessibility, incomprehensibility, independence, incommunicability, etc.

A few devoted nuns, now having inkpots and quills in their cells, made copies of the precious manuscript and distributed them in secret to the friends of the house. One copy was shown to the dear Abbess of Lys, whom Angélique had helped in her reform, as a great favour and just to show her how special she was.

When she returned to Lys, the Abbess unsuspectingly and most indiscreetly showed it to her Archbishop, hoping he would admire it. Alas, he was none other than the Archbishop of Sens, Octave de Bellegarde, one of the three superiors of the Institute of the Blessed Sacrament, who mistrusted Angélique and greatly disliked Monseigneur Zamet, and wanted an excuse to pick a quarrel with him— (or at least, that is what the Jansenists make out). In order to discredit him, he began to find fault with "*Le Chapelet Secret.*" He was frightened! He was scandalized! He was secretly glad to expose this spirituality of that Arnauld clan of which people made such a fuss. So he sent the manuscript to the Sorbonne and asked eight learned doctors to examine it. Their report was that it contained several extravagancies, impertinencies, errors, blasphemies and impieties which had a tendency to turn souls away from the practice of the virtues of faith, hope and charity, to destroy the way of praying instituted by Jesus Christ and to introduce opinions contrary to the love which the Lord has shown us.

When their verdict was passed on to Angélique and Agnès, they did not worry one scrap. Not for one instant did they doubt themselves. They rejected the censures of the doctors, they made fun of the Sorbonne, and showed immense surprise that anybody should make such a fuss about a manuscript which was the quintessence of the purest spirit of Christianity, too elevated, it is true, for the vulgar mob.

Monseigneur Zamet realized that he was in a difficult situation. He was beginning to foresee the doom of his Institute, when, all of a sudden, a completely unexpected champion arose. It was the obscure, unknown, retired Abbé de Saint-Cyran who until then had hardly directed anyone, let alone women.

Saint-Cyran read it through quickly and wrote a masterly defence of it to show how harmless, nay how orthodox, it was. The *"Chapelet Secret"* was eventually sent to Rome, and the Pope admitted that it was not blasphemous, but advised that it was not suitable for general use.

Of course Angélique and Agnès were most gratified that Saint-Cyran had taken such a risk on their behalf. And Monseigneur Zamet was so relieved that he did not know how to prove his gratitude. One day when he was asking Saint-Cyran's advice on his duties as a Bishop, Saint-Cyran told him that he should not come to Paris so often, but should reside more in his diocese. He fell straight into the trap.

"But who will look after my nuns of the Saint-Sacrement in my absence?" he said.

Saint-Cyran did not reply.

Monseigneur Zamet looked at Saint-Cyran's austere face. He recalled his habits of study, his piety, his impeccable reputation, his love for the poor, and, impulsively, not knowing how much evil he was letting the nuns in for, he said: "I wonder if you would be good enough to direct them in my absence."

At first Saint-Cyran protested, but finally, very reluctantly consented. Monseigneur Zamet returned to Langres with a quiet mind.

And now Angélique, who had previously been frightened of him, declared that she had found the director chosen among ten thousand.

The minute he appeared on the scene, he ordered that the Office in choir should be short, and that to avoid distraction, the nuns should not sing a High Mass. All this was not his province, and it really was very disloyal of him to interfere. Little by little, Angélique poured forth her complaints against Monseigneur Zamet. First, how much she disliked the way he taught the nuns to speak clearly. And Saint-Cyran agreed that this really was quite unnecessary, for anyway, nuns should hold their tongues.

And then she complained about Mademoiselle de Chamesson, the distinguished aristocrat who had been made novice-mistress, though she herself had never passed through a novitiate.

Up to date, very cleverly, Angélique had treated her with circumspection and tact, for she sensed the power that lay in her hands. However, a grumbling rivalry gnawed at the relationship, and Angélique was only waiting for a decent pretext to turn her out.

Angélique sent for her, spoke highly of Saint-Cyran, and suggested that she should go and see him. She fell straight into the little spider's web. She went to him, and with admirable humility complained that she had been made novice-mistress, although she herself had never passed through all the trials of a novitiate. He suggested to her that she should renounce her charge. She did so, and looked very sulky about it.

And it was here that Angélique awaited her, prepared to pounce. To start with, she and all the other sisters sent her to Coventry. In a small enclosed space, where the nuns got no breath of fresh air, no exercise, one can just imagine what hell that would be. They used to look askance at each other if Mademoiselle de Chamesson laughed at the jests she heard wafted up from the street. How unrecollected! Tut, tut!

When Angélique's cronies commiserated with her for having to endure such a nun, she replied: "Our Lord had to bear the society of Judas." (Can presumption go further, to put oneself in the place of Our Lord?)

However, a tale-bearing nun is always to be found in most convents. Mademoiselle de Chamesson told tales about Saint-Cyran to Monseigneur Zamet. From then on, the Bishop became his declared adversary; and moreover, he became very cold to Angélique. At last she saw that collaboration between them was impossible. When he had safely returned to Langres, Angélique did something very astute. Although she had three Superiors over her, she appealed to the only one whom she knew she could master—the Archbishop of Paris, Monseigneur de Gondi—and asked him to send her back to Port-Royal of Paris, and simultaneously to send Dame le Tardif to be Prioress in her place at the Saint-Sacrement. She kept that very quiet from the other nuns.

When Dame le Tardif appeared at the door in the coach, the coachman was asked to wait for a moment, and Angélique returned in the same coach to Port-Royal of Paris.

The first thing she did when she returned to Port-Royal was quite shocking in its insincerity, ingratitude and lack of good breeding. Instead of writing herself to Monseigneur Zamet to tell him she believed he ought not to direct the community any more, and then thank him or find a kind word for what he had tried to do, she slipped out of this responsibility—which, after all, was hers —and put her sister Agnès under obedience to write to him and say that he was not to come to the Abbey again; he harmed the nuns because he led them too gently.

One can understand why Monseigneur Zamet was so deeply wounded and disillusioned that he never came to Paris again. He took refuge in complete silence. Unfortunately, this silence told against him in the end, and one had to wait a long time before a biographer like M. Prunel was found to vindicate him.

Jansenists have always blamed him for the report he had to write to Cardinal Richelieu on Saint-Cyran, forgetting that he was within his rights. After all, Saint-Cyran was the usurper, who had behaved with great disloyalty.

"Saint-Cyran found it easy, because of the moods of the nuns who naturally are partial to change and novelty, especially Mère Angélique Arnauld, then Superior of the said monastery of the Saint-Sacrement, whom the Abbé de Saint-Cyran ordered to keep secret the thoughts which he communicated to her, and to hide them from me.

"The said Mère Angélique acquired such a taste for the discourses of the Abbé and filled her mind with them so much that she could hardly speak of anything else but the primitive Church, the Canons, the customs, the early Christian Councils, the Fathers, principally St. Augustine, of whom she spoke even to women who came to call on her, who mocked her afterwards, as it was extraordinary and useless conversation for them."

17. *"GOOD THINGS OF DAY BEGIN TO DROOP AND DROWSE"*

AND so when Angélique in 1636, on February 10th, returned from the rue Coquillière to Port-Royal of Paris, she created an uproar in the community. They did not all wish to take Saint-Cyran for a confessor. She had imposed Monseigneur Zamet on them by saying that his arrival was providential, and now, she had changed her mind again and said that he was no good: she wanted to impose a man of whom many were afraid. The nun who put up most resistance was her own sister, Marie-Claire, who thought that Monseigneur Zamet was a saint. In this, of course, she was upheld by the lady boarder, Madame de Pontcarré, who was now well settled in, and a great trouble to the community. How Marie-Claire could break the Rule to that extent, one does not know, but she would slip over to Madame Pontcarré's apartments and join a nucleus of resistance to Angélique.

Now if it had been her little sister, Madelon, Angélique might have settled the whole affair by a few good blows on the face, but she could not do that to Claire, who had loved her so passionately that she had avoided Angélique, in order to mortify that love.

So Angélique handed over the responsibility of quelling the rebellion to Agnès. She did it quite well. She forbade the nuns to hold any correspondence with Monseigneur Zamet, and stopped the meetings in Madame de Pontcarré's apartment.

After this, Angélique set about imposing Saint-Cyran on the community. Dame de Ligny has written:

"I have to say that Mère Angélique had very much desired that

213

we should all be under the direction of Monsieur de Saint-Cyran, and she had tried to inspire us with this desire gently . . . but her responsibility and her zeal obliging her to speak strongly, she did it in such a way that the most recalcitrant did not dare to resist."

Is it not easy to picture the scene! Angélique beginning with gentle persuasion, and later taking stronger measures against the refractory ones, including her own sister. Angélique was bent on getting her way, by fair means or foul.

In the end the nuns, against their instinct, against their judgment, perhaps against their consciences, were forced and herded into the confessional of this terrifying priest. (How good that at the beginning of the present century the Pope freed souls from this heavy burden, allowed religious to seek confessors of their own choice and forbade all Superiors, either directly or indirectly, to question their subjects on matters of conscience.) Still Marie-Claire held out, until one day, on the feast of the Assumption, her brother Robert came to the parlour and begged her to kneel down with him and pray about it. She did so, and rose declaring that she had been illuminated and she had changed her mind.

Instantly she asked to see Saint-Cyran, but he kept her waiting a long time. Now Sainte-Beuve in his *Port-Royal* describes all this unbearable anguish as if Saint-Cyran were behaving admirably and Marie-Claire were the culprit. How stupid it all is, how lacking in French logic and clarity! This is the true position. Saint-Cyran looked upon Marie-Claire as a sinner almost beyond redemption. For what reason? Simply because she had not wished to take him as a director and his pride was hurt. And for that, he tortured, for months on end, this poor girl dying of consumption, dying almost in despair. It is an ugly, twisted story, grandiloquently related.

On the feast of St. Louis, 1636, she wrote to him very humbly, as if she were a criminal.

He refused to see her for five months—till February 1st of the following year. Let us picture him on this 1st of February, the eve of the Purification of Our Lady, 1637, as he leaves his house on foot, attended by his naive disciple, M. Lancelot.

It is a damp Parisian day and, always careful of his health, Abbé de Saint-Cyran has smothered that vast steel-like dome of a brow

with a large ecclesiastical hat. He had just given M. Lancelot three
pastilles from Verdun. He always did things in threes, it was a kind
of nervous pious tick of his. True, he said he did it in honour of the
Blessed Trinity, but he reminds one more of poor Samuel Johnson,
feeling obliged to knock the wall with the back of his hand when
he walked in the street. He must have been suffering from some
kind of anxiety neurosis. He even washed his face, his teeth, his
hands three times every morning in honour of the Blessed Trinity.

He saw two or three little children on their way to afternoon
school, playing at shuttlecock.

"Ah," said Claude Lancelot, "do they not remind you of the
times you played shuttlecock with Monseigneur Jansen?"

"Indeed," said Saint-Cyran affably, "That was our way of taking
recreation after profound study. I think it helped to keep us in
health, although," he added hastily, "sickness is the natural state of
Christians. In sickness, you are as you always should be, exempt
from all the passions which assail you during life, without ambition, without avarice, in continual expectation of death."

A coach rumbled by on the cobbles, and a beautiful woman appeared at the window. Saint-Cyran turned his eyes away, almost
with horror. "A necessary evil," he murmured quoting his friend
Jansen on women. ("A man who tries to save the soul of a woman,
is always in great peril himself.")

The coach rumbled along the rue d'Enfer, the beautiful lady
within quite unwitting that she had been consigned to the eternal
flames.

Abbé de Saint-Cyran added in sombre tones: "Many are called
but few chosen."

They passed by the fine chapel of the Carmelite nuns.

"Pause!" exclaimed Saint-Cyran. "Consider the diabolical ex-
travagance of it all, when the poor could be helped. Look at that
building there. Does it not sin against the poverty of Jesus Christ?"

Just then a poor woman who had hobbled in from the market-
gardens nearby with little bunches of snowdrops, came up to him
to sell her flowers. Her feet were bare and she looked frozen. As
usual, Abbé de Saint-Cyran had no change. M. Lancelot offered
to buy him a bunch or two, but he refused.

"No, my good friend, I thank you. Spring flowers displease me. They pass too quickly and are lost without bearing any fruit." The good Lancelot slipped a few sous into the woman's icy palm and said: "Keep your posy, my good woman."

And then, to distract Saint-Cyran's attention, he said: "I heard Monsieur de Séricourt begging you the other day to teach him to pray, but I could not hear your reply."

"Ah, because I gave my reply with action, rather than with words," answered Saint-Cyran. "I told him he must pray like this."

He stopped in the middle of the rue d'Enfer, joined his hands, lowered his head and said: "I told him he must do this, for it is enough to place ourselves humbly before God and consider ourselves happy that He looks at us."

After a while, M. Lancelot asked: "Do you think all worldly conversation is evil?"

"Indeed I do. Evil, evil everywhere. We are sunk in a morass of sin. The Church is in need of reform, dire need."

Saint-Cyran glanced up at the church of the Oratorians, next door to Port-Royal, in fact only separated from it by the rue d'Enfer. He exclaimed: "Look at that place! You should have seen the way the Oratorians directed those poor nuns of Monseigneur Zamet's. No grandeur, no depth, no call to repentance in their teaching. It was all little devotionettes, and far too much piety towards the Virgin Mary. The primitive Church would not have allowed that."

Abbé Bremond has said: "He has created . . . an atmosphere, propitious to the contagion which is about to spread. Displeased with everything, speaking ceaselessly of reform, of the early Church, he has developed in that little world anxieties, rancours and aspirations just like his own."

When he reached the gates of Port-Royal, Madame de Pontcarré was about to leave in her coach. She gave him a frigid look, but he did not even bow. He made a mental note to advise Mère Angélique to turn her out and to indemnify her for her building expenses. Those fashionable *dévotes* should never come near a place of repentance like this.

The first person to seek his advice in the convent was Angélique.

She complained of continual dryness in prayer. He said: "Doubt-less a sign that God has withdrawn His grace from you." (Oh, pestilential doctrine!) And later, in the confessional, he refused her absolution.

The second nun to come to him was Anne-Eugénie Arnauld, bowed and fragile. She said: "*Mon Père,* Mère Agnès asked me if some sister in the children's room could not sweep a little flight of stairs near it, and I said no, thinking that they had enough to do. I said so to the Abbess, and she seemed content."

"Why did you not sweep that flight yourself?" he asked.

She replied, "I was afraid that the dust would get into my throat, and that this would prevent me from singing."

He replied, "A great loss your singing would be."

Anne-Eugénie replied timorously: "Our Mother had not specifi-cally told me to do it."

"*Eh bien,*" he answered, "did the Eternal Father precisely tell His son to suffer all that He suffered during His Passion? Try to bend your will to obedience. Send me your sister Marie-Claire."

Anne-Eugénie was touched by these inane words and joyfully went to sweep the stairs in order to repair her fault.

What was that chattering of teeth, that trembling, on the other side of the half-open door? It was Soeur Marie-Claire, whom he had at last consented to see after five long months. He said: "I neither desired nor designed to see you. I had come with some other intention. But, having come to the church, I find myself inspired to ask for you. . . . Today is the feast of Saint Ignatius, martyr. A remarkable saint. *Eh bien,* what do you want? I am here to heal you. Show your wounds."

Afterwards he said to her, "I praise God to see you returning to Him in truth. It is a grace whose rarity you do not sufficiently appreciate. Of a thousand souls, hardly one will be saved. I had thought you were beyond conversion. If you had died, you could not have claimed a great place in heaven."

He warned her of exaggeration: "There is more humility in con-fessing oneself simply. One must come alive to repentance. That is the reason why I have made you wait so long. I have left you to live. You have been living a spiritual life for the last five months.

. . . I cannot leave you in your freedom of conscience. . . . I who know your wounds, I want to heal them. I am the physician who has to apply the remedy. . . . The way is narrow. It is sheer deceit to make a broad way. . . . May your repentance be accompanied with silence, patience and abstinence. I mean by that, the spirit which brings separation from all things."

As she began weeping, he said: "I do not want a grief which shows in the senses. Beware of your tears."

She said in a broken voice: "I am not worthy to be anything else than a lay sister. I want to be the servant of the last of the community for the rest of my life."

He said, "I will allow that for three months. You will become a lay sister this Lent. You will do the manual work, but without excess, so that you will be able to persevere. It is against humility to want to do extraordinary things. We are not saints to do as the saints have done. One must hold oneself humbly in mediocrity and live in a certain disguise, so that people will see only ordinary things in you. You will make yourself just like the lay sisters in all things, only you will try to be the most humble."

And so this poor sick child was now sent to do the work of a lay sister, with all its heavy carrying and lifting, its walks through long stone passages, up and down stairs, the heavy jugs of water to lift, the scrubbing and cleaning with cold water when one's hands were a mass of bleeding chilblains, the raking of ashes.

As ever, she was helped by her devotion to Our Lady. On the feast of the Annunciation, she came to Abbé de Saint-Cyran and asked for his blessing. And he said about Our Lady, "*Sa grandeur est terrible.*" ("Her greatness is terrible.") And so, he tried to blast away from that young mind all the poetic flowers which the great St. Bernard had sprinkled around Our Lady in that great Cistercian Order which had formed Claire. He tried to destroy the hope of the faithful who believe that on their deathbed the Queen of Heaven comes to fetch away to safety the souls who have been devoted to her in life.

Bereft of her sweetest, strongest support, she allowed her malady to take its insidious hold of her. The tell-tale red patches deepened on her cheekbones, and when once she started to cough, she could not stop. In the refectory, she would only eat what the sisters had left on their plates, all mixed up together in a nauseating mess. At night she sweated in fever and never slept. And whatever rest she snatched was broken, because orders had been given to rouse and fetch her if anybody were taken ill in the house.

At last she admitted defeat and fell headlong. They had to pick her up and take her to the infirmary. Happily her deathbed was not attended by her tormentor, for by then Saint-Cyran had been thrown into the Vincennes prison by Cardinal Richelieu. It was Saint-Cyran's successor, Père Singlin, who came to her deathbed. She cried out to him: "*Mon Père,* will I be saved?"

When her death agony began, she made him recite several prayers to Our Lady. Her face became calm again and she said: "Ah yes, it is a great thing to die in hope of eternal life." She thought of Our Lady, and whispered: "Alas, what would I do without her?"

She died on the 15th of June, 1642, raising in her feeble hands the crucifix which she was clasping, and crying very loud, twice: "Victory, victory!"

Her heavenly Mother had not failed her. At the end Marie-Claire had forgotten that "the grandeur of Mary is terrible." Saint-Cyran had not been able to extinguish this, her last joy. She had called upon her in her great pains, and the Virgin Mother of perfect tenderness had come to her.

She was buried the selfsame evening. She was the first to be buried in the old Cistercian fashion, in entire religious simplicity. In Monseigneur Zamet's time, they had adorned the corpses with flowers and beautiful linen and surrounded them with many candles. But this time they went back to rigorous monastic usage.

Three years previously, Catherine Le Maître, whom Monseigneur de Genève had called his "so dear Catherine de Gênes," now a widow, had been clothed at Port-Royal. In 1629 she had an extraordinary dream, which was prophetic to such an extent that one could almost call it a vision. She dreamt that she saw the nuns of Port-Royal in a most beautiful habit, a white scapular with a scarlet cross on the breast. Indeed, eighteen years later, the nuns adopted this habit, which we now see in Philippe de Champaigne's canvasses. She died on January 22nd, 1651, not having been able to bear the death of her son, M. de Séricourt, in the previous October. She had been ill of tuberculosis at the same time as Marie-Claire.

In 1638, two years after Dame le Tardif had come to it, the Saint-Sacrement house in the rue Coquillière was closed for good.

Now it was Angélique de St. Jean who wrote the latter end of Dame le Tardif's story, and although she did it with great charity, there is a suspicion, here and there, that Dame le Tardif's great sufferings at the end of her life were looked upon as expiations of her former mistakes. This is what happened when she returned to Port-Royal.

One day she was cleaning under a cupboard in the sacristy when she got up too quickly and knocked her eye on the edge of the cupboard. She lost the sight of that eye; very soon the other eye was affected and she became totally blind, with terrible headaches and a fearsome sensation of being continually on the edge of a precipice. She would grope her way along the corridors, hoping that somebody would help her to get to chapel. "And so," says Angélique de St. Jean, a little too smugly, "did God purify her for the mistakes she had made." She asked for permission to seek spiritual consolation and material aid from Anne-Eugénie, and this was allowed. Her deathbed, however, was singularly mystical.

The nuns were singing around her, and all of a sudden they heard an invisible choir of angels mingle their voices with theirs. It was all inexpressibly consoling. (Perhaps it was Heaven's way of intimating that Dame de Tardif was a good nun!)

18. *MÈRE DE CHANTAL AGAIN*

IT WILL be recalled that Monseigneur Zamet had forbidden Angélique to correspond with Mère de Chantal. However, when he was
safely out of the way, and Saint-Cyran in charge of the community
in the rue Coquillière, Angélique, who always knew how to twist
her directors round her little finger, arranged things in such a way,
that, not only did the correspondence begin again, but Mère de
Chantal actually came to stay at Saint-Sacrement, and it is recorded that they had long, frank and affectionate conversations
together.

No doubt Mère de Chantal told Angélique of the extraordinary
thing that had happened when she went to venerate Monseigneur
de Genève on his bier. After she had covered his face with white
taffeta and asked for permission to kiss his hand, she bent her head
and put this blessed hand on it. And he stretched out his hand as if
he were alive and pressed her head, as if he were giving her a
fatherly caress. The nuns witnessed this miracle.

Since June 1632, Mère de Chantal had been enduring terrible
mental afflictions, temptations and doubts, accompanied by a continual distaste for holy things. It is thus that God safeguarded her
humility. This venerable old nun who had already been bereft of
all human affections, who had founded so many houses, who was so
much admired by everybody that whenever she appeared in the
streets the crowds practically lifted the coach off its wheels, was
now driven to the brink of despair and was counting the days to
death. And this inner trial lasted for four years.

In the year that the temptation began, Angélique resumed her correspondence with her. Angélique's letters can be found in the Bibliothèque Nationale. They were published in 1742.

Angélique showed a rare sympathy throughout. In order to comfort her friend and show her that, like Mary, she had been given the better part, she went as far as saying: "I believe that all my life is nothing but lying and hypocrisy. With this, I have a fear of God which is servile and horrible, and such an apprehension of Death and Hell, that it seems to me I have no love for or real trust in Him."

Mère de Chantal to Angélique: "*Mon unique Mère*, help me and see to it that I am helped."

Angélique, in spite of twenty years' spiritual darkness, seemed to understand by intuition of love all that her friend had gone through, and she wrote prophetically: "Oh, happy suffering in which not all souls are allowed to live in this world. Perhaps you only live for that, and when the interior trouble of which you complain comes to an end, you will cease to exist. For a little I would believe that your happiness depends on your troubles."

In 1641, the year before Marie-Claire's death, Angélique had the great grief of losing Mère de Chantal. A nun with the gift of second sight had predicted that she was soon to die, and Mère de Chantal was enchanted: "Oh, *la bonne nouvelle!*" she cried.

She caught a chill, travelling in winter, and died in December. Her chaplain spoke to her of the love of God and His goodness. She trembled and cried: "Oh, how sweet this thought is!"

Her chaplain, hearing her sigh, said: "Ah, *ma Mère*, those great pains that you endure, they are the clamourings which precede the coming of the Spouse. He comes. Do you not want to meet Him?"

"Yes, *mon Père*," she said. "I am going. Jesus, Jesus, Jesus."

"Do you not hope that your blessed Father, François de Sales, will come and meet you?"

"Oh yes, certainly," she replied. "I put my trust in that, for he promised me that."

The news of her death must have been a terrible blow to Angélique. Now she felt indeed that she was without a mother, for the

poor blind woman who had struggled along in the convent, her
mother by the flesh, had been no more to her than a shade.

When St. Vincent de Paul heard of her death, he tells us that he
saw her soul mounting to heaven like a globe of fire.

Angélique Arnauld, now struggling alone on earth, had need of
her friend's prayers.

> "There's husbandry in heaven:
> Their candles are all out."

The earlier generation of Port-Royal des Champs began to die
off. Those early days of enthusiasm seemed like a dream. The
principal actors in the play faded away like shadows—Dame Elisabeth de Mauternes, dismissed for immorality, the evil monks of
Port-Royal des Champs, Père Basile, now an apostate. Dame
d'Estrées hurtling herself to final impenitence and doom. Forgotten
the good priests of those early days—Père Gallot, so holy and
learned; Père Archange, now written off as a casuist and quite forgotten; Dame de Soissons, Abbess of Maubuisson, leaving her
Abbey in financial ruin, her deathbed surrounded by thieving
novices who even took away her cloak; Dame Suireau, her successor, tormented by illness; and all those young nuns of Maubuisson, coming to die at Port-Royal. Poor little Madelon, now Soeur
Madeleine de St. Christine, her mind clouded, sitting alone in one
room absorbed in her prayers all day. Her mother, Madame
Arnauld, now Soeur Catherine de St. Félicité, blind and a cypher.
The lay sister with toothache who had escaped and then been
locked up in some other convent far away, now quite forgotten.
Dame Morel with her love for gardens. Monseigneur de Genève,
who had died too soon, so little known, too late loved. Madame
Acarie at Pontoise, whom Angélique had missed by one day, now
a fair remembrance in a sweet-scented tomb. The Carmelites next
door, living lives of such grace and beauty, but completely un-
heeded by Angélique.

There was still her sister Anne-Eugénie, now very bent from her
life of continual prayer. She was to die in 1653, and that death was
to cause Angélique great grief, for her duties having called her to
another deathbed, she had been obliged to leave her alone.

And what a fearsome end! Anne-Eugénie, whose life had been so pure, so holy, now trembled at her departing as if she were the greatest of sinners. How terrible a thing was death at Port-Royal!

"But I have offended God so much," cried the dying Anne-Eugénie. Angélique could never recall that scene without feeling heart-piercing grief. Once, when speaking of it to the nuns in conference, she wept, and said: "I believe that God allowed me such an encounter in order that it should be an affliction for the rest of my life, for I do not think I can ever be consoled about this."

19. *JANSENISM BEGINS*

In 1638, the year of Louis XIV's birth and Jansen's death, Richelieu—who had been apprehensive because Saint-Cyran had shown
his independence, first by refusing promotion at his hands, sec-
ondly by contradicting him about Monsieur's marriage—suddenly
said that he considered Saint-Cyran too dangerous to leave at
liberty. He decided in the month of May to imprison him in the
fortress of Vincennes, that prison which had housed Calvin's disciples. To the Parisians of that day, Saint-Cyran was, to all appearances, a political prisoner; there was as yet no mention of heresy.
Else Mère de Chantal would not have written to him.

Angélique wrote to Mère de Chantal, "They dare to compare
him to Calvin. He bears all this with admirable virtue." In spite of
being forbidden writing materials, he managed to write a good
many letters of spiritual direction in prison. An account of his ac-
tivities and sufferings would be boring, save to mention that he
thought it necessary to provide the women prisoners with longer
chemises—for decency!

Cistercian hospitality was always proverbially openhearted, but
during the time that Saint-Cyran was in prison, when monks or
priests came to Port-Royal asking for refreshment, if the lay sister
told Angélique that she had surmised from their conversation that
they were anti-Saint-Cyran, quickly Angélique ordered the white
bread and the good wine to be taken away from their table, to be
replaced by coarse black bread and servants' cider.

(Ah yes, as her brother had said: "You have a gift for inspiring fear. It is the gift of the rebel angels.")

Saint-Cyran had passed two of the five years of imprisonment when Jansen's *Augustinus* appeared, an astonishing book, packed with learning. It follows Baius in seeing no sufficient distinction between nature and grace, thus necessarily misconceiving the Fall. After the Fall man is fundamentally evil in himself, a slave to concupiscence; he has not only lost the freedom to do good but the power to abstain from evil; he is under compulsion to sin, unless he be one of the small number to whom God has decided to give grace. The book spread rapidly in France and the Low Countries; the Jesuits emerged as its great opponents; the war that was to last well over a century had begun. In 1642 Urban VIII condemned the *Augustinus* in the Bull "*In eminenti*." To Saint-Cyran, of course, the condemnation meant nothing save that Rome must be taught a lesson.

The following year, Richelieu being dead, the Abbé was allowed out of prison, his health gone.

In the meantime, the hermits of Port-Royal des Champs were questioned about their theological orthodoxy. These were relations and friends of Angélique who had retired there to lead a life of prayer, study and repentance. (Incidentally, they drained the marshlands and made the place more habitable when they returned from Paris.) Robert d'Andilly, who had gone there after the death of his wife, was able to cope with the inquisitors—with veiled sarcasm and pretence of innocence.

In February 1641 Madame Arnauld, who had long been infirm, started to fail. When her twentieth child, *le grand Antoine Arnauld*, asked for a last message she sent word that she begged him to uphold truth without fear, even at the cost of a thousand lives, and that he should always remain humble.

In her agony she was heard to murmur ardently: "My God, draw me to Thee," and: "How sweet are Thy tabernacles." She thanked God that all her children were on the way of salvation. She had said she had been the daughter and the mother of a person whom she had carried within her. It is strange to think that she always called Angélique "*ma Mère*," and Agnès also. Because they were, or had been, abbesses, she always used to kneel before them, just like the other nuns.

Antoine Arnauld wrote to Saint-Cyran in prison about his mother's death. Pride peeps forth under his guise of family piety, for he sees her as among the elect, and says that he is no less a child of her tears than St. Augustine was a child of the tears of St. Monica!

And so Antoine Arnauld began to stir up the trouble for which he seemed predestined by the last words of his dying mother. Encouraged by Saint-Cyran, he started writing a book called *La Fréquente Communion*, which was to popularize, for the general public, the principles found in Jansen's *Augustinus*, posthumously published. If one wants to put one's finger on the two events which really brought Jansenism to birth, one can say that they were, first, the imprisonment of Saint-Cyran, which made all his friends feel important and persecuted, and second, the publication of *La Fréquente* (as it was called), which became one of the most fashionable and widely discussed books of the century.

In the first instance, Antoine had composed it at the request of the Princesse de Guemenée, a penitent of Saint-Cyran's whose rigorous conduct concerning Holy Communion was criticized by her more lenient friend, the Marquise de Sablé, at that time directed by a Jesuit. The book is too controversial and too fiercely in the right. Not in vain is Antoine Arnauld the son of an impetuous barrister of passionate pleadings. In reading it, one must remember that the excesses of the seventeenth century are not ours. It was quite necessary to prevent these impetuous people from running to a duel or a house of ill fame, directly after leaving the altar. The book was a tremendous success, and was mentioned in the letters of Madame de Sévigné seven years later. It was read by Christians in the world who would never have opened the heavy, dusty tomes of Jansen.

Angélique, who loved this youngest brother of hers like a son, and whose eyes used to fill with tears when she thought of his enemies, said that her mother had bequeathed to her the tender love which she felt for this Benjamin; she could have had no presentiment of the harm this book would do to her name, and that it would eventually lead to the destruction of Port-Royal.

In his memoirs, Rapin has said that Jansenism spread in France because smart women, who liked the flowered airs of *La Fréquente*, got involved in it. By mentioning this book in a drawing-room, one could join in the conversation of high society. It was the fashionable thing to do.

It had one great evil effect: libertines who read the book gave up all hope of reforming themselves. Its rigidity bred fatalism: "What is written is written." "If I am to be damned, I might as well be hanged for a sheep as a lamb. What's the use of trying?"

And then the great court ladies whose fashions, then as now, always reflected the latest craze, began to wear sleeves and collars "*à la Janséniste.*" With a little decisive air they spoke about St. Augustine and grace. The servants of one lady told her man of business: "Madame cannot speak to you. She is working on the affairs of the Church."

The Jesuit Père Nouet started crying "Wolf! Wolf!" when he saw Antoine Arnauld. In the pulpit he called him a scorpion. Bishops called him "the fox who ravages the vineyard of the Church."

Antoine Arnauld employed all that art of writing which, says Robert d'Andilly smugly, he had learned so naturally by hearing his own relations talk. In spite of this, he entirely lacked humour and imagination. Imagine a man of thirty-five, Doctor of the Sorbonne, coming to tell us, amongst other things, that we must receive public penance for our faults, stand barefoot at the church door! He affirms that daily Communion must only be given to saints, and, in the same breath, he says that he, M. Arnauld, receives Holy Communion every day!!

If this book helped a handful of people, in making them more respectful towards this great Sacrament, there were ten thousand who would be harmed, because it would draw them away from Holy Communion altogether. (It is not surprising that in 1656, some time after Saint-Cyran's death, M. Arnauld was censured.) When Saint-Cyran had heard in prison of the condemnation of the *Augustinus* of his friend Jansen, he had fallen into a terrible fury, saying: "One should show them their duty. . . . They are doing far too much." (*They*, of course, refers to the Pope and the Bishops.)

On February 6th, 1643, when Saint-Cyran came out of prison, almost the first thing he did was to go to the parlour of the Paris Port-Royal, where all the community was assembled. And there, as we know, he suffered a humiliating disappointment, when one of the nuns had that terrible fit of the giggles referred to before. But he had lost his health, and on October 11th he died. His funeral was attended by many high ecclesiastics; he was buried at St. Jacques du Haut Pas.

When the news of his death was broken to Angélique, she raised her eyes to heaven and said: "*Dominus in coelo.*"

A stone was put up in his memory at Port-Royal of Paris. (But the nuns who later ousted Angélique's nuns took away the stone and used it for a sink to wash up on.)

Saint-Cyran had bequeathed his heart to his great friend Robert d'Andilly. His faithful disciple, Lancelot, who was on the watch, asked the guards if he could mind the Abbé's corpse whilst they had some refreshment. In their absence, he took a knife and sliced off the hands. He says so himself. He took a chemise dipped in Saint-Cyran's blood, and the hands in a little box, and brought these relics to Angélique. "These hands," he said, "which had written so well." And Angélique put them in a special relic-room which was very soon to get most overcrowded.

As Saint-Cyran had himself predicted, he could do harm even after death, for he had begun a cult, he had formed a nucleus of disciples now strong in the aura of public persecution; some of them understood the teaching of the *Augustinus*, all of them were inoculated by Saint-Cyran with the despairing doctrine of the small number of the elect, all decrying, as he did, whatever might bring charm to life—poetry, family affection, liturgical ceremonies, recreation allowed to nature.

The Jesuits, ever on the watch near the door of St. Jacques du Haut Pas, noted the coaches of great court ladies who would slip in there, unobserved, as they thought, to pay their respects to his tomb. And on Saturday mornings, the tomb having been previously scrubbed, a Mass was said, *not* as for the dead but as for a confessor of the Church, in white vestments. The poor people in the neighbourhood were given sweetmeats and tracts about Saint-Cyran's holiness. It was really becoming quite a scandal. The Church, of course, always forbids any public honour to be given to a dead person before she has pronounced on his holiness.

In 1646 Robert d'Andilly retired to Port-Royal des Champs, which then was filling up with hermits who had been impressed by reading *La Fréquente Communion*. Now red-cheeked with white hair streaming, Robert turned to gardening and translating St. Teresa to console himself for leaving the world he had loved so much and for losing his wife. Very soon Port-Royal des Champs began to blossom as the rose. He was especially good at espalier fruit, and occasionally would send a basket of choice pears to the Queen Mother. (A friend of hers would tease her at table, saying: "You can eat the pears of Monsieur d'Andilly, they are not Jansenist.") When his Le Maître nephew also decided to become a solitary, he wrote to his father a letter which began: "*Monsieur mon père*, God having made use of you to bring me into the world . . ."!

In May 1647 Angélique left Paris and returned to Port-Royal des Champs, for the Archbishop had now given her leave to use both houses, the Paris house being greatly overcrowded. About that return, Angélique wrote to the Queen of Poland, "It is a marvel to see the silence, the modesty and devotion, even of the valets who are preparing the place for us, with as great affection as if we were angels whom they were awaiting."

Angélique took with her seven professed choir nuns and two lay sisters. She was welcomed by the hermits singing a *Te Deum;* the bells were rung and a bonfire was lit.

In December of that same year, the new habit with the red cross on the white scapular was adopted with great ceremonial. On June 11th, Angélique came to Paris for the day to see the consecration of the new church. Previously she had written about it to the Queen of Poland, who had been French and a great friend of Port-Royal. "This new church is so pretty that I'm almost ashamed. . . . All those who see it say it's a little masterpiece." "Our church is according to all who see it the prettiest and the most devotional in Paris, although it is among the most simple. Our choir is very

beautiful and convenient. There are eighty chairs." Agnès adds:
"*Il résonne à merveille*"—"it echoes beautifully"—which only proves
how she still loved Divine Office to be well sung. After the consecration, Angélique returned with pleasure to her cradle, Port-
Royal des Champs.

Agnès was very sad at this renewed separation from her sister,
and she missed Port-Royal des Champs. She had written about it:
"That holy place is closer to my heart, it seems to me, than any
other. One truly feels that God is there in a special way. If our sisters of Paris felt that, I think they would ask God for the wings of
a dove to fly to it and rest there. . . . One breathes therein quite
a different air from Paris. It is perfect silence. One hears only the
birds."

Now the hermits being homeless, some of them went to Les
Granges, the great farm on the hill overlooking Port-Royal, others
went temporarily to Paris. Angélique's nephew, Antoine Le Maître,
who had left a brilliant career at the Bar, after being greatly impressed by the deathbed of his d'Andilly aunt, went to Les
Granges.

All the hermits were happy to consecrate their strength and time
to the service of "those daughters of Port-Royal who are our ladies,
our mistresses and our queens." The Duc de Luynes, who had
made a vow of chastity after the death of his wife, was among the
hermits. He was very useful to the nuns, for he was both wealthy
and generous.

For some time past, Angélique had complained about her de-
clining health. She was threatened with dropsy, which even she
admitted was hard to bear. In 1649, her digestion was destroyed to
such an extent that she could only digest human milk, and had to
have a wet nurse. And it is not surprising, when one thinks of
the strain she endured in the Fronde.

20. *MÈRE ANGÉLIQUE GIVES HOSPITALITY DURING THE FRONDE*

ONE OF the big "ifs" of history: would Louis XIV have persecuted Port-Royal, had the Fronde rebellion not made him afraid of independent groups of people?

The word "fronde" means catapult. This insurrection was so called because of the stones thrown at the windows during the troubled era which was a forerunner of the Revolution in the following century. The first Fronde, or rebellion of 1648-9, was an insurrection of the Parliamentary Officers against the Stewards, whom they accused of despotism.

But this first Parliamentary Fronde was nothing to the Fronde of the nobility, which lasted far longer—from 1650 to 1653. During that last time, Port-Royal des Champs took refuge in Paris for greater safety, or at least they moved to Paris in the April of 1652.

The great criminal in the eyes of both Parliament and the nobility was Cardinal Mazarin, whom people suspected of being the *cher ami* of the Regent, Queen Anne of Austria, a proud Spaniard who was now reacting against the long indifference of her late husband, Louis XIII. At the so-called dangerous age, she suddenly met this good-looking man whose black eyes caressed her, whose wit amused her. In the end she could not do without him, and she did everything he told her to. True, he was not as hard as Richelieu had been, but he was subtle and flattering and most self-apologetic.

Louis XIV was never to forget the revolution of the people. The royal family fled from Paris, pamphlets insulted the Queen and

the Cardinal, crowds invaded the palace and forced the Regent
to show them the little ten-year-old King in his bed. They all
clamoured to be delivered from the Cardinal. Turenne, seduced
by the beauty of Madame de Longueville, took up arms against
the King and started negotiations with the Spaniards. The magis-
trates insulted the Cardinal, calling him "this thief, this mounte-
bank, this old clothes man, this Italian impostor." The populace
blamed him for the high price of wheat.

Then a terrible thing happened. The grand Condé, the support
of the court, suddenly turned against the King. His pride had
been slighted by the Cardinal. And then all the Amazons took up
arms against the King. Madame de Longueville, Madame de
Chevreuse and, arrayed in cuirass and feathers, the grande Mademoiselle herself commanded an army and, joining with Condé,
opened Paris to the army of the Princes. But when the people saw
her firing the cannon of the Bastille on the royal troops, and Condé
so unbearably conceited, when they saw the Spanish flags in his
ranks, they sensibly began to prefer Cardinal Mazarin with all his
faults.

So at length, in October 1652, Louis XIV made a victorious entry
into Paris. The Cardinal was prudent enough to stay away for
some time, for he was still being called "the greatest bit of filth of
the century."

Louis XIV realized how the unpopularity of too strong a minister
can alienate a kingdom from its king. He resolved to rule by himself without a principal minister, and he decided to tame and
domesticate his warlike nobility.

The King kept Mazarin on afterwards, but henceforward he
looked with suspicion at any section of his people which showed
too great an independence. Port-Royal itself had to suffer from
these suspicions. What was this group of hermits and enclosed
Cistercian nuns who seemed to be so independent of him, so popu-
lar, who were always getting themselves talked about? And when
at length he crushed them with the full support of his Jesuit confessor, all he had suffered during the Fronde leaped back to his
memory.

In that sad spring of 1649, Angélique wrote to a nun: "All our miseries would arouse your compassion. War is a terrible plague. It is a marvel that all the animals and the people are not dead from having been locked up together for so long. We have the horses underneath our room, and, facing it, in the Chapter House, and in the cellar, there are about forty cows belonging to us and to the poor people. The courtyard is full of hens, turkeys, ducks and geese, inside and out. And when we did not want to receive them they said, 'Take them for yourselves if you want them. We would prefer you to have them, instead of the soldiers.' Our church is so full of wheat, oats, peas and beans, cauldrons and ragged clothing that you have to walk over them in order to get into choir, which itself is full of the books of our *messieurs*. In addition to this, there are ten or twelve nuns who have taken refuge with us. All the maidservants of the farm are inside, and all the menservants outside. The barns are full of lame people, the wine press and the lower part of the poultry yard are full of cattle. In fact, without the great cold, I think we would all have caught the plague. Everything has become extortionately expensive here, everything having been destroyed. In fact, it fills one with terrible pity to see this unfortunate countryside. I had not meant to tell you all this, but I am so filled with pity and anxiety about it all, that I have told it to you almost without realizing it."

Dame de Ligny, who describes Angélique's activity during the Fronde, said that the Abbey resembled a Noah's Ark. She comments on Angélique's holy improvidence: she even distributed alms from the provisions which had been made for the needs of the house, even the fruits prepared and cultivated so carefully by her brother Robert.

And this in spite of her lassitude, she did with a marvellous look of joy, as if she were quite well in health.

Many nuns took refuge from neighbouring convents. Nuns from the Abbey of Gif who had heard all sorts of strange accusations against Port-Royal, began to see, as they thought, that they were groundless, and several asked to remain. Perhaps they would have changed their mind had they read the new book by the Jesuit, Père Brisacier, in which Jansenism was attacked with terrible violence.

In April, 1652, during the more terrible second Fronde, Angélique, thinking it was unsafe to remain at the Champs, brought all her nuns back to Paris in the old carriage.

As Angélique and her nuns neared Paris, they saw that all the villages around were absolutely deserted, most of the inhabitants having taken refuge in the woods. Others had died of hunger or been slaughtered by the mercenary troops of the princes. Abbeys had been pillaged, and nuns who had not been able to flee in time had been terribly ill-treated. Angélique heard that the house of her brother Robert at Andilly had not only been pillaged by the soldiers of Lorraine, but almost demolished. The trees were uprooted and all the poor peasants maimed. She turned to her little group of cowed-looking nuns, who dared not look out of the carriage window when Angélique was there to watch them, and said:

"Now that we are going to Paris, where we will probably be inundated by troops of nuns asking for shelter, we must remember that God will give a special blessing to the nuns whom we receive. I don't know why all nuns become like sheep before me, but it is so. Perhaps we will lead many new nuns into the ways of truth and pure religious observance. I am sure that many will come to join us."

And alas, here her hospitality was not pure and unfeigned as commanded by the Apostle, but it had propaganda as its aim.

She continued, "Now we will organize everything in Paris, just as we did at the Champs. What a good thing I had the idea of putting labels on everybody's possessions to avoid confusion. We'll have to lay in a good stock of food, particularly some salt meat for those nuns who don't keep the fast as we do, and some sheets for nuns who are allowed to use them. Now you lay sisters must have a good soup always on the hob."

"Yes, Reverend Mother," they said, kissing the hem of her habit.

"That broth must be good, strong and well-seasoned. We must get some great soup cauldrons and fill them with minced meat, bread and cabbages. That's the only way to keep everybody healthy."

One lay sister said genially, "Ah, *ma bonne Mère*, as I said to Monseigneur le Duc de Luynes, '*Mon bon Monsieur*, your arms are guns and muskets, but the big soup cauldron of our poor people

is our great cannon.' I think it was miraculous the way we were
able to feed two hundred poor people."

They all smiled. Angélique continued: "Our *Messieurs* will bring
flour from the country for us, for I'm sure it will be too expensive
in Paris. Yes, the poor are all important, as I have written to Her
Majesty the Queen of Poland. All she does for the poor is worth
more than if she spent her days in church."

Angélique should really have been a St. Vincent de Paul sister.
If she could have been trained to cleanliness in her personal habits,
she would have been incomparable.

Inspired when a child by the example of her mother's care for
the poor of the parish of St. Merri, she loved the poor all her life.
As a young Abbess at Port-Royal des Champs, she used to collect
beggars outside the Abbey gate, and whilst they were taking soup
prepared by the other nuns, she would get a little boy to read
aloud to them out of some good book. At Port-Royal of Paris she
had told her pupils so often to pray for the poor. She herself had
spent every available free moment in making clothes and underlinen for them.

Just then they were overtaken by some poor peasants fleeing;
all their worldly goods were piled up in a cart which they were
pulling themselves, as their ass had been slain by the soldiers.

"Ah me," cried Angélique, "I hope all their children are safely
with them. I shall never forget the day at Port-Royal when the doctor came back with a child he had found in the arms of its dead
mother." Angélique had no money to give them, so after a moment's
hesitation, she took off her own shoes and flung them out of the
window.

Just then they were caught up by a very grand coach with
postilions and outriders. Angélique glared with angry disapproval:
"Think of it! The luxury! In these terrible times, people still go to
the theatre. Some give so little heed to their neighbours, that they
are just as eager for their amusements as in times of peace. The
court and the Tuileries are as gay as ever, I am told. Supper parties
and all manner of frivolities go on as usual."

To distract her mind from this, her *bête noire*, the lay sister said:

"How we will miss *Messieurs les Solitaires* who used to spend their nights baking bread for us."

"Ah well," replied Angélique shortly. "I know we'll all be very overworked. We'll have very little time for sleep, let alone for missing anybody. We'll have to bake the bread ourselves and see that there's a plentiful provision."

Another pathetic little cart of fugitives passed them, piled with old men and ragged clothes, a truckle bed and tiny, howling children.

"Thank God they have escaped the brigands infesting the countryside!" exclaimed Angélique. "And now I have nothing else at all to give them."

She added: "Oh, God will drop into a sulphur pit those who have refused to wipe away the tears of poor Lazarus. I thank God that amongst all my many faults, He has not made me avaricious like so many of the great ones of the earth."

Angélique got to the Paris Port-Royal on the vigil of the clothing ceremony of Soeur Euphémie, Pascal's sister. Since it was the eve of the feast of the Trinity, the lay sisters had already prepared all the food for the great day, so as not to miss the sermon. And it was just as well, for on that very night before the clothing, there was a sudden knocking at the door, so loud that it awoke all the nuns. They clustered frightened in the corridors. Who could it be? Could it be those terrible bands of mercenary troops?

One old nun started trembling. One poor young novice remembered the incident of the nun chased by a soldier. She had climbed up the enclosure wall, clutching her crucifix, and he had shot her. This novice had even heard Angélique speak of procuresses waiting for fleeing nuns at convent doors. They began to wish they were at Port-Royal des Champs again, where the *Messieurs* would protect them, for they kept watch all night, sword in one hand, prayerbook in the other. They had even built lookout towers near the enclosure walls. So when Angélique heard that great clamouring at the door, she said:

"No, I shouldn't open. I will look through the Judas and see who they are."

She peered through and saw a multitude of nuns clustering in the courtyard.

"It's all right," said Angélique to the lay sisters, "you may open."

Looking more dead than alive, the nuns fleeing from Etampes fluttered in. They looked very much alarmed when they saw Angélique, for they had heard many terrible things about Port-Royal. They had been told that all Mère Angélique's nuns were bullied and oppressed to such an extent that they had become imbecile. But they were quickly reassured by Angélique's warm welcome of almost passionate tenderness.

She confessed that she pitied them, as if they had been her own sisters. And her daughters made them very welcome, too, bringing whatever could be found for their comfort. Quite soon, one met nuns burdened with pillows, blankets and mattresses, all delighted to have this opportunity of practising charity.

"Now what about supper?" said Angélique.

The lay sisters came forward.

"*Ma Mère*, we prepared tomorrow's meal beforehand, because of Soeur Euphémie's ceremony."

"Good. We will have something to give other guests. I'm sure Soeur Euphémie will not begrudge this to our Etampes sisters."

During 1652 she entertained nearly five hundred nuns of different Orders.

All this tremendous activity seemed to suit Angélique; her health was restored and she wrote to a friend, "I get younger every day, and you would be frightened to see me in our anxieties, trotting in the way I did when I was twenty-five."

A visiting nun exclaimed: "Oh, how fortunate you are to have such a Mother!" As Angélique had expected, several visiting nuns never left Port-Royal again.

People in the outside world became envious, and after that famous evening of May 25th when the whole sisterhood from Notre Dame d'Etampes had come, somebody told tales to the Archbishop of Paris, saying that Angélique had broken the enclosure. He replied with warm approval and gave a general permission to begin again whenever she judged it necessary.

Others, hearing that she had received great alms from the

Queen of Poland, began whispering that Port-Royal kept back the alms and gave them to feed the rebellious troops. They even spread the whisper that *les Messieurs de Port-Royal* were in league with that terrible Oliver Cromwell in England, and favoured the rebellion of the Prince de Condé.

And now the Jesuits began to attack. At the beginning of the year, they had a grotesque almanack engraved, representing heretics led by Jansen, winged like a devil, flinging himself into the arms of a Calvinist.

Soon more sinister rumours began spreading, that Mère Angélique was being charged with heresy.

Just then Paris was filling up with all the Stuart exiles who had lost everything to follow their king. One must confess that Angélique showed universal charity to them. She spoke compassionately of that demoiselle Maitland who had to beg to keep alive, of that chevalier Digby who had no bread, and she tried to help them as much as she could. It was when she thought of such people that the rich hermitages and the high altar of the Carmelites next door infuriated her.

Of the 14,000 livres which the Queen of Poland had sent in May 1652, she gave 4,000 to the priests of Etampes, where everything had been pillaged or burnt.

The state of the hospitals as a result of the war filled Angélique with horror: "There were so many wounded men in the encounter of the Faubourg St. Antoine, that they laid them out on stone tiles without a bed at the Hôtel-Dieu.

"Believe me, Madame, that does not prevent folk from having parties with jams and sweetmeats in the open air in the Tuileries gardens, and people still go to the theatre at the Hôtel de Bourgogne."

As the Queen's emissary, she was glad to lend to poor gentlemen, old or sick or wounded in the wars, whose lands had been ravaged. These squires would return the money after next year's harvest. They could buy or hire cows, or procure clothing, or even house the poor round their castles, for their huts too had been burnt. Only women and children remained on these estates. There were hardly any unwounded men.

A nun from an outside convent came to her one day and said, "*Ma Mère,* it is reassuring to be here. We've heard terrible things about you."

"Oh," said Angélique, disagreeably surprised, for she thought that Port-Royal was held in high esteem by all nuns throughout the kingdom, "what have you heard?"

"It was rumoured," she replied, "that half your nuns were Huguenots, and that many of them denied the Virgin Mary and the saints. That is why it is such a joy for us to recite the Rosary with you, and the Litanies to Our Lady, to live as we do, in mutual affection and in the freedom of the children of God. We had heard that there was no freedom here at all, but that all your nuns were blindly submissive to you, even in affairs of conscience. Your nuns are so kind. We are so much impressed that in the middle of all this hubbub, they all keep the great monastic silence. Look at us! Two hundred in the refectory, and we would have so much to say to one another. And yet not a word."

"Yes," said Angélique, "it makes me blush to think that I talk so much, and my nuns keep silent. You must not praise us, sister." She gave her a nod of curt dismissal, and the sister had to go.

Just then, there was more heavy thumping on the outer door. Angélique, who was passing by, went to peer through the Judas, and she saw some very smartly dressed nuns outside. She ordered the lay sister to open the door. There they were, a sight for sore eyes, wearing gloves and elegantly pleated cloaks. One sister in particular had steel busks in her scapular. After welcoming them, Angélique turned to the nun with the busks in her scapular. She said: "Sister, I could not allow my nuns here to see worldly bad example. At Port-Royal, before the reform, many of my nuns wore gloves and masks, and some even carried fans. But now we have renounced all this."

And then, in order to hide the confusion of this poor nun, who was blushing furiously, she called for refreshments all round.

It looked as if Angélique were at her best when she was on her mettle in times of crisis. She impressed everybody. It was just like the old days when a visiting nun had written to her convent at home: "Madame de Port-Royal has such a great care for her nuns, that she even brings the wood to the dormitory to warm them. She has so great a charity for those who are ill, that it seems as if she herself were the infirmarian."

But instead of redeeming her in the eyes of the outside world, her almost defiant charity put many ecclesiastics to shame, and her name was more venomously attacked than before. They now found more excuses for starting a persecution in earnest.

21. *THE OUTSIDE WORLD*

NOT SUFFERING from her baleful moods or her brusque orders, some people in the outside world were even more apt to hero-worship Angélique than her own nuns.

In parenthesis, nothing reflects those baleful moods of Angélique's so much as the conferences she gave to her nuns in place of recreation. If someone came in unpunctually, Angélique reproved her with glittering eyes. A contemporary engraving shows how formidable she looked: long, clever French nose; Cupid's-bow lips, combining self-satisfaction, sensuality and determination; pouches under the eyes; sarcastic, critical, unquiet eyebrows, going up at the ends; beautifully set eyes in drooping lids; a cleft chin, most determined and authoritative. And yet, this grim, disquieting face has something pathetic, something defenceless about it, so that we who know her sad story of frustration find her almost endearing. But she did not like being loved. She said that nothing made her fear Hell more.

Hell and the Devil were her favourite topics during these conferences: she sometimes frightened her nuns when she talked of the "subterranean regions." She even spoke of deceiving the Devil by assuming a cheerful expression. She expatiates on Eternal Torments—"We will not endure them abed, but in devouring flames which will never end." She gives a graphic description of the punishment of Herod, and how he tore himself to shreds and was eaten by worms. There is a lot more about invisible wolves prowling round convents, about Hell, Purgatory and Limbo. "The numberless multitude of the damned will not prevent the eternal horror of the solitude of Hell." On Hell, she exclaimed: "My God, how I fear it!" She said she wanted to be locked up and treated rigorously, with blows, like a slave, to avoid Hell. She even went so far in unhealthy morbidity as to say that she would like a confessor who would beat her.

Only when she talks of the virtue of poverty does she rise to heights like Léon Bloy in "*La femme pauvre*," for she knew, like Bloy, that nothing in the world is so searching, so searing, as poverty: "But rejoice, ye poor and ignorant ones, without books, without reading, without elevating conversations, as you prepare your vegetables, and bring your pot to the boil. . . . It is for you that the son of God is come. . . ." "For to die of poverty is to die with Jesus Christ and in Jesus Christ. It is to die truly in the kiss of God. . . . This virtue comprises all the others because it humiliates and annihilates the soul much more than any other. . . . Love of poverty makes one choose what is ugliest, coarsest and dirtiest."

Sometimes a nun would timorously voice a weak protest—against uncleanliness, against lack of recreation which drove nuns mad, against ill-treatment, but Angélique always eluded her.

One feels that many a nun must have left these conferences far from comforted.

To Euphémie Pascal, sister of the great Pascal, Angélique was perfect. In May 1653, in Port-Royal of Paris, Soeur Euphémie was in great distress of mind, as her illustrious brother would not hand over her share of their father's inheritance for her dowry. Angélique, noting the extraordinary sadness in her face, left choir before Mass began, and calling her away, made every effort to allay her pain:

"But because the space of time was too short to satisfy her charity, immediately after Mass, she made a sign to me to follow her, and placing me near her, she held me for a whole hour with my head clasped to her breast, embracing me with the tenderness of a real mother. And there I can say with truth, she did all in her power to charm away my distress."

Secretly, Angélique's attitude was: let us show the wicked world

how disinterested we are at Port-Royal. It acted like a charm—
Pascal gave up the money, and eventually joined the hermits of
Port-Royal des Champs, where he composed the immortal *Lettres
Provinciales* against the Jesuits. But Pascal, possessing "to a high
degree of intensity, the feeling for the human person,"[1] and Angélique, having no real respect for human individuality—these two
were not meant to understand one another. Angélique deplored
the mockery of his *Provinciales*. She wrote to the Queen of Poland:
"I assure you, Madame, that I am just as impatient as your Majesty
with the author of the Provincial letters. He raises up terrible enemies against us."

After a great mystical experience in November 1654, Pascal came
to the Champs in January 1655, and wrote there *Le Mystère de
Jésus*, the manuscript of which still exists. When Pascal started to
write in defence of his new friends, his identity was kept secret for
fear of the police. When we look at his wonderful death mask today and admire that long, jutting-out, intelligent nose, that mouth
as if closed on a secret, we wonder how any disguise could ever
have concealed this supreme genius.

Oh, Port-Royal des Champs, in which *Le Mystère de Jésus* was
conceived!

"Jesus will be in agony until the end of the world: one must not
sleep during that time. Be consoled: thou wouldst not seek Me, if
thou hadst not found Me.

"I thought of thee in My agony. I have spilt such and such drops
of blood for thee.

"I love thee more ardently than thou hast loved thy sins.

"Thou wouldst not seek Me, if thou didst not possess Me. Be not
therefore anxious."

In the *Mystère de Jésus* Pascal is, as it were, prolonging the sublime ecstasy of that November night in the rue des Francs-Bour-
geois-Saint Michel.[2] No greater prayer on the Agony of the Garden
has ever been composed.

It is a pity this great genius could not give conferences to those
Hell-satiated nuns, in place of Angélique.

[1] Sainte-Beuve.
[2] Rue Monsieur Le Prince.

In December of 1656, Pascal went back to his house in Paris, and Soeur Euphémie wrote him a bantering letter: "They have congratulated me on the great fervour which elevates you so much above all common manners, that you put brooms in the rank of superfluous furniture. . . . It is necessary that you should now be, for at least several months, as clean as you are dirty. . . ."

Each morning as they dressed, the hermits prayed: "Give me the grace, Oh my God, to be of the small number of your elect."

These gentlemen rose at one o'clock to sing Matins before the nuns. The memoirs of good Fontaine show us the hermits on winter nights, coming down the hundred steps in a long silent file, carrying lanterns. Antoine Le Maître used to shriek, "Thief! Thief!" at this untimely awakening, and had to be soothed. In the days before they moved to the farm at Les Granges, they used to walk on the neighbouring hill after Compline, because the air was purer. And as they walked, they sang holy canticles, softly for fear of being overheard. They avoided women, for Saint-Cyran had said that a single glance had caused David's downfall with Bathsheba. If a stranger appeared on the scene, they all fled. Antoine Le Maître had made it a general rule to speak to no one. This ferocious purity may have hidden many mysterious repressions.

Indeed M. Hamon, the physician, confessed to Angélique that he was tormented by the flesh, and she had advised him to kill his passions with hard work. They were all a tiny bit eccentric, these *Messieurs*, foregoing fires, even in the dead of winter, and running up and down stairs with heavy blocks of wood to keep from freezing to death. If one met them out of doors, it was difficult not to giggle. The Chevalier de Sévigné carrying his large umbrella was stoned by small boys; M. Hamon visited his patients riding on his ass, with a little desk installed for the Scriptures, and his knitting at hand. As he was long and thin and dressed in black, a poor woman meeting him in lonely country took him for a ghost. The Duc de Luynes was so myopic that he used to bow low to all the peasants and then peer at them in case they were holy hermits. After the death of his first wife, he made a vow of chastity, but, much to the horror of the nuns, married again twice, the last time as quite an old man.

Racine came there as a young pupil, and used to go for walks on a woodland path which still exists, with his dog Rabotin. He composed long poems about the beauties of Port-Royal. "Holy dwellings of silence./Place full of charm and attraction," laying stress on the fruits cultivated by Robert d'Andilly—the blushing peach and that little sun, that sweet apricot *nonpareil* whose colour is so charming, and the espalier pears.

It is very painful to leave these hermits of Port-Royal des Champs. They deserve a whole book of their own. M. Hamon has been called "the magic king in rags," and someone else has said that he lived the beautiful mystical dream of a monk of the Middle Ages. No one knows what changed him from the rich fashionable physician in the parish of St. Merri to the beggar in tatters, the servant of poor nuns whose infirmary he visited twice a day. He slept on a plank in a miserable garret, and at night used to write a commentary on the Song of Songs.

He bullied his patients, and Angélique had to ask him to deal more tactfully with them, "to endure with compassion their little contrarinesses." He was a great talker: often Angélique had to warn him to stop talking. She would send him away abruptly when she judged that he had said enough.

In order to eke out her slender finances, and much against her will, Angélique was still obliged to take in lady boarders at the Paris Port-Royal. Great court ladies who had led tragic lives sought peace near the precincts of the cloister. Often these were introduced by her brother, Robert, who was more interested in a soul if it were housed in a beautiful body. On the whole, these beauties did not take their retreat very seriously.

Angélique supervised them as strictly as she could. One Christmas, she had three of them together at Port-Royal. After her meal she suddenly bethought herself that they had been talking together for a very long time. "A headdress, collar or a new fashion must inevitably crop into the conversation. One must try to banish these evils which should not be allowed in Christian intercourse."

The Princesse de Guemenée, like the others, had a history of unexampled brilliance and sadness. Her great beauty had excited jealousy at court. She never persevered in her project of retreat.

She had "attacks of adoration" and then would return to the world.

The second great lady of the trio was Anne Geneviève de Bourbon, Princesse de Longueville, who had her own house at Port-Royal des Champs. She was a great friend of La Rochefoucauld, the author of the *Maxims*, and she too had had great tragedies in her life. She is the only court lady of whom Angélique speaks highly: "She was pure gold, through and through. Cold, prudent, humble, gentle, devout. Nothing in her of the false flighty ones who only produce fine words."

The third of the trio, and the most amusing, was the Princesse de Longueville's great friend, the Marquise de Sablé, who, for all her exquisite sensibilities, neglected her appearance and "looked like a dish of scrambled eggs." Perhaps this is the reason why she attracted Angélique's affection. La Rochefoucauld said that she had an understanding of the inmost recesses of the human heart. As the hypochondriac par excellence, she caused the nuns a great deal of trouble. When the Marquise suspected that any of the nuns had measles or high temperatures, she would send her spies around to find out the situation, and then shriek with fury if it had been concealed from her. If a sick friend wrote to her, she would give the letter to her maid to read aloud to her from the garden, to avoid contagion.

It is not surprising that Angélique, who was often afflicted with the most awful headaches, particularly when she went anywhere near a fire, could sympathize heartily with the migraines of the Marquise. She wrote:

"*Ma très chère,* I send you some liquorice juice which we have made here and which seems to me very good. I should be enchanted if you thought so too, but I beseech you most humbly not to pretend, and to tell me the real truth. . . . Be assured that no feverish air or other ills have gone near this juice."

But Angélique's greatest lay friend, and the one to whom she wrote the most, was Marie de Gonzague, who later became Queen of Poland. Her letters are very confiding, full of severe tenderness and a great concern for the poor of Poland. They are not, however, renowned for any spiritual elevation. Marie de Gonzague had loved the young Cinq Mars, whom Richelieu had sent to the block.

She had to keep her secret and her tears to herself. In desperation she turned to Mère Angélique, who at once put her under the direction of Saint-Cyran. She gave her a cell at Port-Royal, quite poor and humble, where she could make retreats. Angélique was disappointed when she left to marry. She said rather sarcastically, "She has preferred a crown." Matrimony was not in high honour at Port-Royal. One can imagine Angélique's dismay when, having lost her first husband, the aging, plump queen married her brother-in-law. Angélique had been expecting her to return to Port-Royal and become a Cistercian nun.

Angélique's letters, which have all been preserved, often revert to her favourite subject, the poverty of the Poles. She says that there can be no real spiritual life for people reduced to a misery too great: only voluntary poverty was fruitful. What could the poor renounce, when they lived in mud, cold and filth, and had no shoes? And here Angélique made a rare and really practical suggestion. She said she was going to recruit a little company of shoe-makers and tailors to send to Poland. They would have to live in community; the Queen must go to see them often, and give them some little Polish apprentices. This would take some of the savages off the streets and keep them out of mischief. . . . Visitation nuns were also to be installed next door to the Palace. The Queen has only a few steps to make to rejoin her nuns: she was then both Queen and Abbess.

It is in her letters to the Queen of Poland that we get a full account of the miracle of the Holy Thorn in 1656, which caused a temporary lull in the persecution of Port-Royal. It is extraordinary that the miracle was performed on Marguerite Périer, the little niece of that invisible Pascal whose anonymous *Provinciales* were taking Paris by storm. Angélique was not in Paris at the time of the miracle, and so she speaks of it with restraint and caution.

It seems that a friend of the nuns, hearing of their troubles due to being implicated in Jansenism, had lent them a thorn from Our Lord's Crown of Thorns. This was exposed for adoration in a monstrance on the high altar. Marguerite Périer, who had a lachrymal ulcer, apparently incurable, was urged by her mistress to place the thorn on her eye: she was instantly cured. Many physicians testified to this. One can imagine the great hubbub in Paris. Enormous crowds of sick people then queued up outside the chapel to ask for cures.

Later, there was a public thanksgiving. Marguerite Périer, dressed in a white habit, knelt on two cushions in the chapel so that the people could see her. (Later, Soeur Catherine, the daughter of Philippe de Champaigne, was also cured of paralysis by the same holy thorn. We can see her in the great oil painting with Mère Agnès in the Louvre. Her father had painted this as a thanks-offering. There is always a crowd of people looking up at this wonderful picture in the Louvre, with its strange austerity and peace.)

However, the lull caused by the miracle was only temporary. Quite soon the storm that was utterly to destroy Port-Royal loomed and then broke in all its fury over the two houses, the nuns, pupils and hermits.

22. *LAST PERSECUTION AND DEATH*

AFTER THE first condemnation in 1642, Rome had moved slowly,
allowing the Jansenists every opportunity to state their case. It
was eleven years later that the Bull *Cum occasione* singled out the
famous five propositions as heretical. The fourth and fifth are rather
technical, the other three are only too clear:

(1) Some of God's commandments are impossible even for the
just who strive to keep them—the grace by which these commandments would be possible for them is lacking.

(2) In the state of fallen nature, no one ever resists grace [so that
if a man sins, it means God had not given him the grace to resist].

(3) It is a semi-Pelagian error to say that Christ died or shed his
blood for all men.

The main body of Jansenists replied by accepting the condemnation of these doctrines, but denying that they were to be found in
the *Augustinus* (Pascal was too clear-sighted for that, he rejected
the Bull totally). Three years later, in the Bull *Ad sanctam,* Alexander VII defined that "the five propositions have been drawn from
the book of Jansen entitled *Augustinus,* and that they have been
condemned in the sense of the same Jansen, and we once more
condemn them as such."

The Bull of Pope Alexander VII was received in France in
March 1657. During four years, storm clouds gathered, thunder
grumbled nearer and nearer. The storm burst in April 1661, when
the king, whose confessor was a Jesuit and who disliked individual-
ism, decided to uproot the principal seat of resistance—Port-Royal.

251

He was as harsh in this as in his persecution of quietism and Fénelon. The Bishop had issued a Formulary[1] which each nun was enjoined to sign, declaring that she rejected as heretical five propositions in the *Augustinus*. This the Port-Royal nuns refused to do, claiming that they had never read the work: and indeed Angélique never had. *Les Messieurs* were more specific: they continued to affirm that indeed those five propositions were heretical, but that they were not to be found in the *Augustinus*. All of them put loyalty to a friend of Saint-Cyran's before obedience to the Holy See. They refused to give credence to the expert advice of their bishops, and said it was all a huge Jesuit plot.

Angélique herself called Jansenism "the phantom heresy" and refused to take it all seriously. Then Louis XIV, with his Spanish hatred of heresy and his realization that an orthodox Church was the chief support of the Monarchy, struck.

Saturday, April 23, 1661. Angélique was sixty-nine, with barely four months to live. Bad news from Paris. The pupils and novices were to be dispersed. She was just getting painfully into her coach when, seeing her brother, Robert, she said to him: "Take courage."

He replied: "I have plenty."

She answered: "My brother, my brother, let us be humble. Let us remember that humility without firmness is cowardice, but that courage without humility is presumption."

She upbraided him for his lack of humility. At all the great moments of her life, she always spoke like a Plutarch heroine, or like her father at the Bar.

Farewell, Port-Royal des Champs, where she had spent over sixty years of her life, a long farewell to the holy mountain of Mollerets, seen in a dream, a mountain which symbolized the blessed Jerusalem.

For the last time her weary eyes glanced at the field where she had first seen the mare with her colt, that day when she had de-

---

[1] The Formulary. "I submit sincerely to the Constitution of Our Holy Father, Pope Alexander VII, and I condemn in heart and speech the doctrine of the five Propositions of Cornelius Jansen, contained in his book entitled *Augustinus,* which the Pope and the Bishops have condemned; which doctrine is not that of St. Augustine, which Jansen has ill-interpreted, contrary to the true meaning of that holy Doctor."

cided to elope. Farewell, the chapel in which others had known
spiritual consolation, but where she had suffered long aridity, after
the first glowing moment of her March conversion.

The Arnaulds had found the Abbey in a state of decay and desti-
tution, and now it was flourishing, and so greatly renowned that it
was praised throughout the length and breadth of the kingdom.
Would their humility suffer? Was this persecution sent to them
to teach them lowliness?

She rode away like a mediaeval chatelaine surrounded by her
tenants. An Englishman, Francis Jenkins, who was an enthusiastic
hermit, interrupted his digging and watched her leave.

When she arrived in Paris, she found all the pupils, Marguerite
Périer among them, in floods of tears at the idea of having to go
home for ever. She brought calm at once by exclaiming: "What? I
think there's crying here. How now, my children, what's all this?
Eh, what? Men are active? Ah well, they are flies. Are you afraid
of them? You hope in God and you fear something." (She flapped
her hands in the air, as though she were driving away flies—a
characteristic gesture.)

After the children, came the problem of the seven novices. They
refused to take off the new habits, as ordered by the King. When
they consulted Angélique, she did not hesitate. She said that each
novice was to decide for herself. And then she put their lay clothes
at hand, so that they could wear them if they wished. So all the
novices left in their habits, but, as a token of respect to the King's
orders, they were draped in long thick cloths to cross the courtyard and get into their coaches in front of the crowd now gathering
in the street. Robert had followed Angélique from Port-Royal des
Champs. He wanted to support her. He was, as Sainte-Beuve said,
"the master of ceremonies of the persecution." He received each
novice in turn, offered his arm and handed her back to her family.
And this he did seven times.

Angélique kept repeating, "When I consider the dignity of this
affliction, it makes me tremble. What? Has God judged us worthy
to suffer for truth and justice?"

Her thoughts turned to humility: "We need all that has happened to us to humiliate us. It would have been dangerous for us

to remain any longer in our abundance. There is no other house in France which has been so greatly endowed with spiritual blessings. They are speaking of us everywhere. Believe me, it was necessary for us that God should humble us. If He had not brought us low, we would perhaps have fallen. Affliction, grief, and troubles are more necessary for us than bread."

"All that they plan to do to us, I care as much about as this fly." And again she would make the familiar gesture of chasing a fly, and thus inspire everybody with courage.

The police appeared and started walling up the doors of the enclosure, on the garden side.

"They are going to hide Heaven!" the nuns exclaimed, and Angélique replied:

"You must not say that, my children. Let us pray to God for them and for ourselves."

And all the time she felt terribly oppressed, for her dropsy was increasing.

On May 15th, before she lost her strength completely, she began writing an appealing letter to the Queen Mother. But Anne of Austria, hearing that these nuns of Port-Royal, in disobedience to their Archbishop, still refused to attribute the five heretical propositions to Jansen, was horrified, and exclaimed: "Eh, what, nuns disobedient to their Bishop?" and refused to help them.

At the end of May, the nuns began a novena, or nine days' prayer, for help. Every afternoon they would walk in procession, barefoot, around the church, holding lighted tapers. The procession would finish in choir, before the great screen of relics. On the last afternoon of the novena, each sister carried a relic, a tiny piece of bone or a drop of blood in a little flask, or a fragment of a habit. Angélique had the signal honour of carrying a fragment of the True Cross, given by Queen Marie de Médicis, and enclosed in a very heavy wooden cross. Completely exhausted by dropsy, she stumbled under the weight of this cross. However, she reached the choir and there fell headlong. Her daughters brought her to her cell and put her down on her hard paillasse. Weeping, they surrounded her, for they felt the end must be near.

Angélique asked them to close the curtains around her bed. She wanted to be alone with her thoughts.

"The time has come, my sisters, to keep the Sabbath"—*Sabbatiser*, the rest that follows labour.

Perhaps she was thinking of Abelard's beautiful hymn, "*Quanta Qualia*," about the long Sabbaths of eternity.

She choked, and was so much oppressed that she was unable to lie in her bed. She had to sit on the edge, gasping for breath. The dropsy made her enormously stout, and her skin began breaking all over, causing her to cry out in agony when she was moved.

They brought a chair for her and she deplored the luxury of it. Then they carried in a second couch for her to use during the day. They wanted to surround it with fustian, but she would only allow them to put a cloth sheet on the side closest the wall. She wanted to die in great poverty.

Alas, she began to be greatly afraid. The fears of a lifetime crowd around one's deathbed. She would say to her nuns, "Believe me, my children, we don't know what it is, this thing, death. We don't think of it. All that I have imagined about it is nothing compared to what it is in reality, to what I realize at this hour."

One day a nun watching by her side heard her murmuring: "Hope in God. He will know how to rescue you, when you are in the whale's belly."

This obscure pronouncement frightened the poor nun, and trembling she asked:

"Will I go in there?"

"Oh, no," replied Angélique, showing panic for the first time. "Only drag me out of it, and I will look after your affairs as I should."

June passed, and then began the long hot July afternoons. On Monday, July 25th, the King's Attorney, accompanied by the Civil Lieutenant, appeared at half-past six in the morning, on foot, having left the coach some distance away in order to take the nuns unaware. They wanted to look at the house and the wall from the outside to make quite sure that there was no secret getaway from the back. Putting the porter and the extern sisters under arrest, they went to Madame de Sablé's lodging and woke her up. Then they

called on the Chevalier de Sévigné and others. They took a ladder
in order to look over the garden walls. This inspection was a kind
of surrounding of the monastery before the great siege. As a result
of it, they had the garden walls heightened.

It is so easy to lose oneself in pity, and miss the point of the whole
affair. One finds the obstinacy of these pious, holy sisters unpardon-
able. Pleading ignorance, they refused to refer to a competent
authority. Allowing for the fact that the dogma of the Pope's In-
fallibility in matters of doctrine and morality had not yet been
promulgated, we, with Sainte-Beuve, are irritated by all these
"evasions, these airs of humility and ignorance with which they
try to wrap round and cover their thought." For fidelity to the
friend of a friend, they are prepared to be thrown out of the bosom
of the Church and die without the Sacraments.

Even the sick Angélique was not left alone by the police. Racine
recorded this for us:

"At this time M. de Contes and M. de Bail who were beginning
their visit, having come into her room, M. de Contes asked her how
she was, and she answered him with great composure.

" 'Like a nun, monsieur, about to die.'

" '*Eh quoi, ma Mère,*' cried M. de Contes, 'you say that as if it
were a thing of no importance. Does death not frighten you at all?'

" 'Monsieur,' she said, 'I have come here to prepare myself to die,
but I had not come here to see the things that I see.'

"At those words, Monsieur de Contes shrugged his shoulders
without replying.

" 'Monsieur,' said the Mother, 'I understand you. Here is man's
day, but the day of God will come and reveal many things.' "

It was very difficult to keep the atmosphere of the sick room
quiet, for during her agony, the Attorney was questioning the nuns.
Soeur Angélique de St. Jean, her niece, replied in her usual proud
fashion. Soeur Euphémie Pascal, so near her own death, replied
so sensibly that the Attorney praised her. He asked her, amongst
others, this habitual question: "If Jesus Christ has died for all men,
how is it that there are so many who are eternally lost?" And she
replied:

"I confess to you, Monsieur, that this often troubles me, and that ordinarily, when I am saying my prayers, and particularly in front of a crucifix, this comes to my mind, and I say to Our Lord within myself, 'My God, how can it be, after all You have done for us, that so many people perish miserably?' But when these thoughts come to me, I reject them, because I do not believe I must probe the secrets of God. That is why I content myself with praying for sinners."

He replied, "That is excellent, *ma fille*," and went on to ask her what books she read.

It is very hard for us in the twentieth century to visualize the effect which these outsiders would have on these cloistered nuns, so many of whom had left the world a long time ago. The very idea of signing the Formulary made them shake. When the Archbishop came to see the house, one nun was seized with such a trembling in her entrails and legs, followed by an attack of giddiness, that she had to leave the room. She could not eat, then she had a terrible headache which prevented her from going to Vespers. The next day, the same trembling, and the beginnings of insomnia and a long neurasthenia. If only Angélique had said one word, "Obey," all would have been well.

Although apparently so inhuman in her detachment, Angélique was heard to whisper, "*La pauvre Marquise.*" So she was remembering her boarder, that troublesome Marquise de Sablé, who had been such a nuisance to her, realizing how lost she would be without her.

All that time the devoted niece, Soeur Angélique de St. Jean, would rush back to her cell and write down a relation of all she had heard her say, in case, of course, it would be used for future beatification. Port-Royal was always taking copious notes in view of canonizing its hermits and nuns. Angélique was not unaware of this. After all, she had known that they used to slip into her cell and take copies of her letters to the Queen of Poland. She kept saying: "Silence. The best part of persecution is humiliation, and humility is kept in silence."

Seeing that other nuns were on the lookout for all her last words, she tried to speak very little and to say nothing remarkable. She said, "They love me too much. I am afraid that they are going to tell all sorts of fairy tales about me."

She hated the idea of nuns saying: "The late Mère Angélique said this, the late Mère Angélique said that." She had a more austere idea of a Christian end: "The true preparation for death is to renounce oneself entirely and to lose oneself in God."

She would cut short all the human tendernesses of her nuns by saying: "I beg you to bury me in the courtyard, and that after my death, you don't go in for so much banter."

And then Angélique, who had lived such a penitential life, at the end was seized by an unspeakable feeling of horror. She had to endure all the anguish of a real spiritual agony.

Ah, the Place de Grève, the criminal she had seen as a child! Yes, she felt like that before God. Like a criminal at the foot of the gallows, waiting for the execution of his sentence. She looked utterly destroyed and consumed.

She had prepared for this terrible hour all her life, and now here it was, more hideous than she had ever dreamed.

Agnès wrote about this horrible fear to her brother, who replied that she was indeed passing through a fearsome Purgatory, ". . . and it seems that it is the heritage of souls who are stronger and more solidly established in piety." Pride again! We see those Arnaulds, always wishing to put their nuns in the very highest place.

And then suddenly fear vanished. Père Singlin, her confessor, seeing her for the last time, exhorted her to trust. She said: "I will then not see you again, *mon Père*, but I promise you that I will be frightened of God no more."

However, this fear came back and persisted in spite of herself, though it left her at the very end.

When the confessor told her that the rank which God had bestowed on her of Mother of the whole house, gave her the right to bless them, she lowered her eyes and struck her breast three times without answering.

Trouble in breathing had yielded after three weeks to profound drowsiness from which by the doctor's orders she was continually aroused. This was torture to her mind and body, and she was in a state of continual exhaustion. She only accepted the invalid chair because it would serve other patients.

To one who spoke of a covering against the draught, she said, "My God, will they always find these pretexts? That does not affect my malady, and I am not afraid of cold. One must confine oneself to what is necessary."

On the afternoon of July 25th she was seized with violent shivering which lasted for two hours. She saw they were greatly depressed at this, and looking at them very tenderly she said, "That is nothing extraordinary. I have been expecting this coldness. Death comes in no other way."

The day after, on the feast of St. Anne, she received Holy Communion at two in the morning. The sight of her face aroused devotion in the onlookers.

On August 4th she was *in extremis*. A nun said: "Mother, you forget us and pray only for yourself."

Angélique clasped her hands and said in a penetrating voice: "My God, have pity on us all. I say upon all, my God, upon all."

She said "Adieu" several times. And then; "My children, I am going."

At eight in the morning of the next day, she lifted her eyes to the Cross in front of her bed and said: "Oh Jesus, oh Jesus, You are my God, You are my Judge, You are my strength, You are my all."

She said this so earnestly that she seemed to be pouring out her whole heart. She received Viaticum with a fervour which made her face glow with a heavenly serenity. Seeing the nuns in tears, she said: "Adieu, my children, let us go to God."

She said a few words of comfort to all who were beside her. Turning to a sister who had always served her and who was now in floods of tears, she said: "How human you still are."

At about nine o'clock on the evening of August 6th, the Feast of the Transfiguration of Our Lord on Mount Thabor, all her former restlessness changed into a kind of lethargy, and she passed quietly away.

Her nuns laid her body in front of the choir grille. The people of Paris came in great crowds. Through the bars, women passed bits of linen, and the nun on guard placed them for a second on

Angélique's scarlet cross. Mothers presented their children for her blessing. The maimed, the lame, the blind, brought by an extern sister, passed by in silence.

Alone of all the hermits of Port-Royal, her eldest brother, Robert, hidden behind a pillar, was praying, tearless.

The annalist of the hermits, M. Fontaine, then in hiding, wrote: "From our little lodging we heard the lugubrious sound of the bell ringing during her funeral. And if we did not hear the sad groans which accompanied this sound, we could well imagine them. We tried from afar to mingle our sighs with theirs, and God saw the grief of His servants which His hand kept in retreat and in silence."

Her heart was brought to Port-Royal des Champs. The nuns used to carry it about in procession. She was buried in the choir of Port-Royal of Paris.

Her niece Angélique de St. Jean had a special gift for making wax masks of people who had just died. The one of Angélique was probably her handiwork. It remained in Port-Royal of Paris from 1661 to 1668. The nuns used to pray before it during the persecution. And then the nuns who signed the Formulary stayed on in Paris. The others, after brief imprisonment, were sent to the Champs, and they took the mask with them. After various peregrinations during and after the Revolution, it has returned to the Champs.

If the mask is seen in its case, instead of in misleading photographs, one can realize what her mouth looked like, before some of her front teeth had gone and the lips had fallen in. Anyway the lower lip collapsed and jutted out on death. One is struck by the nobility, the beauty, even the peace of the face. It is not hard; the features are small and good. She looks like a soul who has suffered intensely.

The contemporary obituaries written on Mère Angélique were very enthusiastic. They called her "a nun veritably illustrious and praiseworthy, the most beautiful, the purest, the holiest figure of Port-Royal."

Or again, they speak of "her heart faithful to her Spouse, capable by its range of understanding, not only of embracing an abbey, but the whole Church. . . . All that she has done is, however, less than what she was."

Her sister Agnès with her usual pride wrote to the Chevalier de Sévigné that she boldly gave her the title of saint.

The great criminal of this tragedy was Angélique's father. He was so unscrupulous, so forceful, that there was no resisting him. Angélique dared not hold her own and make him see that she had no vocation to be a nun. He was the kind of man who swept all before him, and through sheer avarice made Angélique become a nun without a vocation.

She seems to have fallen between two stools as a human being. She was never a mystic and yet she was not a practical woman. Although extremely overactive, she never really achieved much. She could have asked her father to drain the marsh. She could have made the place more healthy. But all she thought about was dragging those poor nuns into greater austerities, hardships for which they had never bargained when they entered the Order. Quite soon, she found that she had a personality magnetic and compelling, and that she could influence nuns to do all she wished. And although they did not share the inner vision which had been hers after the first sermon, still she expected them to live up to her standard. She was unable to control her animal overactivity. She was the sort of person who would do anything to avoid an hour's hard thinking or reading. No, she must instead go and do jobs which were not hers as Abbess—laying fires, scrubbing floors, washing dishes.

Even her great redeeming quality, her love for the poor, was tainted with self-consciousness, while her hospitality to nuns during the troubles of the Fronde was smirched with this *arrière pensée*: "Ah yes, we are going to show them what we nuns of Port-Royal are like."

Angélique had the great privilege of meeting the remarkable Mère Madeleine de St. Joseph. And yet, whenever she mentions the Carmelites, it is only to criticize them. It is essential for the true contemplative to have the receptive mind, the listening ear, the appreciative eye: all these she did not possess. Her autobiography is full of denigrating criticism of a very disagreeable kind.

Ah yes, the old Albigensian heresy, which is as old as the world, that heresy which aims at an inhuman purity and condemns marriage and all natural things, was twisted right round that heart of hers. She talks so often of the evil of the world. She is obsessed with evil.

As one says farewell to her unquiet spirit after many months of research, one almost breathes with relief, one sings a great Alleluia of thanksgiving for the glory of the world: for all the learning and beauty of the Renaissance, then pouring in from Italy; for all the works of art of that stately, noble century; for the city of Paris itself, slowly filling with those lovely Florentine domes, like Val de Grace for example; for the society life of the times, which was growing more and more refined under the influence of the Précieuses and their drawing-rooms, wherein the ideal of Platonic love was beginning to permeate society; for Palestrina, for the music of the seventeenth century, that music which filled her with dismay; for the canvasses of Claude Lorraine, Poussin and the peasant interiors of Le Nain, singing the "still, sad music of humanity."

All the beauties of art and nature are so many facets of the love of God for us, that passionate, exclusive, devouring, consuming love. Closing her eyes to His creation, Angélique turned away from God's Heart.

It is not surprising that the Jansenists were among the chief enemies of the great seventeenth-century devotion to the Sacred Heart of Christ. Souls must become very small, like St. Margaret Mary, to enter in spirit through the narrow wound of Christ's side and understand the immensity of His love.

The love of God in all its plenitude was more real to Pascal at the end of his life, when he became in the words of his curé, "as a child."

Angélique's Purgatory must have begun when, with a gasp of amazement, she realized that she had painted God in her own image, that He was a father who ran swiftly to meet the prodigal son, who made no reproaches but speedily called for the robe and the ring and set him down by a festal board of joy, Love's feast and banquet. God's courtesy! It takes generosity in a soul to know how to receive those amazing gifts with childlike simplicity. There was a spark of generosity in Angélique, but not enough humility.

And now her weeping is stilled forever. And may she, who had denounced mirth, "laugh in the latter day," like the wise woman in the book of Proverbs.

APPENDIX

From 1660 till 1706, three Archbishops of Paris spent themselves in trying to induce the Port-Royal nuns to sign the Formulary. Monseigneur Hardouin de Péréfixe, formerly Louis XIV's tutor, even fasted and prayed for them. Day after day, he came to Port-Royal of Paris and Port-Royal des Champs to exhort them: but without success. By August 1664, his patience was at an end. Armed with a list of twelve of the most recalcitrant and obstinate nuns, he suddenly appeared with six coaches and a crowd of ecclesiastics. He had the convent surrounded by the guard.

The day is so dramatic that it deserves a whole book of its own. The non-signing nuns were sent away to solitary confinement in other convents. Those who signed remained. Soeur Angélique de St. Jean, tall, thin, beautiful and cold, about whose dangerous nature Mère Angélique had been so anxious, was to spend several months at the Annonciades. As she was about to leave Port-Royal on the arm of her father, M. d'Andilly, somebody asked her for her name, and after replying, she added proudly that it was "almost like confessing the name of God, to confess the name of Arnauld." Eventually some of the prisoners signed and then a few retracted. In the end the most obdurate were sent away to Port-Royal des Champs. And here they vegetated, cut off from the outside world, without a breath of intellectual fresh air, without a glimmer of intellectual light. Seeing themselves as the elect, suffering martyrdom, they trembled with joy. Cut off from the living, they walked with the dead—their dead. At night, hand in hand, they wandered about in the darkness of their graveyard, digging up the bones of "their saints." Mère Angélique's heart, they carried in procession.

Although they were most expressly forbidden to approach the holy table, they used to borrow the lay sisters' veils (they were not under this interdict, as they could not read) and tried to cheat about receiving Communion. But quite soon the priest realized what was happening, and insisted that before he communicated a nun, she must lift her veil, and if he saw that it was a choir sister, he passed her over.

Almost all the twelve prisoners have written a relation of what they call their "persecution"; the one by Angélique de St. Jean is tremendously interesting, a masterpiece of intellectual pride. Mère Agnès, who had survived all her other sisters, was by then extremely old; she had had three strokes and was nearly blind. She retracted after signing. A hermit, M. de Saint-Marthe, used to leave Paris on winter nights, climb to the top of the wall of the Champs by a stepladder, and preach consoling discourses to the forty-five captive nuns in the garden. Racine tells us that by his efforts no one died at Port-Royal without the Last Sacraments. They were forbidden to sing Office any more, and thus nobody came to hear them as in the old days. Their main devotion was to process round and round in the cloisters. They turned and turned in those dismal damp cloisters, like lost souls.

Years passed, and by 1705 there were only twenty refractory nuns left at Port-Royal des Champs, old and infirm, and a few of them helpless invalids. Louis XIV then ordered that these survivors should be taken away to other convents to be properly looked after before death.

The Abbess of Port-Royal of Paris, who had signed the Formulary, came to the Champs to make her legal seizure of the Abbey. The bell tolled, its knell was echoed by the encroaching hills, and the nuns trembled with fear. On the next day, this Abbess went to St. Cyr, and Madame de Maintenon said to her sneeringly: "Do tell me, did you find that the church at Port-Royal des Champs had that unction it is said to possess?" At the end of November, although sickened by the chill atmosphere, her very limbs swelling

with the damp, the Abbess returned with a hundred carts to take
away the furniture, clothing, relics, altar ornaments, everything
which the soldiers on guard had not already stolen. Some objects
were auctioned on the spot. A few may still survive in the neighbourhood to this day.

And so at last Port-Royal des Champs was empty for the first
time since its foundation. Even so, it still had a magnetic attraction,
and became a place of pilgrimage. Strange shadows could be seen
at night secretly gliding among the tombs, making holes in the
ground, and burying the hearts of men and women who had loved
Port-Royal and who had wanted to be entombed in its earth.

Angélique had once written to the Queen of Poland: "If I were to
leave Port-Royal, the stones would follow me." This time Louis
XIV took good care that there would be no stones. Four years later,
in 1709, he sent men to demolish and entirely destroy the place,
although it was crumbling of its own accord and jackdaws nested
in the hollows of the arches, and in the niches. All the varieties of
peaches planted by Robert d'Andilly died off and were choked by
the encroaching brambles and nettles. The marshlands appeared
again. All stank of desolation and decay.

And yet, even when the buildings and gardens were destroyed,
the place still fascinated. So Louis XIV decided to destroy the very
tombs. Families were given three months in which to take their
corpses away and bury them elsewhere. This is what Jansenists call
"the desecration of the graves." Quite soon afterwards one could
recognize in the village inns of the neighbourhood, stones engraved
with the faint effigies of abbesses: they now served as tables spread
with wine and sausages for yokels.

But people still went to Port-Royal. The French looked upon it
as a stream of the nation's life-blood. In 1842 Madame Sophie Gay
wrote a letter to her daughter Delphine about this deserted place,
beloved by great thinkers. "I am a firm believer in the influence of
aspect on ideas. It is certain that in the valley of Port-Royal you
must think of God more than of men."

In the mid-nineteenth century, M. de Silvy brought the site and
planted the outline of the cloisters with trees. He built a little
museum in which today we can see among other treasures Mère

Angélique's death mask. We can gaze at the suffering face of this abbess who was the mother of a spiritual family destined to national glory but spiritual doom, one who like Lucifer had been created by God for great fame, but who lost all through pride.

1955 Paris: Bibliothèque Nationale. Sorbonne
      Versailles: Bibliothèque
1956 Port-Royal des Champs. Port-Royal de Paris.
      British Museum.
      Bodleian

BIBLIOGRAPHY

1. Fontaine (N.). Mémoires pour servir à l'histoire de Port-Royal. Utrecht. 1736. 2 vols.
2. Lancelot (Cl.). Mémoire touchant la vie de Monsieur de Saint-Cyran. Cologne. 1738. 2 vols.
3. Tallemant des Réaux (G.). Les historiettes. Pp. G. Montgrédien. Paris. 1932–4. 8 vols.
4. Gazier (C.). Ces Messieurs de Port-Royal. Paris. 1932.
5. Hartmann (G.). Anciennes maisons de la rue du Renard. "La Cité." 1907.
6. Vergé du Tallis (O.). Chroniques de l'Abbaye Royale de Maubuisson. Paris. 1947.
7. Mémoires et Relations sur ce que s'est passé à Port-Royal des Champs depuis le commencement de la réforme de cette abbaye. 1714. 1 vol.
8. Mémoires pour servir à l'histoire de Port-Royal. 1734. 2 vols. (Tome III in 1737.)
9. Relation écrite par la Mère Angélique Arnauld sur Port-Royal. Ed. Louis Cognet. 1954. Grasset.
10. Lettres de Mère Angélique Arnauld. Utrecht. 1742–4. 3 vols.
11. Lettres de la Mère Angélique Arnauld. (Pub. by Mlle Rachel Gillet, with an introduction by P. Faugère.) Paris. Duprat. 1858. 2 vols.
12. Dall (G.). (=Mme Lebaudy). La Mère Angélique d'après sa correspondance. Paris. Perrin. 1898.
13. Arnauld (Mère Agnès). Les Constitutions du Monastère de Port-Royal du Saint-Sacrement. Mons. G. Migeot. 1665. (Pub. by S. de Pontchâteau.)
14. Gazier (A.). Jeanne de Chantal et Angélique Arnauld. Paris. Champion. 1915.
15. Histoires des persécutions des religieuses de Port-Royal, écrites par elles-mêmes. Ville-Franche. 1753. 1 vol.

16. Pinault (N.). Histoire abrégée de la dernière persécution de Port-Royal. 1750. 3 vols.
17. Berliet (J.). Les amis oubliés de Port-Royal: Saint François de Sales et Sainte Jeanne de Chantal. Paris. 1921.
18. Depoin et Dutilleux. L'Abbaye de Maubuisson.
19. Hallays (A.). Le Pèlerinage de Port-Royal. Paris. Perrin. 1908.
20. Brégis (Soeur Eustoquie de). Modèle de foi et de patience dans toutes les traverses de la vie ou Vie de la Révérende Mère Marie des Anges Suireau, Abbesse de Port-Royal et de Maubuisson. 1754. 2 vols.
21. Monlaur (M.R.)=(Mme Reynès). Angélique Arnauld. Paris. Plon. 1901.
22. Jaccard (L.F.). De l'institution ecclésiastique au dix-septième siècle.
23. Cognet (L.). La mère Angélique et St. François de Sales. Paris. Sulliver. 1951.
24. Ricard (Mgr.). Les premiers Jansénistes. Paris. Plon. 1883.
25. Mémoires pour servir à l'histoire de Port-Royal et à la vie de la Révérende Mère Marie Angélique de Sainte Madeleine Arnauld. 3 vols. Utrecht. 1742.
26. Arnauld d'Andilly (Mère Angélique de Saint-Jean). Exercices de piété à l'usage des Religieuses de Port-Royal. Au Désert. 1787.
27. Knox, Ronald (Mgr.). Enthusiasm, Chapter 9.
28. Delatour (M.A.). "Un pèlerinage à Port-Royal," in Revue de Paris. 1839.
29. Magne (E.). "Quelques pénitents mondains de Port-Royal de Paris," in Revue de Paris, March 15, 1924.
30. Gazier (C.). "Les premières conquêtes mondaines de Port-Royal," in Le Correspondent, Sept. 25, 1930.
31. Joly (H.). Génies sains et malsains. Paris. 1928.
32. Gazier (A.). "Racine et Port-Royal," in Revue d'Histoire littéraire de la France, Jan. 15, 1900.
33. Entretiens ou conférences de la Révérende Mère Marie-Angélique Arnauld. Bruxelles. 1757.
34. Arnauld (Mère Agnès). L'image d'une religieuse parfaite et d'une imparfaite, avec les occupations intérieures pour toute la journée. Paris. 1665.
35. Prunel (L.). Sébastien Zamet, sa vie et ses oeuvres. Paris. Picard. 1911.
36. C. Grolleau et G. Chastel. L'Ordre de Cîteaux. Paris. Gasset. 1932.
37. Vies intéressantes et édifiantes des religieuses de Port-Royal et de plusiers personnes qui leur etaient attachées. s.l. 1740–52. 4 vols. (Pub. by Abbé J. Leclerc.)
38. Macaire (L.). Déposition de la Mère Angélique Arnauld sur les vertus de St. François de Sales. Paris. Picard. 1906.

39. Carmel de Clamart. La Vénérable Madeleine de Saint Joseph. Clamart. 1935.
40. Saint-René Taillandier (Mme). La tragédie de Port-Royal. Paris. Plon. 1950.
41. Bremond (H.). Histoire Littéraire du Sentiment religieux en France. Paris. Bloud et Gay. 1916–1933. 11 vols.
42. Bremond (H.). Sainte Chantal. Paris. Lecoffre. 1912.
43. Mémoires de la Mère de Chaugy sur la vie et les vertus de Ste. J. F. de Chantal. Paris. Julien Lanier. 1853.
44. Bougaud (Mgr.). Histoire de Sainte Chantal. Paris. Poussielgue. 1909. 2 vols.
45. Bordeaux (H.). St. François de Sales et notre coeur de chair. Plon. 1924.
46. Relation de captivité d'Angélique de Saint-Jean Arnauld d'Andilly. Gallimard. 1954.
47. Pascal (B.). Oeuvres Complètes. La Pléiade. 1954.
48. Sainte-Beuve. Port-Royal. 3 vols. La Pléiade. 1953–1955.
49. Arnauld d'Andilly (R.). Mémoires. Hambourg, 1934. Journal inédit (p.p. A. et C. Halphen). Paris. 1857–1909. 5 vols.
50. Guilbert (P.). Mémories historiques et chronologiques sur l'abbaye de Port-Royal des Champs. Première partie. Utrecht. 1758–59. 2 vols.
51. Delavaud (L.). Le Marquis de Pomponne. Paris. Plon. 1911.
52. Racine (J.) Abrégé de l'histoire de Port-Royal. Very many editions.
53. Rapin (R.). Histoire du Jansénisme. Paris. Domenech. 1861. Mémoires. Lyon-Paris. 1865. 3 vols.
54. Thomas du Fossé. Mémoires. Utrecht, 1739.
55. Cognet (L.). La Réforme de Port-Royal. Paris. Sulliver. 1950.
56. Frencken (J.). Agnès Arnauld. Nimègue-Utrecht. 1932.
57. Gazier (A.). Histoire générale du mouvement janséniste. Paris. Champion. 1922. 2 vols.
58. Orcibal (J.). Jean Duvergier de Hauranne, Abbé de Saint-Cyran, et son temps. Paris. Vrin. 1947–49. 2 vols.
59. Varin (P.). La verité sur les Arnaulds complétée à l'aide de leur correspondance inédite. Paris. 1847. 2 vols.
60. Zamet (S.). Lettres spirituelles. P.p. L. Prunel. Paris. Picard. 1911.
61. Pinthereau (P.). Le progrès du jansénisme. Avignon. 1855.

DATES

1204 Mathilde de Garlande founds Abbey of Port-Royal des Champs.
1230 Consecration of Abbey Church, built by architect of Amiens Cathedral.
1236 May. Abbey of Maubuisson begun.
1567 St. François de Sales born.
1572 Ste. Jeanne de Chantal born.
1576 St. Vincent de Paul born.
1582 St. Teresa of Avila dies.
1585 Jacqueline's (Angélique's) parents marry. They have twenty children between 1588–1612.
1585 Jansen born.
1591 Sept. 8. Jacqueline (later Angélique) Arnauld born at Tours.
1593 July. Henri IV abjures Protestantism.
1594 Monsieur Arnauld makes speeches against the Jesuits, and they are expelled from France.
1596 Simon, Jacqueline's favourite brother, born in Paris.
1597 Angélique d'Estrées enthroned as Abbess of Maubuisson.
1598 Jacqueline made coadjutrix of Port-Royal des Champs.
1599 April 10. Gabrielle d'Estrées dies.
1599 September. Jacqueline clothed at St. Antoine de Paris, and goes on to Saint Cyr.
1600 June. Jacqueline goes to Maubuisson and is named Angélique as a compliment to the Abbess.
1602 July. Angélique Arnauld goes to Port-Royal des Champs. Sept. 29. Is consecrated as Abbess.
1602–7. Lives un-converted at Port-Royal des Champs.
1604 First Carmelite nuns come to France.
1605 M. Marion, Angélique's grandfather, dies.
1607 Marie-Claire Arnauld comes to Port-Royal des Champs as a pupil.
1607 Angélique plans to elope in summer and falls ill.
1608 March. Angélique is converted by a sermon.
1609 Angélique reforms her Abbey.
    Sept. Day of the wicket gate.
    Oct. Père Archange visits her.

1610 May. Renews her profession, hitherto invalid owing to falsification of age.
1610 May 14. Henri IV assassinated.
1610 Annecy Visitation founded.
1610 Agnès Arnauld ill at Port-Royal des Champs.
1611 Agnès clothed.
1612 Madame Arnauld has her last child, Antoine.
1613 Robert Arnauld marries.
1614 St. Teresa beatified.
1614 Marie-Claire comes to Port-Royal des Champs as a nun.
1615 April 12. A chariot of postulants from Chartres.
1615 Sept. 8. Anne-Eugénie's vision in St. Merri.
1618 Feb. Angélique d'Estrées turned out of Maubuisson.
1618 Feb. Angélique Arnauld becomes Abbess of Maubuisson.
1619 May 1. Paris Visitation founded.
1619 April, June and August. Angélique meets St. François de Sales.
1619 Monsieur Arnauld dies.
1619 Angélique d'Estrées attempts to overthrow Angélique.
1620 Ste. Jeanne de Chantal at Maubuisson.
1621 Dec. St. François dies.
1621–1628 or 1630. Angélique has no director.
1622 Feb. Dame de Soissons comes to Maubuisson.
1622 Madelon Arnauld comes to Port-Royal des Champs.
1622 Molière born.
1623 March 3. Angélique leaves Maubuisson. Epidemic at Port-Royal des Champs.
1623 Pascal born.
1624 Angélique de Saint-Jean, niece, is born.
1624 Madelon makes her vows.
1625 The Arnaulds buy Port-Royal of Paris. Angélique moves.
1625 May. Angélique meets Saint-Cyran.
1625 Ascension Day. Dom Boucherat dies.
1626 Madame de Pontcarré builds at Port-Royal of Paris.
1626 Spring. Angélique twice meets Paris Carmelites.
1626 end. Dame Agnès composes "Chapelet Secret."
1627 Port-Royal under jurisdiction of Archbishop of Paris.
1627 Angélique meets Mgr. Sébastien Zamet.
1627 Bossuet born.
1627 Dame Suireau goes to Maubuisson.
1628 Angélique deposes on holiness of St. François de Sales.
1629 Madame Arnauld professed.
1630 July. Angélique resigns and has a bad time till 1633.
1633 Angélique elected Superior of Saint-Sacrement, rue Coquillière, under Augustinian rule.
1635 Saint-Cyran becomes director at above.

1635 Mère Agnès becomes Abbess at Port-Royal of Paris.
1635 Community gives up Augustinian rule and returns to Cistercian.
1636 Feb. 10. Angélique returns to Port-Royal of Paris, and Dame Le Tardif goes to rue Coquillière.
1637 Angélique renews correspondence with Mère de Chantal.
1638 Louis XIV born.
1638 Saint-Sacrement closed, and Saint-Cyran put in prison by Richelieu.
1638 July. Hermits go to Port-Royal des Champs and are questioned by police.
1638 Jansen dies.
1639 Mère Agnès re-elected.
1639 Princesse de Guemenée becomes lady boarder at Port-Royal of Paris.
1639 Racine born.
1640 Catherine Le Maître (née Arnauld) becomes novice.
1640 Madame de Sablé boarder at Port-Royal of Paris.
1640 Jansen's *Augustinus* posthumously published.
1641 Feb. 28. Madame Arnauld dies.
1641 Dec. Ste. Jeanne de Chantal dies.
1642 Marie-Claire dies.
1642 Pope Urban VIII condemns *Augustinus*. Bull, *"In eminenti."*
1643 Oct. 11. Saint-Cyran dies.
1643 Madame de Gonzague boarder.
1643 May. Louis XIII dies.
1643 Antoine Arnauld's *Fréquente Communion* published.
1644 Angélique de Saint-Jean professed.
1647 Dame Suireau leaves Maubuisson.
1647 Angélique leaves Paris and goes to Port-Royal des Champs.
1647 Dec. New habit for nuns.
1648 Madelon dies.
1648 June 11. Church at Port-Royal of Paris consecrated.
1649 Angélique very ill.
1649 Charles I executed.
1648–9 First Fronde.
1648–56 Port-Royal at zenith of its fame.
1650 Monsieur Hamon at Port-Royal of Paris.
1651 Fénelon born.
1651 Catherine Le Maître dies.
1652 April. During Second Fronde. Port-Royal des Champs moves again to Paris. Level of chapel floor at Port-Royal des Champs raised.
1653 Jan. Death of Anne-Eugénie. Paris nuns return to Port-Royal des Champs.
1653 Pascal visits his sister at Port-Royal of Paris.

1653 Pope Innocent X condemns Five Propositions from *Augustinus* in Bull *"Cum Occasione."*

1654 Dec. Angélique writes her memoirs at Port-Royal des Champs.

1654 23–24 Nov. Pascal's *Memorial* in Paris.

1654 Coronation of Louis XIV.

1655 Jan. Pascal stays three weeks at Port-Royal des Champs.

1656 24 March. Miracle of Holy Thorn at Port-Royal of Paris. Schools closed at Port-Royal des Champs. (Racine, aged sixteen, was pupil there.)

1656 16th October Bull *"Ad Sacram"* of Alexander VII.

1656 Arnauld censured and excluded from Sorbonne.

1657 Grande Mademoiselle visits Port-Royal des Champs.

1656–7 Pascal's *Lettres Provinciales*.

1658 Dame Suireau dies.

1659 *"Précieuses Ridicules"* acted.

1660 Bossuet preaches at Versailles.

1661 July. Louise de la Vallière becomes Louis XIV's mistress.

1661 April. Paris Port-Royal schools closed.

1661 April 23. Angélique comes to Paris.

1661 May. Angélique falls ill.

1661 August 6. Angélique dies.

1662 Pascal dies.

1662 St. Teresa canonized.

1662 Jan. Catherine de Champaigne cured by miracle.

1664 Aug. 24. Mgr. de Péréfixe, Archbishop of Paris, imprisons Port-Royal of Paris nuns who refuse to sign Formulary. The two houses separated.

1665 Port-Royal des Champs under an Interdict. Angélique de Saint-Jean goes to Port-Royal des Champs and writes account of her captivity.

1668 Temporary truce called *"La Paix de l'Eglise."*

1679 Patroness, Princesse de Longueville dies, and persecution of Jansenists begins again.

1684 Death of Angélique de Saint-Jean.

1705 Only twenty-five left at Port-Royal des Champs, and youngest is sixty.

1709 Port-Royal des Champs razed to ground. Nuns dispersed.

1713 Bull *"Unigenitus"* of Clement XI.

1715 Ste. Jeanne de Chantal's canonization postponed because of association with Saint-Cyran probably.

1715 Death of Louis XIV.

1793–98 Port-Royal of Paris becomes prison under Revolution.

1814 Port-Royal of Paris becomes Maternité.

1824 Ruins of Port-Royal des Champs bought by M. Silvy.

POPES DURING ANGELIQUE'S LIFETIME AND AFTER

Gregory XIV. 1590–1.

Innocent IX. 1591.

Clement VIII. 1592–1605.

Leo XI. 1605.

Paul V. 1605–21.

Gregory XV. 1621–23.

Urban VIII. 1623–44.

Innocent X. 1644–55.

Alexander VII. 1655–67.

Clement IX. 1667–69.

Clement X. 1670–76.

Innocent XI. 1676–89.

Alexander VIII. 1689–91.

Innocent XII. 1691–1700.

Clement XI. 1700–1721.